A Parent's Guide to Everything!

THE
ONLY
BABY
BOOK
YOU'LL
EVER
NEED

ADVICE ON:
Diaper Rash,
Late-Night Feedings,
Swaddling, Teething,
Vaccinations, Potty
Training, Picky Eaters,
Tantrums, and More!

Includes expert advice from Marian Borden,
Ellen Bowers, PhD, Vincent Iannelli, MD, and others

Adamsmedia
Avon, Massachusetts

Published by
Adams Media, a division of F+W Media, Inc.
57 Littlefield Street, Avon, MA 02322. U.S.A.
www.adamsmedia.com

Contains material adapted and abridged from *The Everything® Baby's First Year Book, 2nd Edition* by Marian
Edelman Borden with Alison D. Schonwald, MD, FAAP, copyright © 2010, 2002 by F+W Media, Inc., ISBN 10:
1-60550-368-1, ISBN 13: 978-1-60550-368-4; *The Everything® Father's First Year Book, 2nd Edition* by Vincent
Iannelli, MD, copyright © 2010, 2005 by F+W Media, Inc., ISBN 10: 1-4405-0600-0, ISBN 13: 978-1-4405-0600-
0; *The Everything® Guide to Raising a Toddler* by Ellen Bowers, PhD, copyright © 2011 by F+W Media, Inc., ISBN
10: 1-4405-2585-4, ISBN 13: 978-1-4405-2585-8; *The Everything® Mother's First Year Book* by Robin Elise Weiss,
copyright © 2005 by F+W Media, Inc., ISBN 10: 1-59337-425-9, ISBN 13: 978-1-59337-425-9; *The Everything®
Organic Cooking for Baby & Toddler Book* by Kim Lutz and Megan Hart, MS, RD, copyright © 2008 by F+W
Media, Inc., ISBN 10: 1-59869-926-1, ISBN 13: 978-1-59869-926-5; *The Everything® Toddler Book* by Linda Sonna,
PhD, copyright © 2002 by F+W Media, Inc., ISBN 10: 1-58062-592-4, ISBN 13: 978-1-58062-592-0; and *The
Everything® Toddler Activities Book, 2nd Edition,* by Joni Levin, MEd, copyright © 2012, 2006 by F+W Media, Inc.,
ISBN 10: 1-4405-2978-7, ISBN 13: 978-1-4405-2978-8.

ISBN 10: 1-4405-7335-2
ISBN 13: 978-1-4405-7335-4
eISBN 10: 1-4405-7336-0
eISBN 13: 978-1-4405-7336-1

Printed in the United States of America.

10 9 8 7 6 5 4 3 2 1

Illustrations by Eulala Conner.

Cover images © 123rf.com.

This book is available at quantity discounts for bulk purchases.
For information, please call 1-800-289-0963.

CONTENTS

Introduction. 13

PART 1: PREPARING FOR YOUR NEW BABY. 15

CHAPTER 1
So You're a New Parent! 16
Parenting Styles 16
When Parents Have Different Opinions. 19
How to Handle Advice from Others 21
Just for Dads: What Kind of Dad Will You Be?. 23
Just for Moms: Common Myths of New Motherhood 27
The Changes Are All Worth It 29

CHAPTER 2
Baby Gear and Other Preparations 30
What Gear Do We *Really* Need? 30
Get Your Home Ready 41
A Medical Decision to Consider: Cord Blood Banking 43
Financial Considerations 45
Baby Names 48

CHAPTER 3

What to Expect at the Hospital......................... 50

Meeting Your Baby 50
First Visitors 52
Newborn Tests and Procedures 53
Common Problems 55
Rooming-In 57
Bringing Baby Home 57
Baby Basics 59
Early Health Problems 60
Caring for Siblings 63
Just for Dads: Supporting a New Mom................................64

CHAPTER 4

Understanding Your New Baby......................... 66

Your Baby's Temperament..66
Your Baby's Body 68
Infant Reflexes 71
Early Sleeping Patterns..73
Crybabies..74
Babywearing 76
Settling a Fussy Baby..78
Could It Be Colic?...84

PART 2: FEEDING 87

CHAPTER 5

Breast and Bottle Feeding 88

Benefits for Baby and Mom 88
The First Feeding 91
Troubleshooting 97
Breastfeeding Post-Cesarean 98
Milk's Here 99
Gearing Up 100
Breastfeeding Fashions 101
Maintaining Your Milk Supply 102
Breastfeeding Hills and Valleys 102
Baby's Breastfeeding Quirks 106
Call a Doctor If 107
The Joy of Pumping 108
Breastfeeding after Mom Goes Back to Work 110
Bottle Feeding 112
Choosing a Formula 115
Preparing Formula 117
Top Ten Bottle-Feeding Mistakes 118
Feeding Baby a Bottle 119
Timing the Introduction of a Bottle 120

CHAPTER 6

Start on Solids 122

Time for Mush 122
First "Real" Food 124
Gearing Up 126
Life after Rice 127

Homemade Baby Food 128
Baby Food Safety Tips. 130
Meat and Dairy. 130
Be on the Lookout for Allergic Reactions 131
All about the Cup. 132
Finger Foods 133
How Much Food Should I Offer My Child? 138
Recipes to Try at Home 140

CHAPTER 7
Toddler Foods 156

Toddler and Preschool Patterns and Portions 156
Special Bodies, Special Needs. 158
Healthy Appetites 160
Broadening Culinary Horizons 161
Food Struggles 165
When to Wean from Breastfeeding. 170
Recipes for Toddlers 172

PART 3: SLEEP TRAINING. 189

CHAPTER 8
Sleep Like a Baby. 190

Sleep Basics. 190
Night Feedings 191
Where Will Your Baby Sleep?. 192
Sleeping Through the Night. 194
Back to Sleep. 196
The Day-Night Transition. 198

Sleep Strategies 198

Sleep Programs. 200

Daytime Naps 205

Avoiding Common Sleep Problems. 206

Just for Dads: Your Role in Baby's Sleep. 208

CHAPTER 9

Helping Toddlers Sleep 210

Counting the ZZZs 210

Knowing When Your Child Needs Rest 212

Sharing Sleep Space with Your Toddler 214

Winding Down 217

Teaching Healthy Sleep Skills 218

Handling Specific Types of Toddler Sleep Issues 222

From Crib to Toddler Bed. 224

Exhausting Work 229

PART 4: DIAPERS AND POTTY TIME 231

CHAPTER 10

Diapering 101 232

Wet Diapers 232

The Scoop on Poop 233

Cloth vs. Disposable Diapers 233

Gearing Up for Diapering. 238

Diapering, Step-by-Step. 239

Diapering Tips 240

Diaper Rash. 241

Intimate Care 243

CHAPTER 11

Potty Training..**246**

The Parents' Mindset 246

Signs of Readiness...247

Seeing Is Believing..250

On Your Mark ... .251

Get Set ... .253

Go!...253

Teaching Hygiene..254

Rewards and Praise..255

Tracking Progress...256

Up with Undies, Down with Diapers! 257

Bedwetting 258

Bowel Problems 258

PART 5: SAFETY FIRST! **263**

CHAPTER 12

Safety Basics..**264**

Childproofing the House 264

Poison Control 266

Choking Prevention 268

Recalls and Product Alerts....................................269

Sunscreen 270

Insect Repellents 271

Pool and Water Safety 272

Kids and Pets...273

First Aid 274

CHAPTER 13
Babyproofing for Experts.............279

Room-by-Room Safety.................279
Other Important Safety Measures.................282
Lifesaving Skills.................284
Medication Safety.................288
Car Safety for Toddlers.................289

PART 6: MEDICAL CARE AND BASIC BABY HYGIENE.............291

CHAPTER 14
Choosing a Pediatrician.................292

The Selection Process.................292
Solo versus Group Practice.................295
Making Your Choice.................296

CHAPTER 15
Well Visits.................298

Preparing for Your Visits.................298
Well-Child Visits.................299
Recommended Vaccinations.................301
Alternative Immunization Schedules.................304
Early Intervention.................305

CHAPTER 16
Sick Visits.................306

Infant Alert: Sick Visits During the First Month.................309
Childhood Fever Basics.................311

Medicines 101. 314
Common Medical Problems 317
Infections and Other Problems. 324

CHAPTER 17

Keeping Your Baby Clean 328

Gearing Up 328
Into the Tiny Tub 331
Bath-Time Tips. 332
Graduating to the Big Tub 333
Baby Hygiene 101. 333
Beginning Tooth Care 335
After Teeth Arrive 336

PART 7: DISCIPLINE AND ENCOURAGING INDEPENDENCE. 339

CHAPTER 18

How to Discipline 340

Little Disciples 340
Teaching about No-Nos 341
Dangerous Situations 345
Time-Out. 347
Spanking. 348
Handling Tantrums 350

CHAPTER 19

The Road to Independence 355

The Roller Coaster Years 355
Playing with Your Baby and Toddler 357
A Growing Trust.. 364
The Problem with Praise..365
Praising Accomplishments 367
Stranger Anxiety 367
Comfort Objects 368
Feelings 101 369
Developing Initiative...370
Delaying Gratification..371

APPENDIX

Developmental Guidelines 375

The First Year **375**
Age Twelve to Eighteen Months...378
Age Eighteen to Twenty-four Months................................. 380
Age Twenty-four to Thirty Months 382
Age Thirty to Thirty-Six Months and Older...........................383

Index..385
About the Experts 399

INTRODUCTION

As you navigate the speed bumps of parenting a baby and toddler, you'll probably want some direction along the way. In *The Only Baby Book You'll Ever Need,* you will find advice that is thoughtful, practical, and simple: from how to survive the first few days back home (accept all offers of help, but organize them!) to what to do once your baby's mobile (babyproof!). You'll find realistic suggestions on identifying your own parenting style. You'll find tips on the myriad ways to feed your baby—from breast- and bottle feeding to starting solids. Oh, and what about getting that cherub to sleep? You'll find sleep information from A–Zzz in Chapters 8 and 9.

Dealing with medical issues, big and small, is one area where you'll likely want some guidance and reassurance. From the mundane well-child pediatrician visits to a scary bout with the flu, it's all covered here.

Just when you think you're in a parenting "lull," you'll hit another developmental milestone that throws you for a loop. Perhaps it's moving your baby to a toddler bed or potty training her. Or your eighteen-month-old went from the most adventurous eater to the pickiest. Or maybe it's facing a two-year-old who suddenly wants to do *everything* "by myself!" Regardless what the stage is, you'll find answers in these pages. As you're going through the suggestions, remember no one trick works for *everyone.* You might have to try several ideas before you find the one that works best for you and your child.

More than anything, *The Only Baby Book You'll Ever Need* is a one-stop source for all things parenting, from newborn to about age three.

As you shepherd your little one through this special stage of life, try to relax, smile, and enjoy it! Yes, it can be stressful and exhausting at times, but it's also incredibly rewarding and downright awe-inspiring to see how much your helpless newborn will grow in just her first few years . . .

PART 1

PREPARING FOR YOUR NEW BABY

Chapter 1

SO YOU'RE A NEW PARENT!

There is not simply one correct way to raise a child. Every child and every family has unique needs. It's helpful to have a general idea of how you'd like to parent, but your methods will adjust and change to accommodate your child's individual qualities and requirements. Be leery of any person or parenting program that claims a one-size-fits-all method is the answer to all your problems—it's not true. With some patience and persistence, the right path for your family will present itself in time.

PARENTING STYLES

You've probably received endless "advice" from well-meaning friends and family on how to raise your baby. Despite what anyone tells you, your parenting style must be developed over time—by you. However, you can still pick up tricks from existing parenting styles, including those that seem like fads. You can also take advice from friends and family—but with a grain of salt; a few of their methods might work for you, but others might not. Simply keep an open mind and consider your baby's unique characteristics when making these decisions.

Following are descriptions of some of the most popular parenting styles. Again, you might find that no one style works perfectly for you. If that's the case, don't be afraid to pick and choose certain tenets of each that work for your family.

Attachment Parenting

The words *attachment parenting* might conjure up images of a child being dependent on his parents forever. Actually, this is the opposite of the outcome this method produces. Attachment parenting is a technique in which parents read the baby's cues to figure out what he needs. By learning to recognize the needs of your baby and meeting those needs, he will develop into a confident child with a healthy attitude, who is not afraid to venture out into the world. Here are some characteristics of attachment parenting:

- Baby's needs are met immediately.
- Physical punishment is not used.
- Parents read signs from baby to learn how to best handle situations.
- Babies are seen as unique individuals.

The baby builds self-confidence because his parents always promptly meet his needs. To facilitate this relationship, the baby must always be in close proximity to one or both parents. For this reason, many parents who follow the attachment parenting model co-sleep with their children, at least for some part of their lives. Attachment parenting subscribers usually breastfeed their babies as well.

Baby wearing is another component of attachment parenting. Dr. William Sears says that babies who are worn in slings are better able to relax, sleep, eat, and play. He feels that baby wearing is a natural extension of pregnancy.

Fussy babies especially love being worn, as the positioning close to the parents' bodies helps keep them calm. Even if other parts of attachment parenting don't work for you, you might consider wearing your baby if he ever gets fussy. This is also a great way to discreetly nurse your baby.

Pediatrician-Directed Parenting

Some parents who like to have guidance as they develop their parenting methods prefer to follow the advice of the pediatrician. The guidelines your pediatrician follows likely come from the American Academy of Pediatrics (AAP).

Pediatrician-directed parenting might be a great way to start if you are unsure of how to proceed with your new baby. The problem with this method is that you are effectively letting someone else raise your child. Try this only as a starting point, and then as you gain confidence in your ability to raise your baby, start making your own decisions. As you grow confident that you can meet the needs of your baby, you will be able to transition into your own style of parenting. At this point, your pediatrician will become a resource rather than a leader.

Scheduled Parenting

Parenting by the clock, or scheduled parenting, means that your child consistently does everything at a certain time of day. Supporters of this method believe that if you find a predictable schedule for your baby, then he will grow confident and thrive. These infants are usually crib sleepers, with scheduled times for eating, playing, and sleeping.

Unfortunately, real life doesn't work like this for most parents. The fear of falling off the schedule can lead to some serious issues for some parents and babies. One of the biggest problems of scheduled parenting can be feeding issues, particularly early on in your baby's life. Newborn babies have very small stomachs. They are not designed to hold large amounts of food. Therefore, they need to eat small, frequent meals. Scheduled feedings can lead to weight gain issues, including problems with malnutrition and dehydration.

As with any other decision concerning your baby, you need to figure out what works for your family. Don't worry if you can't manage the scheduled-parenting method—it's not for everyone. But if you find that some of the method's tips are helpful, go ahead and incorporate them into your parenting style.

WHEN PARENTS HAVE DIFFERENT OPINIONS

The first step to dealing with differences between your and your partner's parenting theories is recognizing that they exist. You must realize that each person has a different view of things, and that each person's opinions have merit. Start early in the pregnancy to calmly educate each other about the style you think works best, why it works, and how you think it works. Remember to be open to suggestions from the other side. Your best chance for success lies in finding a common ground.

Start a conversation with your spouse about the topic. Some questions to begin with might include:

- What did you like best about your parents' parenting methods?
- What would you do differently from your parents?
- Describe your philosophy toward meeting your baby's needs.
- Are there things you definitely want to do as a parent?
- Do you see yourself as a partner in raising your child? Or would you prefer a more laid-back role?
- Should only one parent be the disciplinarian?

- Do you believe in spanking children, and if so, for what offenses? When is your child old enough for spanking?
- What are your beliefs about punishing children?
- What is the best style of communication with your child?
- Do you think yelling is necessary?

As you explain your ideas to one another, create examples and even act them out to demonstrate your rationale. Ask your partner to do the same. If you have gotten your information from a certain source, share the book, website, or other resource. Thoroughly explaining each of your opinions will make it easier to compromise. Remember, parenting is a team effort. The earlier you compromise to establish a parenting style, the better. This will save you and your child stress later on.

Parenting Pointer

Be aware of tactics you use in discussing parenting issues with your spouse. Avoidance, arguing, and ignoring are not conducive to meeting your final goal. Active listening, honest dialogue, and serious compromise are necessary from both sides to make change happen.

Once your baby is born, parenting really begins in earnest. No longer are these questions of philosophical debate. Where will your baby sleep? Will you respond immediately to her needs? Conflict here can be very uncomfortable. Be prepared to have differences, but be sure the major kinks are worked out before your baby is born. Conversely, you can also agree to put some decisions on hold. Don't waste your time and energy arguing about the age at which your baby will be allowed to date when she's still in the womb. Agree to wait and see what kind of person your baby develops into. These questions might have much clearer answers in fifteen years.

HOW TO HANDLE ADVICE FROM OTHERS

As soon as you share news of your pregnancy, words of advice will probably start flowing in from all directions. During pregnancy, excess advice may be easy to shrug off, as your baby has not yet arrived. But once the baby is born, you may be a little more likely to worry. If someone suggests that holding your baby too much will spoil her, you may begin to second-guess your choice to use the attachment parenting method.

Listen only to advice that seems to be practical. Think about how it might apply to your life. Does it make sense? How would you feel if you applied it? Does it go against any of your major beliefs about parenting? If an idea seems to meet all your requirements, consider trying it out. Remember, you can always scrap the idea if it doesn't work for you.

Grandparents

Unfortunately, the stereotypical new grandparents you see on sitcoms might actually turn out to be a reality for you. Your and/or your partner's parents might actually hover over you with advice, citing thousands of their own experiences when you two were little. Though they probably mean well, this unending "guidance" can drive you crazy. But unlike strangers with bad advice, you can't just ignore them and walk away.

Keep a couple of things in mind when dealing with unwanted advice from the baby's grandparents:

- They probably mean well.
- They probably aren't aware of the new technologies, products, and knowledge available to parents today. Don't be afraid to try to educate them—they may actually enjoy it.
- Listen to their advice; use what you can and discard the rest.
- Divide and conquer: If it is your spouse's parents who are driving you nuts, ask him to step in. Be willing to do the same if your parents act up.

- Remind them that ultimately, you are the baby's parents and your word is law.
- Most important, do not feel guilty for discarding advice that doesn't work for you.

Of course, not every set of grandparents will overwhelm you in this way. You may be lucky enough to have parents who offer to babysit and visit with the baby with no strings attached. If this is the case, enjoy it! And don't take this to mean that your parents can't offer advice if you need it. Feel free to ask, even if they aren't offering it up on a daily basis.

Friends

Your friends may also fall into the well-meaning category, but that doesn't make hearing their incessant advice any easier. Sometimes, however, friends are well connected, up-to-date parents themselves and have great advice to offer. In this case, listen to their advice, but heed it only if it fits your own parenting ideals.

Parenting Pointer

Beware childless friends with theories. You might find that the parenting theories you hold before you have kids will fly out the window when your little ones actually arrive. This is probably the same for many of your friends who don't have children. Still, these people just want to help, so be gentle if and when you must refuse their guidance.

If your friends have kids, they probably have some ideas that are similar to yours, and that might be what drew you together in the first place. Separate out the helpful advice using some of the same principles you use with grandparents. Try to laugh off or ignore what doesn't work for you. Be kind but remind friends to give you your space in parenting.

Parenting differences can seriously affect your friendships. If you and your friends have very different styles, it will be apparent and may cause tension. Try not to let parenting differences ruin your friendship. Agree to disagree and go on from there. This usually works well for all involved.

Strangers

One day, you might be standing in line at the grocery store holding a huge package of diapers. The lady behind you might tap on your shoulder and tell you that the brand of diapers you've chosen always leaks. Is this helpful? The answer probably depends on how much sleep you got the night before.

....

Parenting Pointer

Beware of the quick fixes people offer you with regard to parenting. Very rarely do they work, and they may undermine what you are trying to accomplish. However, the more tired you are, the more gullible and desperate you may become. Always bounce ideas off someone who has had more sleep before trying them out.

....

Advice from strangers can be very helpful or downright awful. How you choose to deal with it will depend on many factors, including the nature of the advice and your mood when you receive it. Try to be kind to nosy strangers offering tips or tricks, even if you don't find them helpful. They might be exhausted new mothers just like you.

JUST FOR DADS: WHAT KIND OF DAD WILL YOU BE?

After a baby is born, well-wishers tend to pepper mom with all sorts of questions about the delivery, the baby, and her parenting decisions. As a father, you might feel like a third wheel in your own family, though no one *wants* you to feel this way. Still, the waters of fatherhood can be choppy early on, and they can leave you doubting whether you'll ever feel comfortable in your role as dad. If you're feeling unsure, know this: Not all good dads are just naturally good at fatherhood. It takes some work to be a good father, and the first step is to be prepared. It all starts with knowing what it takes to be a good dad, and then deciding what kind of dad you will be.

Parenting Pointer

When does it hit you that you're a dad? For some new fathers it is while they are still expecting the baby. For others, it happens quickly once the baby is born or when they first hold their baby. But sometimes it doesn't happen until later, and that's okay too. If you are not feeling at all like a dad, try spending more time bonding with your baby.

The New Dad's Role

Knowing what role to take that first month after his baby is born can be difficult for a new dad. The role of the new mom is well defined, but dads don't always know what's expected of them. And different families will have different needs and expectations, which can make things even more confusing.

When you're trying to determine your role, it can help to simply have a talk with the new mom to figure out what your family needs from you. Should you try to stay home from work for a few weeks? Should you help care for the baby—for example, taking over some feedings and changing diapers—or should you just help around the house? If mom wants to spend most of her time bonding with her baby, having dad take over some extra household chores can be extremely helpful.

Dealing with Negative Emotions

A dad's role also can be shaped by his feelings toward his new baby. Although you might expect that all fathers would feel love, pride, and joy toward their baby, some instead feel resentment and jealousy, because they may no longer have their partner's full attention. If you find yourself having any of these feelings, do what you can to help overcome them before they harm your relationship with your child. You can either find someone else to watch the baby so you do have some special time alone with your partner or you can make an effort to get more involved and do more things together with her and your baby.

Changes Dads Should Expect

First-time dads who think that their lives won't change much are in for a very big surprise. Having kids may not change everything, but it will change a big part of your life. You won't be able to go out each night, watch every sporting event on TV, or spend all of your free time playing golf.

Other changes that you can expect this first year can include:

- Needing to be more flexible with your time
- Being less spontaneous
- Getting by with less sleep
- Having less time alone with your partner

Of course, there are plenty of positives, too. Chief among them is having the unconditional love of your baby. Remember that having a baby is not all about the things that you are going to give up or have less time to do. It just makes things easier in the long run if you go into this new time of your life with a good idea of what to expect.

Prioritizing Your Time

Just because you should be more available to help at home and with your baby doesn't mean that you can't still make time for other things that are important to you. As with other busy times in your life, you just have to set your priorities and give up or cut back on some of the less important things you used to spend time doing. Take a good look at your usual schedule, and see which things show up more often than they should. Do you really need to go for a drink after work with the guys, spend several hours on the Internet, or watch television *every* night?

Your priorities still can (and should) include some time for yourself. This means that in addition to your new role as the helpful father, you can probably still play your usual rounds of golf if, for example, you give up watching sports on TV in the evening. Or if you like working out at a health club regularly, switch your workouts to the early morning so that you can head home right after work to take over caring for your baby. As long as your top priority is your family, you should be able to balance the rest of your time to fit in the other activities that are important to you.

Qualities of a Good Father

Being a good father means different things for different families, but it usually isn't about how much money you make, all the things you can buy your family, or how successful you are at work. It's more about being available and supporting your family with your love and attention.

....

Parenting Pointer

Being a good father can be harder if you didn't have a strong role model to lead the way for you. But unless you want your kids to have the same problem once they begin to have kids, learn to be a good role model of fatherhood for them.

....

Being an equal partner when it comes to taking care of your baby is one of the most important qualities of a good father. Others include:

- Understanding your family's needs
- Offering unconditional love
- Having patience
- Being generous with your time

- Setting a good example
- Staying calm and learning to teach when you discipline (instead of simply relying on physical punishment to stop bad behaviors)
- Being responsible with your family's money

Parenting Pointer

How you were raised is going to be one of the big influences on the type of father that you will be. What role did your own father have when you were growing up? Was he simply a strict disciplinarian, or did he take a more active role in your care? Was your father even around very much? For good or bad, the type of father you had is likely to influence what kind of father you will become.

JUST FOR MOMS: COMMON MYTHS OF NEW MOTHERHOOD

As if you needed another challenge on top of learning to be a mom and getting to know your baby, there are a bunch of myths about new babies in circulation. By ridding yourself of some erroneous bits of information, you can streamline your life and make your days and nights more pleasant.

Myth: Babies Should Sleep Through the Night

Lack of sleep is an oft-cited reason to dislike the first months of new motherhood. Sleeping like you did prior to pregnancy is not going to happen for a while. However, there are a couple of key things to remember about nighttime sleep when you're a new mom.

For one thing, no one actually sleeps deeply through the night. If you look at what sleep researchers have known for years, the truth is that everyone passes through different cycles of sleep each night. These are periods of both light and deep sleep. Many adults have minor waking episodes at night. When your baby wakes you up with crying, it might not be much different from those experiences.

Second, in many cases, it is dangerous for babies to sleep through the night. This is because a baby has a tiny stomach that cannot hold enough food to get her through the night. By waking to feed, even in small amounts, babies get what they need to survive and thrive. In the beginning, most babies wake up two or three times each night. By three months of age, this has gradually decreased for most families, though it is not uncommon to have a baby who is still waking up once a night even at nearly nine months of age.

Additionally, waking to feed your baby a few times a night gives you the opportunity to meet some of her other needs. This might include changing a dirty diaper or moving your little one into a better sleeping position. Some mothers are also anxious about sleep periods that last too long, so night waking can ease these worries.

Myth: You Will Lose Weight Right Away

You will probably be sad to know that you'll most likely wear maternity clothes home from the hospital. Though you lose a lot of weight when your baby is born, you may also suffer from some swelling, particularly if you have intravenous therapy in labor or postpartum. You will have stretched your abdominal skin, which will take a while to return to its original shape. Remember, it took you nine months to put on the weight, so you can't expect to lose it overnight. However, you will see the most dramatic changes during the first six weeks after birth.

The good news is that breastfeeding can burn up to 1,500 calories a day. It also taps stores of maternal fat that were established in your body specifically for breastfeeding during pregnancy. This makes breastfeeding the natural way to shed unwanted pregnancy pounds.

Myth: The First Six Weeks after Birth Are Unbearable

Surely you have heard this one. Everyone says those first six weeks of little sleep, endless feedings, a sore body, and other physical issues will nearly kill you. Truthfully, many women actually find the first six weeks interesting and pleasant.

Many of the sweetest moments you will share with your baby come during late-night feedings and other supposedly "terrible" moments. Don't expect the first six weeks postpartum to be miserable; you may end up pleasantly surprised to find these few weeks go more smoothly than you thought.

Myth: After the First Few Days You Should Feel Like Your Old Self Again

Giving birth is hard work. You will likely feel drained from pregnancy and birth for weeks to come. You'll probably also be a bit overwhelmed by the task of shaping your parenting theories, not to mention tired from a few sleepless nights. While the physical issues are normal and simply take time to heal, your new role as a mother will take the place of certain other activities you enjoyed as your "old self."

It will take at least six weeks for the majority of the physical healing process to occur. During this period of time, your uterus will shrink back down to its prepregnancy size. You will lose the majority of your weight, though it will take additional work to strengthen and tone your muscles. Your hormones will start to level out, and your body will heal any wounds incurred during the birth process.

THE CHANGES ARE ALL WORTH IT

There are a million beautiful moments, exciting events, and fun changes that take place during parenthood. Probably the most thrilling part is watching your baby grow. Along with the excitement, however, come challenges. Most families go through at least a few rough times during the first year of their baby's life, and you will need to work through each one with patience and confidence.

It's true that your life will never be the same again—but it'll be better! Always remember, there is not a correct path for you to take, but you must simply find your own way.

Chapter 2
BABY GEAR AND OTHER PREPARATIONS

Expectant parents have a lot of work to do to prepare for the baby besides considering the more philosophical "what kind of parent will I be?" questions. For small creatures, newborns need a lot of gear! This is also a good time to think about important medical topics, like cord blood banking, newborn screening, and whether to circumcise your baby boy.

WHAT GEAR DO WE *REALLY* NEED?

One ironic part of having a tiny newborn baby is all the equipment that goes along with him. There is an incredible selection of products to buy, all of which claim to make your life with a new baby easier. From car seats and cribs to slings and swings, the choices can be overwhelming. How will you know which ones are right for your family? Also, how do you know if you're getting good deals? This section will help you sort out what you need and how to get it.

Your Baby's First Car Seat

Shopping for a car seat, with so many different brands and types available, can be very confusing. You will find many brands and styles of seats that fit the AAP's guidelines for a safe seat, so in the end your choice will come down to personal preference and proper fit in your vehicle. Just be sure to read the manufacturer's instructions so that you install and use the seat correctly.

....

Parenting Pointer

Car seats have always been hard to use, and most experts estimate that 85 percent of parents use them incorrectly. LATCH (Lower Anchors and Tethers for Children) is a relatively new system that is installed in new cars and car seats to make them much easier to install and use.

Infant-Only Carriers

Your first car seat will probably be an infant-only seat. This seat is designed for young infants and uses the rear-facing position that is safest for them. (Keep in mind that rear-facing car seats cannot be used in a seat with an air bag.) One of the best features of an infant-only seat is that after installing a detachable base into the back seat of your car, you can just snap the seat into the base when you are ready to go. When you reach your destination, detach the seat and use it as a carrier to transport your baby. Without this type of seat, you will have to buy a separate carrier, use a sling, or simply carry your baby around in your arms to transport him when not in the car.

Parenting Pointer

Every year, the AAP publishes a car-seat guide for parents. It is available free online at *www .healthychildren.org.* You can also find other useful information on this site to guide you in your first year of parenting.

Many infant seats can only be used for babies weighing less than twenty-two pounds. If you use an infant seat and your baby reaches twenty-two pounds, you will have to get a convertible seat and use it in the rear-facing position for a while, or get a newer infant-only seat with a higher weight limit. Many infant seats can now be used rear-facing until a baby is thirty to thirty-five pounds.

Convertible Car Seats

This type of seat is "convertible" because it can be used in both the rear-facing and forward-facing positions, accommodating newborns, infants, and most toddlers. These seats can be used until a child weighs about forty pounds. There are even some with higher weight limits that can be used as a belt-positioning booster seat for children weighing sixty-five to eighty pounds. While this means that you might be able to use just one car seat until your child is three years old (and therefore buy only one), a convertible seat might not fit your newborn well and it can't be used as a carrier.

Parenting Pointer

Where exactly to put the car seat is another common source of confusion. Although it sometimes depends on how many other kids you have seated in the car and where the seat fits best, in almost all cases your baby will be safest in the middle of the back seat. In addition to keeping her away from side-impact collisions, it protects her from any danger from side air bags.

Bassinets, Cradles, Co-sleepers, and Cribs

The crib is the classic place for a baby to sleep. However, there are many other options nowadays for places for your baby to sleep. Some are long-term options, while some are appropriate for only certain age ranges.

Bassinets and Cradles

Bassinets and cradles are typically used for the first few months of your baby's life. Many families choose to use them in order to keep the baby closer to them while they sleep. These are smaller than a standard crib and don't allow the baby much room to move.

....

Parenting Pointer

Be sure to check out any antique or heirloom bassinets or cradles prior to use for your baby. There are certain safety features that your baby's new bed should have. Check out the Consumer Product Safety Commission (CPSC) website for more information: *www.cpsc.gov.*

....

These short-term options are very useful for the first couple of months. Since you will have your baby close to you during the night, these items can make night feeding much easier on your family. Unfortunately, you need to discontinue the use of these products when your baby reaches a certain weight or gains the ability to roll over or sit up.

Co-sleepers

If you would like to co-sleep with your baby, this product enables you to have your baby very close by for ease of feeding in the night. A co-sleeper allows you to expand your bed to make a safe place for your baby to sleep next to you.

Most co-sleepers come in portable and wooden varieties. The wooden ones can be converted into benches or desks as your child grows. The sleeping area in a co-sleeper is larger than a cradle or bassinet, but slightly smaller than a crib. The co-sleeper tends to cost less than your standard crib.

Cribs

Cribs tend to be the largest-size sleeping area of all the baby sleeping items available. They come in a large variety of shapes, colors, materials, and styles. Some cribs are able to convert into toddler beds or day beds as your child grows.

Because of the size of a crib, most cribs are housed in a nursery or room other than your room. You may decide to keep your baby's crib in your room and move it later or begin your baby's night life in another room. Cribs can also be used for naps or for playtime while you're working on something else in the room.

If you have a nursery in your house, your crib will likely be the centerpiece of the room. The crib can be your expression of creativity in the room, or you can choose a simple crib that will allow you to change the look and feel of your baby's nursery as often as you like.

Portable cribs are also an option and provide a great middle ground. They are smaller than normal cribs, so some families use them as a daytime solution, for naps and such. You may also decide to use a portable crib continuously if you are strapped for space. Some portable cribs have bassinet attachments to help you get more use out of them.

Strollers

Strollers are the ultimate way to get your baby out and about. From getting exercise to simply strolling through the mall, a stroller can help you get out of the house and enjoy other activities. The key is choosing the right stroller for your lifestyle, or purchasing multiple strollers for different needs.

Standard Strollers

Strollers nowadays come in a wide range of price and quality. You'll see strollers that will allow your infant carrier car seat to snap in, strollers with large rubber wheels, and strollers that fold down very flat. Your best bet is to go to a nearby store and try out a variety of styles to decide what features are most important to you. Do you live in the city, and need a compact stroller that you can fit through sidewalk traffic? Do you plan to take frequent walks on uneven ground, therefore needing large, sturdy wheels? Will your stroller be stored in a garage, or does it need to fit folded in your car's trunk? Asking yourself these types of questions will help you decide which features you really need. From there, you can decide which add-ons (parent trays for a bottle of water for you, storage bins, car seat adaptability, etc.) you'd like to pay for.

Umbrella Strollers

Umbrella strollers are great for fast and furious shopping trips and quick strolls. They are very portable and also easy to store in the car, for those unexpected walks in the park on your way home from the grocery store.

Umbrella strollers are safe to use before your baby can hold his head up well, however—his head is not supported well enough in a simple umbrella stroller. While umbrella strollers are ultra-lightweight and easy to use, they are not usually sturdy enough for heavier toddlers or older children, either.

Double Strollers

Double strollers are a wonderful invention! They work great not only for families with multiples, but also if you have an older child who wants to tag along. You may also consider a double stroller as an investment if you want more children in the future. Having the extra storage space is never a bad thing!

There are a few different types of double strollers:

- **Side-by-side stroller:** This stroller works well if you have two young kids who like to talk or play. It also works out well for one child because you can put purchases or coats in the extra seat.
- **Tandem stroller:** This stroller has one seat in the front and one in the back. Many are made so that one or two car seats will snap right into the stroller. This can make the transition from car to stroller very easy, particularly with a sleeping baby. And if you have a toddler as well as an infant, your older child can sit up front and look out while your baby snoozes in the back.
- **Other variations:** The other main variation on a double stroller allows one child to sit or stand on a small platform built behind a normal-looking stroller seat. These are lightweight strollers. They are designed for one small child and one older child.

Carriages

The old-fashioned carriage is coming back into style. These buggies are usually for babies who want to lie down and not sit up. For this reason, carriages are perfect for newborns and little ones who can't yet sit up. Most carriages have a wide enough berth in the compartment to hold two small babies, if you have multiples.

....

Parenting Pointer

Storage space is a must in a stroller or carriage. After all, you need a place to store your diaper bag and/or purchases when you're out. Be sure whatever stroller you have enables you to carry your stuff without dragging anything on the ground or tipping over the stroller.

....

The downside to carriages is their lack of flexibility. Most carriages don't fold and go very easily. They also do not expand to accommodate a sitting older baby. This can make them more of an expensive toy for you than a practical solution for travel and getting out and about.

Swings and Things

Swings and other baby carriers can be great ways to help contain your baby for short periods of time. These carriers also offer a way to help soothe your baby, usually via movement. The main difference between the options is in the way the motion is created—by the baby or a battery.

Swings

Swings come in many shapes and fashions. In fact, you can find them in such a variety of styles and colors that there is surely one to match your nursery. These infant seats are much like light car seats, suspended from a metal frame. A battery pack tends to power the motion for the swing.

Swings can be used to help soothe a baby to sleep, or as an easy way to entertain a tyke while you get a small task done. It can be a blessing to have something to entertain the baby for a few minutes while you cook dinner or pay bills or even read a few pages of a book. Just be sure not to leave your baby unattended in a swing.

Bouncer Seats

Bouncer seats are usually cloth seats fitted to metal frames. Most of these seats include a safety strap that goes between your baby's legs and secures at the waist. Because these seats recline, they can be used even for small babies.

Bouncer seats are great for use with little ones. They can entertain and comfort at the same time. As your baby gets older and learns cause and effect, she'll begin to learn that when she moves, the chair bounces. Most models also have a toy bar across the front for even more hours of fun. Other models have battery packs to allow for vibration—some children like this, and others don't.

Stationary Jumpers

Stationary jumpers are much like the old walkers of the past. The good news is that they are not as dangerous as walkers. (The AAP has warned against the use of walkers.) This circular-based toy has a seat in the middle, and the seat rotates 360 degrees, giving your baby access to a variety of fun toys.

Be cautious with any type of carrier or bouncer. It should always be placed on the floor, as opposed to a table, bed, or other surface that is off the ground. This prevents the motion from carrying the bouncer onto the floor and tossing your baby.

In the stationary jumper, your baby can stand and learn to use her leg muscles; however, some say that it isn't good to allow babies to bear weight on their legs before a certain age. Be sure to check with your pediatrician before buying a stationary jumper.

Slings and Carriers

Babies love to be held, and adults love to hold babies. But parents have busy lives and can't sit around holding their babies all day, no matter how much they'd like to. For this reason, parents need a way to hold their babies while getting other things done, from vacuuming the floor to talking on the phone. Luckily, a sling or carrier can help you hold your baby and keep your hands free for other tasks.

Slings

Slings are pieces of fabric that hold your baby on your body, distributing the weight from shoulder to hip. They can be used from the newborn period until your child weighs about thirty-five pounds. There are several different types of holds that can be used with the slings, depending on your preference and the baby's age.

Parenting Pointer

Because baby rests so close to your body in a sling, it's very important to be sure he is positioned correctly and has proper air flow around his face. Consult your product's manuals and your pediatrician ahead of time to be sure you know how to use a sling safely.

Some slings have padding; others do not. Some slings are simply long pieces of material that must be wrapped around your baby in a particular fashion, while others are fitted to a certain shape but offer flexibility in sizing.

Front Packs

Front packs are just what they sound like: backpacks for the front of your body. There are many varieties available, all with different systems of snaps and buttons to help you position your baby. Your baby can face either inward or outward.

Parenting Pointer

Slings and other carriers are not just for moms! Many dads love using these items to hold their babies and bond with them. One family might even have two slings or carriers—one for mom and one for dad—if their sizes differ or just for convenience.

The main complaint about these types of carriers is that they can be difficult to learn to use. However, once you learn to use them, they are a snap. Some women don't like them because using a front-pack carrier makes them feel pregnant again. Ask a friend if you can try on her carrier or sling before selecting one for your personal use.

Clothes

Everyone loves cute little baby clothes, and people will be lining up to give them to your baby. But before long, you'll have nowhere to put them all, and your laundry duty will spin out of control. Too many baby clothes means clutter, and you don't have time to deal with clutter as a new parent.

Although many of the clothes that your baby will wear are easy to recognize—like undershirts, bibs, and hats—others can be more confusing. The following definitions might help:

- **Onesie:** a one-piece, short-sleeved outfit without legs that snaps in the crotch area and is usually worn under other clothing
- **Romper:** a one-piece outfit with short legs that snaps on one shoulder and in the crotch and inner legs
- **Coverall:** a one-piece outfit with long pant legs and either short or long sleeves; may be footed and have snaps that either go all the way down from the neckline or just from the crotch to the feet
- **Nightgown:** a one-piece outfit with an elasticized bottom for newborns to sleep in
- **Sleeper:** a footed, one-piece, full-body outfit with a zipper or snaps that extend from the neckline to one pant leg
- **Sleepsack:** a cotton or fleece bag that baby can use instead of a blanket to keep warm but still sleep safely
- **Receiving blanket:** a light blanket used to swaddle a baby

Remember, babies grow quickly! Hesitate before you buy a ton of clothes that fit her right now, or before you give away clothes that are currently too big. Remember, your baby may grow at a different rate than other babies and might need to wear sizes that are above or below her age level. Consider the weather at the time of year your baby will be born, and choose several outfits that will match the temperature.

GET YOUR HOME READY

Many of the things you will do to childproof your house can wait until your baby is getting around on his own (see Chapter 13), but there are a few things you should take care of immediately to keep your baby safe. These include checking the temperature on your hot water heater and eliminating secondhand smoke.

Hot Water Heater Temperature

Younger children, especially newborns, are very sensitive and their skin can burn easily. Also, they usually are not able to quickly pull away from scalding water or let you know if the water is too hot, so it is important to protect your child from hot water to prevent scalding burns. The best precaution is to turn down the temperature of your hot water heater to no hotter than 120°F, before you even bring the baby home.

Be sure to test the water before you use it near your baby each time, especially if you are lowering her into a bath, and never leave your kids unsupervised in the bathroom or kitchen.

Eliminate Secondhand Smoke

One of the healthiest things that you can do, for your baby and yourself, is to make your home smoke-free. If you smoke, the best time to quit is now, before your baby is born and you bring her home.

If you had been planning to just smoke outside, understand that really isn't enough to keep your baby healthy. Many studies have shown that babies whose parents smoke are more likely to have ear infections, allergies, and asthma, and are at greater risk of Sudden Infant Death Syndrome (SIDS). This is true even if the smoking isn't done directly around the babies. Your doctor or a good website, like *www.quitsmoking.about.com*, can help you stop smoking before it's time to bring your baby home.

Fire Safety

It's obvious that infants depend completely on you or another older family member to get them out of the house if there is a fire. Having working smoke alarms installed properly throughout the house can help you create an early warning system in case of such an emergency. A fire escape plan will help you handle an emergency situation as calmly and efficiently as possible, and allow everyone in your family to make it to safety. As you install smoke detectors in your house, consider going the extra step and installing carbon monoxide detectors as well. Otherwise you may not know this harmful gas is in your house until it's too late.

....

Parenting Pointer

Carbon monoxide is a colorless and odorless gas that can quickly be poisonous. It is produced by cars and appliances that burn fuel such as charcoal, natural gas, coal, wood, oil, kerosene, and liquefied petroleum. Carbon monoxide detectors are especially important if you have a garage attached to your home or if you have any fuel-burning, nonelectric appliances, such as furnaces, fireplaces, or stoves, in your home. Like smoke alarms, carbon monoxide detectors should be installed near your bedrooms and on every floor of your house.

....

Every floor or level of your house should have a working smoke alarm. They are especially important inside or just outside each and every bedroom. To prevent false or nuisance alarms, don't install a smoke alarm in the kitchen or bathrooms. The manufacturer's instructions and your local building and safety codes can also help you find the best places in your home for smoke alarms.

To make sure that your smoke alarm is in good working condition, change the batteries at least once a year and test the alarm each month. Also, be sure to replace any smoke alarms that could be more than ten years old.

A MEDICAL DECISION TO CONSIDER: CORD BLOOD BANKING

There are few things that you can invest your money in that have the potential to save your child's life. Clearly, buying a car seat, getting your child vaccinated, and having working smoke and carbon monoxide alarms in your home are incredibly important, but none of these will cure her if she gets sick.

Unlike these preventive strategies, storing your baby's umbilical cord stem cells in a cord blood bank does have the potential to save her if she someday gets seriously sick. Once collected, stored, and saved, umbilical cord stem cells can later be used for a stem cell transplant if your child develops a genetic disease or a type of blood disorder or cancer that can be treated with a bone marrow transplant.

In recent years, many for-profit programs that collect and store umbilical cord stem cells have been developed. You probably have seen advertising in parenting magazines and may even have received brochures in the mail describing these services. Because your baby's cord blood must be collected at the time she is born, you will have to think about and be prepared to have her cord blood collected while you are still expecting. It is not a decision you can make later.

The marketing of the cord blood banks that describe a "once-in-a-lifetime opportunity" can be persuasive, but the procedure is expensive. After a one-time "banking fee" of about $1,500 to $1,700, you will have to pay about $100–$150 a year to store the stem cells. Even with payment plans, that is a lot of money for most new parents.

It doesn't hurt your baby to take the blood from the cut umbilical cord, and this blood would just be thrown out if you decided not to save it. That seems to leave money as the main deciding factor. So should you pay to bank your baby's umbilical cord stem cells? If it is something that you can afford and you feel better knowing that you are storing your baby's stem cells in case you ever need them, then signing up with a cord blood bank might be for you.

When making your decision, keep in mind the clinical report on cord blood banking by the AAP, which concluded that "private storage of cord blood as 'biological insurance' is unwise." In other words, the AAP doesn't think that it is necessary for the average parent to store their child's cord blood. However, it may be a good idea if you already have a family member who needs or may need a stem cell transplant due to leukemia, a severe hemoglobinopathy, or other disorder, both because he may be able to use your baby's cord blood for a transplant and because your child may be at increased risk of developing these conditions too. The AAP does recommend that parents donate their babies' stem cells to nonprofit centers, like the National Marrow Donor Program cord blood banks, so that they can be used for stem cell transplants in unrelated recipients.

FINANCIAL CONSIDERATIONS

You may have heard people say that if you waited to have a baby until you could afford it, you'd never have children at all. While there is truth to this statement, there is also something to be said for being fiscally responsible in planning for your children. The first step to success is knowing what expenses to expect and which are the most important. Then, a little planning can mean the difference between an anxious parent and a confident one.

Making a Will

Younger couples often overlook the need to have a will. After all, they don't expect anything to happen to them anytime soon and they probably haven't built up many assets yet. Once a baby is born, the need for a will becomes essential.

. . . .

Parenting Pointer

You should hire a lawyer if you need more than just a basic will. In complicated situations—for example, if you are not married to your baby's other parent, have children from a previous marriage, or already have a lot of financial assets—then a lawyer should help you prepare your will.

. . . .

Without a will, if both you and your baby's other parent die, you have no control over who becomes your baby's guardian. Do you want family members to fight over your baby, have a court pick someone, or have your baby go to a foster home? Or would you rather put some thought into who would best raise your baby, and make sure that they have the legal right to do so?

Unless your financial or family situation is complicated, a basic will is likely to be all you need, and you may not even need a lawyer to do it. There is a wide choice of software and self-help books to help you prepare a simple will on your own, inexpensively.

Sorting Out Maternity and Paternity Leaves

Taking time off from work when you have your baby is only partially a matter of your choice. How much time you choose to take off can be influenced by the rules at your workplace. Other factors would be your health, the health of your baby, your job requirements, the work season, and other details. A combination of these factors will determine how much time you actually take off.

Preliminary Research

Arranging a maternity or paternity leave with your boss can be a daunting task. The important thing is to have a plan before you go speak with your boss. Talk to your company's human resources department or research your rights according to state or local regulations to educate yourself about the process. You might also consider talking to other new parents at work to see what types of job leave they had when their children were born.

Having an idea of the normal leave process before you approach your boss will boost your confidence. This will also show your boss that you thoroughly understand your position. In showing her you care enough to do the research, your boss will see that you value your job and want to coordinate the best possible arrangement.

Family and Medical Leave Act (FMLA)

Federal law on family leave is called the Family and Medical Leave Act (FMLA). You must work at a qualifying company—meaning a business that has a certain number of employees—in order to take leave under this act. And your job must qualify, meaning you have worked full-time in your position for a year or more.

If you have questions about the FMLA, address them to your company's human resources department. If the staff can't help you, go straight to the law itself, which is available on the Department of Labor's website: *www.dol.gov/whd/fmla*.

If you and your place of work meet the requirements, you can take up to twelve weeks of unpaid leave. This time can be used for, among other things, the birth of a baby, an adoption, or the caretaking of a sick immediate relative. The good news about the FMLA is that both parents can use it, and in some cases both of you may choose to take some or all of this leave, while having your job status protected. Dad's work may offer a paternity leave schedule, or he may use part of the FMLA time. Keep in mind that being paid while you're out on leave is a different matter entirely—talk to your human resources department about your company's policies.

Budgeting and Saving

If you plan to take a significant duration of unpaid leave from work, it's wise to accrue some savings to be used while you do not have income. Try to figure out your minimum budget. Decide how long you will be out of work and how much you will need to cover that time, then budget in that amount for the months remaining in your pregnancy. Remember to add about 10 percent extra for emergencies or an early birth. It's great if you have a paid leave, but setting aside some money for this time will create a nice cushion in either case.

....

Parenting Pointer

There are several costs associated with the birth. A normal, uncomplicated vaginal birth can cost about $5,000, including prenatal care. If you require anesthesia, such as an epidural, that might add another $1,200, and a cesarean can cost about $3,000 extra. This total doesn't even include an additional nursery stay for your baby. However, if you are low risk, a less expensive option for birth may be to use a midwife or birth center instead of a hospital.

....

If you will be leaving work for good, or if you'll be returning to work while your partner stays at home, it's a great idea to use those final months of income to build a nest egg. If you are able to bank vacation or sick days, do this too. Spend your final months in the working world thinking about how you can adapt to life on a single income. Talk to others who've done it, and heed their advice.

Preparing for being a stay-at-home parent while you still have the extra income can help pad the pitfalls

BABY NAMES

As you gather the gear you need, figure out financial situations, and consider how to handle any special situations you might have, it can be relaxing to step away and discuss what to name your baby! Choosing a name for your new baby can be one of the most fun things you can do before your baby is born—but it can also be one of the most difficult. How on earth do you even begin to decide on the name your baby will live with for the rest of his life? Do you choose a family name, a popular name, a unique name?

It can be hard for both parents to agree on a name for their baby, but you should be prepared to offer your own favorites and suggestions and try to compromise if you can't decide on a name that both of you like.

Popular Baby Names

Choosing a popular name usually doesn't mean naming your baby after your favorite movie star, singer, or character on TV or in the movies. It means choosing a name that many other people are also going to choose, leading to classrooms with two or three Matthews and several Emilys. Here's a list of the most popular names from a few years ago that you can review if you are looking for (or trying to avoid) a name for your baby that a lot of other babies will have too.

TOP TEN BABY NAMES OF 2012	
Boy Names	**Girl Names**
1. Jacob	Sophia
2. Mason	Emma
3. Ethan	Isabella
4. Noah	Olivia

5. William	Ava
6. Liam	Emily
7. Jayden	Abigail
8. Michael	Mia
9. Alexander	Madison
10. Aiden	Elizabeth

From the U.S. Social Security Administration.

Middle Names

The baby's middle name might simply be a name that you like, or the name of a friend or family member whom you want to honor. Be sure to check if the initials spell an unintended word so that your child doesn't end up with initials like FAT or PIG. If your partner had to make a compromise on the choice of the baby's first name, it might be nice to let her choose the middle name.

Starting Your Own Traditions

Sticking to a family tradition for naming your baby can be a good way to honor or remember your ancestors, but whose tradition do you follow? What if both the mom's and dad's families have a tradition of naming the first-born child after their own grandparents?

In this kind of situation, if you can't reach a compromise, you might come up with your own "tradition." Maybe name all of your children with names that start with a certain letter: Charlie, Chris, and Chad. Or name your first girl after the mom's mother and your first boy after your father. In any case, choosing a name is sometimes the last thing parents do before baby's arrival—in fact, some even make a decision after the baby is born!

Chapter 3
WHAT TO EXPECT AT THE HOSPITAL

If having a baby really changes everything, then get ready, because here is where it all starts. Once your baby arrives, you will soon be very much aware that you're a new parent. Although the first few days can be overwhelming, they are also fun and exciting. This is a time that you will always remember. Knowing what to expect and what is going on with your baby can help make these days even more enjoyable.

MEETING YOUR BABY

When she is born, your baby may cry, whimper, or be quiet, but none of these is a bad sign. The important thing is that the baby is breathing. Once this is ascertained, your baby should be handed to you right away. The best way to keep the baby warm is by holding her to your bare skin and covering her up with warm blankets. Even before the umbilical cord is clamped or cut, you can hold your baby as high on your chest as the cord will allow.

Parenting Pointer

Cesarean-born babies are just as capable of snuggling skin to skin as vaginally delivered babies. If mom doesn't feel up to it during the remainder of the surgery, dad can nestle the baby inside his shirt for warmth.

Your baby will probably feel a bit wet and potentially be tinged with blood. This is the mother's blood—not the baby's blood. You or your partner can take a clean towel and dry the baby while your newborn gazes up at you (new babies can see best from a distance of about eight to twelve inches) and listens to the sound of your heartbeat from the outside. Your baby will probably be wrinkled and may appear reddish or swollen. Don't worry if her head looks a bit misshapen. New babies' heads are designed to change shape as they fit through the mother's pelvis. A normal, round head shape will develop as the skull hardens.

During these first few minutes and through the first hour, your baby will likely be in a quiet, very alert state. You will both be taking in so much during this time. In addition to relief that the labor is over, you will likely feel an instant, overwhelming love for your baby.

Baby Basics

Generally, you can wait to have your baby weighed or bathed until you and your baby are ready to have them done. If you know you want to spend at least one uninterrupted hour with your baby before he is weighed and measured, be sure to mention this desire in your birth plan.

If your baby needs to be seen for emergency reasons, or is taken to the neonatal intensive care unit (NICU) after birth, do not fear. This does not necessarily indicate tragedy, and you can still be with your baby in the NICU once you are both stable. While these first few moments are wonderful and precious, you will still have a sense of connection with your baby if these moments must come a bit later. Your and the baby's health are the most important issues.

First Feeding

Soon after birth, your baby will probably be wrapped in a blanket and handed back to either mom or dad. You may not be thinking about feeding your baby at this time, but if your baby's mother plans on breastfeeding, now would be a good time to start if she is feeling up to it (see Chapter 5 for detailed instructions on baby's first feeding). This is especially important, because after being awake and alert for an hour or two, your baby is likely to sleep most of the rest of his first day and will be harder to wake up for breastfeeding. Even if you aren't breastfeeding, you both should spend the first hour after delivery holding and bonding with your new baby if he is healthy and doesn't have to be taken immediately to the nursery.

FIRST VISITORS

Everyone will be very anxious to meet your new baby. However, knowing there is an audience waiting outside your door can add to the stress of your labor and delivery. Consider telling everyone to wait at home, promising to call at a certain point in labor or just after your little one has arrived.

Immediately after the birth, you may wish to spend some time alone with your partner and new baby. Don't worry about offending those who are waiting to see the new arrival. They've already been waiting for a while, so they can wait a few more minutes. In fact, they probably won't even know the baby has been born until you tell them.

Several factors will dictate when you are ready to see visitors. If the delivery room gets a bit messy during the birth (it usually does), you may prefer not to have visitors come in until it has been cleaned up a little. You might also choose to shower first. And you'll probably want to breastfeed the baby before anyone else comes into the room. In a home birth, you might choose to join the guests who are waiting in another room for a few minutes before retreating again with the baby.

Above all, remember that *you* are the parents. This means you're the boss. Feel free to insist that your guests wash their hands before holding your baby. On the other hand, also keep in mind that it's impossible for you to keep your baby safe from everything. You can take some basic precautions, but there's no need to keep your baby in a bubble. Babies and small children are remarkably resilient, as you'll soon learn.

NEWBORN TESTS AND PROCEDURES

Soon after the birth, the doctor or midwife will want to do a few tests and procedures to make sure that your baby is in good health. You may not like being separated from your little one so soon, but you might feel better about these procedures if you have an idea of what they entail and what they will determine. Once you have this knowledge, if you still feel strongly about delaying or avoiding the tests, discuss this with your pediatrician and be sure to address it in your birth plan.

APGAR Scoring

The APGAR scoring system, named for its creator, Virginia Apgar, is a mnemonic device that covers five different ways of grading a baby at birth. This system is used to determine the baby's basic health status. APGAR stands for:

- **Activity:** muscle tone
- **Pulse:** heartbeats per minute
- **Grimace:** reflex irritability
- **Appearance:** skin color
- **Respiration:** absence or presence of breath

Your baby is given a score of 0, 1, or 2 for each category, with 10 being a perfect score. A score of 7 to 10 is considered normal, 4 to 7 might call for resuscitative action, and 3 or below requires immediate resuscitation. Your baby will be graded one minute after birth and again at five minutes. If your baby is having a rough time getting started, you will also have a third score after ten minutes. This scoring usually goes unnoticed by parents. While you are consumed with the emotion of new parenthood, a nurse or midwife will be keeping a sharp eye on your baby for labored breathing or other signs of stress.

Weighing, Measuring, and Blood Work

You'll probably be very excited to know how much your baby weighs and measures. These numbers stick in most parents' heads forever. Just keep in mind that these measurements do not indicate the health or ultimate body type your child will have. A seven-pound baby can be just as healthy as a nine-pound baby, and one that measures twenty-two inches will not necessarily grow to be taller than a baby born at nineteen inches.

Weighing and measuring is usually done in the first couple of hours of life, but it doesn't need to happen right away. After you have spent some time nursing and cuddling with your baby, you can declare that she's ready to be measured.

You may also be asked to permit a routine blood screening for metabolic disorders such as phenylketonuria, thyroid issues, sickle cell, and other problems.

This is usually done with a heel stick. Feel free to hold or nurse your baby during the procedure to comfort him and ease any pain. Be sure your baby is at least forty-eight hours old when blood screening is done. If performed prior to this time, the results may be invalid and the screening must be repeated. Your baby usually also received a vitamin K shot.

Eyes and Ears

Your state law may mandate eye medication following the birth. Check with your local government to find out what the laws are in your community. The eye ointment is administered to prevent blindness in your baby in case you have an untreated sexually transmitted infection (STI). Even if eye medication is mandated, you can still choose when it's done and what medication is used. For example, erythromycin is much gentler than the silver nitrate alternative. Many parents also wait for an hour or two before using the medication because it can cause blurry vision. This may be a bit annoying for your newborn but not harmful.

Where the ears are concerned, many states now require that hearing screenings be done on newborns. These screenings work best when your baby is asleep. So, during the night, a nurse may tap on your door and ask for the baby. Feel free to send the baby with your partner or bring him yourself for this brief test. Bringing the baby ensures that he will return to your room with you as soon as the test is complete.

COMMON PROBLEMS

Chances are your baby will be born happy, healthy, and without complications. However, there are a few rather common complications to be aware of. It is important to know how these are handled so you can be more involved if one should occur with your baby.

Breathing Difficulties

Some babies will have breathing difficulties at birth. If your baby is born early or via cesarean section, he will be more likely to have these problems. Usually, the doctor or midwife can facilitate breathing by rubbing the baby's skin, possibly by giving him oxygen. This can be done in any birth setting.

All practitioners are also trained to provide CPR on your newborn, if needed. Long-term ventilation and other breathing treatments may be available only at a Level II or III hospital setting. These measures are the least likely to be needed.

Meconium Staining

Once your water breaks, it may become apparent that your baby has passed his first bowel movement while still inside your body. This is called meconium staining. Meconium is seen in cases where the baby is overdue, stressed, or both. If your practitioner sees meconium, she is likely to listen to the baby more frequently during labor to ensure he is not stressed.

As your baby is born, he will be suctioned before he can breathe or scream. This is done to prevent him from inhaling the meconium. Because meconium is thick and tarlike, it can make it difficult for a newborn to expand his lungs. So, removing it prior to screaming or breathing is important.

In the case of meconium staining, you may have to wait a few minutes before your baby is handed to you. Someone may perform deeper suctioning once the baby is completely free of the birth canal, also to prevent inhalation of meconium. Some babies will still inhale the meconium despite all efforts to prevent this. If your baby does this, he may need further tests, including X-rays. In some cases, a baby will also need to stay in the NICU. Your doctor will explain more about this, in the unlikely event that it becomes necessary.

Jaundice

Jaundice is the collection of bilirubin in the blood. This can be discovered through a blood test, but more likely it will be discovered because a baby has turned a shade of yellow. This usually doesn't happen until the first few days after birth.

The best way to get rid of the bilirubin is to encourage as much breastfeeding as possible. Breastmilk, particularly the colostrum it contains during the first few days, acts as a natural laxative, helping your baby to pass the bilirubin. Exposure to natural light through a window can also help.

Extreme cases of jaundice are rare. They are usually treated by breastfeeding and light therapy. Light therapy is usually done by using light blankets. A couple of days are all that is needed to clear up the condition.

ROOMING-IN

Once it has been determined that your baby is healthy, you can usually decide to either have the baby stay in your room for all or most of the time, which is called rooming-in, or continue to have him go back and forth from the nursery.

....

Parenting Pointer

Nursery workers often assume that sleeping mothers don't want to be awakened for nighttime breastfeedings. If you and your partner don't want your baby to get formula and she isn't rooming-in, be sure everyone knows to wake mom up for feedings. You should also alert the nursery that you do not want them to use a pacifier, because that can often interfere with effective breastfeeding.

....

Rooming-in with your baby can make breastfeeding on demand easier for the mother and give her more time to bond with and understand her baby before going home, but it may make it harder for her to get much rest. Rooming-in is also a good idea for dad, so that he can also bond with the baby and help his partner get some rest.

BRINGING BABY HOME

The timing of your baby's discharge from the hospital depends on many things, including how your baby was delivered. Although families often want to leave early (before forty-eight hours), that likely won't be possible if your baby was born by cesarean section. After a C-section, most mothers have to stay in the hospital for at least three to four days, if not longer.

Discharge Criteria

How well your baby is doing also will be a big factor in the decision as to whether she can go home early. Using criteria from the AAP, your baby should be discharged early only if she was born full-term, had a normal physical examination, and maintains a stable body temperature for at least six to twelve hours.

Parenting Pointer

Don't accept an early discharge from the hospital, which usually means leaving less than forty-eight hours after your baby is born, unless *all* parties feel comfortable going home.

Before going home, your baby also will have to be either breastfeeding or taking formula well. If your baby isn't latching on, isn't sucking well, or is taking less than an ounce of formula at a time, then she likely will need to spend a little time in the hospital nursery.

Your baby also probably won't be able to go home early if she is much smaller or bigger than the average baby, is having problems with her blood sugar, develops jaundice early, or shows any signs of illness, or if the mother had a positive Group B strep test.

Before You Go Home

The hospital can be a great resource for you both to learn about breastfeeding, changing diapers, taking a temperature, and so on. Before discharge you also should try to take any parenting classes that the hospital offers.

You likely won't be able to learn everything you want to know about your baby in one or two short days in the hospital, but you should be able to learn the basics. It can be especially helpful for a new dad to perform as much of his baby's care in the hospital as he can. That means changing clothes and diapers, swaddling baby in a blanket, picking her up, and holding and carrying her. Getting comfortable with these very basic procedures, with a nurse ready to step in if you are really doing something wrong, is a great way to learn.

BABY BASICS

The "basics" are going to mean different things to different people. For brand-new parents who haven't been around a lot of babies, simply holding your baby is something that will have to be learned. Learning to take a rectal temperature is another good skill to learn before you go home.

See One, Do One

Reading long, detailed instructions isn't the best way for most new parents to learn about changing diapers or dressing a baby. Unless you have seen or done these things before, even the best instructions are going to seem as if they are written in a foreign language.

A much better approach is the basic "see one, do one" technique of learning baby basics. This means that you watch an experienced person perform each task, and then try it yourself. You'll feel more comfortable doing these things with someone watching, especially if that person can point out things you may be doing wrong.

Basics to Learn

These are some of the more important things that both mother and father should know how to do before discharge, so that you will feel more confident and will be able to be more helpful at home.

- [ ] Recognize proper breastfeeding techniques, including positioning, latching-on, and sucking
- [ ] Prepare your baby's formula and bottles (if using formula)
- [ ] Burp your baby
- [ ] Change a diaper
- [ ] Dress and undress your baby
- [ ] Pick up, carry, and hold your baby

- ☐ Take a rectal temperature
- ☐ Swaddle your baby by snugly wrapping him in a blanket
- ☐ Put your baby to sleep on his back to prevent SIDS
- ☐ If necessary, care for a circumcised penis

EARLY HEALTH PROBLEMS

Your baby should do fine after he goes home if he got a clean bill of health in the hospital. Most of the more common problems that can affect a newborn are easy to uncover while he is still in the hospital, including severe infections, pneumonia, respiratory distress syndrome, and major heart defects.

Still, especially with early discharges, your baby could be born with a problem and not start to show symptoms until after you get home. And then there are problems that don't even begin until after a few days of life. Knowing what to look for should ease your worries and help you recognize when your baby might be having a problem that requires a visit to your pediatrician.

Breastfeeding Problems

The first few weeks of breastfeeding can be difficult, especially for new parents. Afterward, once a mom has a good milk supply and the baby has learned to latch on and suck well, things usually go much more smoothly.

During those first few days and weeks, though, moms might struggle with nipple soreness, a baby who doesn't latch on well or who has a poor suck, and other problems. At these times, instead of just giving a bottle of formula, you should get help.

Getting help is easy if you have friends or family members who have already breastfed successfully. If not, look to your pediatrician or a lactation consultant for some expert advice. It may not be easy, but most breastfeeding problems can be overcome with the right help. It's likely that after you receive help, your baby will soon be breastfeeding without further problems.

Signs that your baby is not breastfeeding effectively might include:

- Wanting to breastfeed fewer than eight to twelve times in a twenty-four-hour period
- Having fewer than two yellow-green stools by three to four days after birth (these follow the black, tarry meconium stools he will have the first two days) or fewer than three to four loose yellow stools by day five to seven
- Having fewer than six full, wet diapers by day five to seven, although urinating less frequently is common until mom's milk comes in
- Losing more than 5 to 10 percent of his birth weight in the first week
- Persistent nipple or breast pain for the mother

Remember that letting your baby breastfeed frequently, at least eight to twelve times a day, is the best way to help mom establish a good milk supply and encourage effective breastfeeding.

Problems with Formula

Although people often think of feeding problems as being limited to those babies who are breastfeeding, formula-fed babies can have problems too. One of the biggest problems is simply not tolerating the formula, which might lead to your having to change to a different type. This means if you are giving your baby a cow's-milk-based formula, you might have to switch to a soy or elemental (amino-acid-based) formula.

Many of the things that parents interpret as problems with food—such as the baby having gas, spitting up frequently, or having loose stools—are actually normal reactions. Although changing the kind of formula your baby drinks is not usually harmful, it can lead to increased anxiety if you think something is wrong. That is why it is usually a good idea to talk to your pediatrician before changing formula.

Another problem that formula-fed babies can have is simply not eating enough or eating slowly. After the first few days of life, most babies will drink about two to three ounces of formula every three to four hours. Talk to your pediatrician if your baby is drinking much less than that or regularly going longer than three to four hours without wanting to eat.

Parenting Pointer

Because the different brands of the same variety of formula, such as Enfamil Premium Lipil and Similac Advance, have the same protein (cow's milk) and sugar (lactose), changing from one to another is usually not helpful when your baby has a real formula intolerance.

Poor Weight Gain

It is expected that a baby will lose weight during his first week of life. This upsets many parents who were happy with their healthy seven- or eight-pound baby and who don't like to see him drop even an ounce. However, your baby will almost certainly lose at least 5 to 10 percent of his birth weight during the first week. This weight loss is mostly because newborns lose excessive fluid they are born with and because at first they can't eat enough to keep up with their caloric needs.

A greater weight loss can be a problem, though. Or it might indicate a problem if your baby loses weight too rapidly. If your baby is already down 5 or 7 percent after just one or two days, then by the end of the week the loss might be well over 10 percent. These babies should be closely monitored every day or two to see whether they continue to lose weight.

After the weight loss of the first week, your baby should start to gain some weight. You can expect a baby who is feeding well to gain at least one half to one ounce each day, so that by the two-week checkup, the baby is back up to his birth weight. Continuing to lose weight or not getting back up to birth weight by two weeks can indicate a problem, especially with feeding, and should be investigated by your pediatrician.

Jaundice

Developing jaundice, which is a yellowish discoloration to the skin, is very common in newborns. This jaundice typically develops on the baby's second or third day, so it may not be seen in the hospital. Jaundice that develops within twenty-four hours of your baby's birth, or that rapidly gets worse, can be a sign of a more serious problem than the typical "physiological jaundice" that most babies have.

Jaundice usually starts on your baby's face and eyes and then spreads down his body as it gets worse. You should notify your pediatrician if the jaundice seems to be spreading quickly or has already reached your baby's arms and legs. Although many babies with jaundice are simply observed until it goes away on its own, some babies require blood testing and treatment with phototherapy and special lights. Because so many people are aware of this problem, jaundice rarely gets to a high enough level to cause serious or permanent problems anymore.

CARING FOR SIBLINGS

In some ways, already having children can make having a new baby easier. After all, it's likely that you already feel comfortable holding a small baby and may already know how to change a diaper. You may also have a lot of the clothing and other baby accessories you will need, such as a crib, changing table, and infant carrier. And mom might already be a pro at breastfeeding.

Having other kids at home can also make things much more difficult. New dads might not be able to stay at the hospital with the new baby as much as they would like because they have to be at home to take care of the other kids. And once you bring the baby home, caring for your other children will leave both mom and dad with less time to spend with the new baby.

Another big problem with siblings is the development of jealousy toward the new baby. There are several things you can do to help prevent this kind of jealousy. These include:

- Preparing siblings for the arrival of the new baby throughout the pregnancy

- Making sure they are being cared for by someone they are comfortable with while you are in the hospital
- Having them at the hospital or at least visiting when the baby is born
- Asking other family members to pay a lot of attention to your other children after you bring your baby home
- Having older siblings help you with simple tasks, such as bringing you a diaper or baby wipe
- Spending "special time" alone with your other children each day, even for just a short time

You should also prepare for and accept regressions in your other children's behavior, although things like tantrums or hitting shouldn't be encouraged, even if your children are upset about the new baby. To be safe, you also shouldn't leave your new baby alone with a younger toddler or preschool-age child.

JUST FOR DADS: SUPPORTING A NEW MOM

Once she gets home with her baby, a new mother is likely to be both excited and exhausted. So many things go on in the hospital that it is often hard to fully recover before being discharged. That is one reason why it is important for mom to rest as much as she can while she is in the hospital and make sure she is ready when she does go home.

During those first few days after you bring your baby home from the hospital, it is going to be especially important for you to help out. What you actually do to help is going to vary depending on your situation. If your partner had a long or tough delivery or a C-section and is still recovering, then you may have to do a lot more than you ever expected.

Even with a quick recovery, you should still help, although that doesn't always mean taking care of the baby. It can sometimes be even more helpful to let the baby's mother spend most of her time bonding with the baby and just take over other household chores yourself. You might care for your other children, do the shopping, clean the house, etc. Helping doesn't always have to mean helping with the baby, unless that is what mom needs.

If you are still overwhelmed with all that is going on, try to arrange for extra help in the house from other family members or friends. You can ask friends to babysit your other kids, or maybe bring over ready-to-eat meals at least a few times each week. (Just remember to return the favor when they have a new baby!)

Chapter 4
UNDERSTANDING YOUR NEW BABY

The first few days and weeks with a new baby can be overwhelming for new parents. Especially if this is your first child, there are a lot of things that will be new to you. You may understand that your baby needs to eat, sleep, and have her diaper changed regularly, but what about all of the other things that are going on with her and her body? Learning to understand your new baby should help you to feel more comfortable caring for her.

YOUR BABY'S TEMPERAMENT

Understanding your baby's temperament can help you to understand why she does the things she does. Does she cry every time you change her diaper or when it is time to go to sleep? Is she fussy a lot or slow to adapt to changes in her routine? Or is she the model "easy" baby who rarely cries and always seems happy?

Basically, you can think of your baby's temperament as her personality. It is something she is born with and not something that is easily changed. Instead of trying to change it, you should try to understand it and adapt to it. Is she easily overstimulated or bothered by loud noises? Then try to keep things calm and quiet around her. Does she adapt poorly to changes in her regular routine? Then try to keep things on schedule as much as possible.

Responding to your baby's temperament is harder if your baby is very unpredictable. Fortunately, your baby's early temperament does not always predict how she will be later. Many infants who are difficult early on seem to outgrow this behavior and become more easy and outgoing later in infancy.

Can You Spoil a Baby?

Instinctively, parents often pick up their baby when she is crying, but should you? It depends on who you ask, but the advice to not pick up or hold your baby very often is now considered rather old-fashioned. Realizing this will help you to respond to family members or friends who incorrectly tell you not to hold your baby so much.

So how much holding is too much? Really, no amount of time is too much. Parents who practice "attachment parenting" even advocate that your baby be in close contact with you for most of the time. Instead of worrying about whether you will spoil your baby, you should trust your instincts as a new mother or father and pick her up when it seems right.

Playtime with an Infant

While you should begin playing with your baby now, it is not what you would usually think of as formal play. Your baby is too young to grab things at this age and can't bat at a hanging mobile or other toy. Instead, she will mainly enjoy hearing and seeing things. They can't be just any things, though, because toys that are too loud or that move too quickly will probably upset her.

More simple toys, like a face drawn on a paper plate, a black-and-white mobile, or some other figure with highly contrasting bright colors, might hold her attention briefly. The best way to "play," though, might be just holding your baby close and letting her see her new daddy's or mommy's face and listen to your voice.

YOUR BABY'S BODY

Getting to know and understand your baby's body can help you to feel more comfortable holding, handling, and carrying him. Can you hurt your baby if you are too rough? Of course you can, but babies aren't easily "breakable" if you do things in a gentle and caring manner.

Floppy Heads

Your baby's floppy head is probably one of the most important things to understand about his little body. If you don't support his head and neck when lifting, carrying, or turning him over, you could very easily hurt him. His poor head control and lack of strong neck muscles can cause his head to quickly fall or flop backward. You should continue to use one hand to support your baby's head and neck until he develops better head control in later months.

The Soft Spot

Your baby's soft spot, or fontanel, is one area of his body that you might be trying to avoid. Many new parents worry that if they touch their baby's head, they might push all the way through the soft spot. Although this part of his head isn't protected by bone, it is still fairly tough and is not easy to push through during the regular day-to-day tasks that you do to take care of your baby. So don't become overly worried about the soft spot when you put on your baby's hat, brush or wash his hair, or simply pat his head. Still, there is no reason to directly push on his soft spot.

....

Parenting Pointer

Your baby's soft spot has a very important function. It is where the different plates of your baby's skull come together. Without this type of system, your baby's head would not be able to mold as it comes through the vaginal canal, and his brain would not be able to grow so quickly during his first few years.

....

Your baby's soft spot can also alert you to when he is sick. A sunken fontanel can be a sign of dehydration, and would be something to worry about if your baby also is vomiting, has diarrhea, or isn't eating well. On the other hand, a bulging fontanel can be a sign of raised pressure inside your baby's head. Babies with a bulging fontanel also are likely to be fussy or have a fever. Without any other symptoms, small changes in the fontanel may be normal. It is also normal if you sometimes see the fontanel pulsate in rhythm with your baby's heartbeat.

Umbilical Cord Stump

Your baby's umbilical cord stump is probably going to be another part of his body that you try to avoid. Until it completely falls off by two to three weeks, it might look strange, could smell or bleed, or even have some discharge. A little care and attention is important though, and can help to prevent any more serious problems from developing.

Parenting Pointer

Your baby's umbilical cord stump might need some type of treatment to prevent it from getting infected. Some pediatricians advise using alcohol to prevent infections; others take a hands-off approach. Be sure you understand the instructions you're given.

First, remember to keep his cord dry. That means no real baths until it falls off. Until then, just continue to give him sponge baths when necessary. It can also help if you leave his cord exposed to the air by not letting it be covered by his diaper or clothes.

Advice on cord care is surprisingly controversial. Many experts now advocate "dry cord care," or basically doing nothing at all and simply watching for signs of an infection. Some others still recommend applying alcohol a few times a day. Just don't overdo it, like applying alcohol to your baby's cord with each diaper change, which might be ten to twelve times each day if you are breastfeeding.

Some studies have shown that applying alcohol too frequently can make it take longer for the cord to come off. Whatever method you choose, call your pediatrician if your child does develop an infection of the umbilical cord stump, known as omphalitis. Signs can include a persistent, foul-smelling discharge and redness around his belly button.

Your Baby's Body in Motion

You might be surprised by the way your baby moves during his first few weeks. Instead of smooth, purposeful movements, your baby will normally make quick, jerking movements. A quivering chin and occasional trembling of his hands are also normal.

One sign that a baby's movements are not normal is if he is not moving both of his arms and legs equally. For example, if he consistently doesn't move one arm, that could be a sign of nerve damage or a fractured clavicle (collarbone). Rhythmic movements, like jerking his arm or leg once every second, can be a sign of a seizure. You should call your pediatrician if you notice either of these patterns of movement or if you have any other concerns about the way that your baby moves his body.

Are Girls Different?

Sure, girls are different, but most of the ways that they are different won't become important until much later. When your daughter gets older, you may have to worry about girl clothes, girl issues, and of course, puberty—matters that are of minor concern during her early infancy.

There are a few things that you should be aware of, though, when caring for a baby girl. The first is that it isn't unusual for a newborn baby girl to have a little vaginal discharge. This discharge will be clear or white, will not have a foul odor, and can simply be wiped away. Keep in mind that the discharge can be a little blood-tinged, and that can still be normal. This discharge is caused by the effects of the hormone estrogen that the baby gets from her mother before being born, and the effect usually wears off by the time she is about two weeks old.

The other big thing that you should understand about your little girl is how to clean and change her. When changing diapers, use a fresh diaper wipe or washcloth to also wipe your baby's vaginal area from front to back. That means going from the top of the vaginal area down toward her bottom. If you go the other away, then you may push up bacteria from her bottom into her vaginal area, leading to infections.

And Those Boys . . .

Dads usually have an easier time understanding a baby boy's body, because they are familiar with all of the anatomy. There are a few things that you might find surprising or different, though. One of the most common is that one or both of your baby's testicles might be undescended in early infancy. They usually descend later on their own, although sometimes surgery is required to treat this condition. Be sure to alert your pediatrician if you think your baby's testicles are undescended.

A circumcised dad might also be a little confused if his son is left intact, just as an uncircumcised father can be confused about a circumcised son. Either way, your baby's penis will not need any special care in early infancy, and you can just wash it like you do the rest of his body when you give him a bath.

INFANT REFLEXES

New parents are often more familiar with their baby's reflexes than they think. Although you may not officially be aware of what they are, or know the names of them, these reflexes involve things you probably notice your baby doing every day. For example, you observe the rooting reflex when your baby looks for the breast or a bottle when she is ready to eat and her cheek is stroked.

Why does your baby tightly grab your finger when you put it into her hand? That's the palmar grasp reflex. The plantar grasp reflex causes the baby to turn her foot and curl her toes downward when the sole of her foot is stroked. In addition to being the easiest to recognize, these reflexes also are often the last to disappear. The palmar grasp reflex doesn't usually go away until your baby is five to six months old. And the plantar grasp won't disappear until even later, when your baby is nine to twelve months old.

....

Parenting Pointer

Infants are born with reflexes that help protect them in their environment. For example, the Moro or startle reflex might protect your baby if something suddenly covers her face. The parachute reflex, in which the arms extend if your baby falls forward, can protect her as she learns to walk. And the rooting and sucking reflex can help her to eat.

....

Observing these reflexes and the time at which they go away can help to make sure that your baby is growing and developing normally. Normally, you won't need to test these reflexes on a regular basis. For most parents, it is just a fun thing to notice. Your pediatrician will be checking all of your baby's reflexes at her well-baby exams, and will pay special attention to them if you have any concerns about your baby's development. There are several other reflexes your pediatrician will check that you may also notice as you watch your baby.

Moro or Startle Reflex

This reflex is one of the easiest for parents to recognize. After your pediatrician stimulates this reflex, your baby should throw her arms and legs outward, cry, and then draw them back in. The Moro reflex also can occur if your baby is surprised or startled by a loud noise or if you quickly change her position.

If your baby doesn't have a Moro reflex or only responds with one side of her body or one arm, it can indicate a problem that your pediatrician will want to investigate. The Moro reflex is present at birth and usually goes away by two months.

Tonic Neck Reflex

This is an interesting reflex when you see it. In response to turning her head to one side, this reflex causes a relaxed baby to straighten her arm on that side and bend her other arm. If you then turn her head to the other side, she will reverse the positioning of her hands. The tonic neck reflex usually goes away by five to six months. This is one of the harder reflexes to see, so don't be surprised if you never see your baby getting into this "fencing position."

EARLY SLEEPING PATTERNS

Although your baby is likely to do a lot of crying and eating, the one thing that he should be doing even more of is sleeping. Babies sleep about sixteen and a half hours a day during the first month of life, and may sleep even more during the first few days.

Baby Basics

Your baby may be sleeping too much if he is missing feedings, is difficult to wake up for feedings, or isn't awake at least briefly for some part of the day. Very young infants will not be able to get enough to eat if they don't continue feeding through the night.

To help your baby sleep, you can try swaddling him by wrapping him snugly in a blanket. And always put him to sleep on his back to help reduce the risk of SIDS. Remember that it will be a few weeks or months before your baby gets into a regular pattern of sleeping more at night. Until then, he probably will sleep and eat on regular two- to four-hour cycles.

CRYBABIES

In your first days at home, dealing with a crying baby will likely take up a lot of your time. All babies cry. Infants cry an average of one to four hours a day. Some infants cry more—a lot more—and some cry less. Your baby may do nothing but sleep the first few days after birth and hardly cry at all. Don't congratulate yourself yet. Crying often doesn't really get going until babies are a few weeks old, and usually peaks at six weeks. A baby's cry makes both moms' and dads' heartbeats speed up, blood pressure increase, and palms sweat. It also activates the breasts of nursing mothers, so hearing your baby cry may soak a mom's shirt with milk.

A crying baby is trying to tell you something. She may be trying to communicate that she's hungry, or that she ate too much and her stomach hurts. She may be saying that her diaper is wet and it feels yucky, or that she liked that nice warm wet diaper on her and now that you took it off she's cold—and mad! She may be saying that she's tired and wants you to rock her to sleep, or that she's bored and wants you to samba dance for her entertainment. She may be saying that she's furious that she can't scoot across the carpet and grab the fireplace tools. When you first hold your baby in your arms, you won't understand any of this.

....

Parenting Pointer

Never shake your baby. It won't make the crying stop and can cause permanent paralysis, seizures, blindness, brain damage, or death. Because babies have large heads and weak neck muscles, shaking a baby causes the brain to bounce about in its skull, tearing blood vessels. If you feel overwhelmed, put the baby in a safe place and walk away.

....

Your job is to figure out how to understand your infant's language, because crying is a language. The sooner you figure it out, the sooner you'll spend more time listening to your baby coo and babble and less time listening to her shriek.

What you shouldn't be doing, at this point, is trying to teach your baby patience. In fact, the faster you respond to her cries, the better; it's easier to calm a baby that's just started crying, before it escalates into hysteria.

Translation, Please

While no one has created a baby-cry/English dictionary, the pitch and rhythm of your baby's cry can provide a clue as to where to begin to look for the problem.

- **Tired:** A whimper or somewhat musical cry, it can be irregular, sometimes accompanied by eye or cheek rubbing. You might think he fell asleep because he got so tired from crying. It's more like that he was crying because he was tired.
- **Sharp pain:** A shriek, followed by a long silent pause and another shriek. You'll definitely hear this one when your baby is vaccinated. It can also mean an air bubble is making his stomach hurt, his foot is caught in the bars of the crib, or he is being stabbed by a diaper pin.
- **Hunger:** Short, rhythmic cries that can sound desperate.
- **Pooping:** Starts out as more of a grunt than a cry, often while eating.
- **Too hot, sick, or feverish:** A whiny cry.
- **Anger or frustration:** Your baby may let out screams of outrage when you take a nipple from his mouth or unfasten his diaper, or for no apparent reason.
- **Boredom:** Progresses from gurgling and grumbling to wailing. The crying usually stops instantly when you pick up a bored baby.

BABYWEARING

Babies are meant to be carried. In some cultures babies are carried as much as 90 percent of the time, and they don't cry as much as babies in industrialized countries (who spend more of their time alone). In fact, researchers have confirmed that extra carrying results in dramatic reductions in crying. If you don't want your baby to let out more than a whimper once in a while, don't put him down.

This isn't as onerous as it may seem. With such options as front packs and slings and backpacks for older babies, your child can be "worn" comfortably for hours, leaving your hands free to do other things.

Carrying Power

Here are some suggestions for holds that might calm or soothe your baby. Don't forget to always support a newborn's head and bottom, and keep the baby as snuggled as possible—a baby that suddenly finds himself surrounded by not much but air may startle.

- **Snuggle:** Hold baby facing you, with his head resting on your chest, supporting his head and neck with one hand and his bottom with the other.

Snuggle

- **Football:** Hold baby on one side of your body, supporting his head and neck with your hand and forearm.

Football

- **Knee rest:** With your legs together, put baby face up on thighs, head toward knees, with his legs bent, holding your hands on either side of his body.

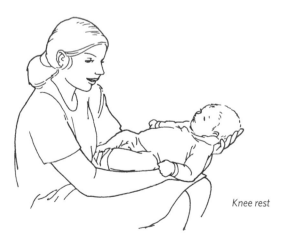

Knee rest

- **Shoulder:** Supporting baby's head and neck, place him so that his head is resting on your shoulder. Support his bottom with your other arm.

Shoulder

SETTLING A FUSSY BABY

Many of the same things that put your baby to sleep when she's tired will soothe her when she's fussy. To create homemade white noise, which soothes lots of babies, turn on the bathroom fan, tune in static on the radio, or run the vacuum cleaner or dishwasher.

Don't be afraid to hand her over to someone else. Your baby will know it if you're getting tired or frustrated, and a fresh pair of arms may solve the problem. If none are available and you're reaching your limit, put her down in a safe place and take a short break. Go into another room and calm down.

Parenting Pointer

When your baby won't stop crying, place her in a front carrier and vacuum. The combination of the warmth of your body, the sound of the vacuum, and the rhythmic motion as you move back and forth across the floor is almost guaranteed to settle her down. (The clean rug is a bonus.)

Even better, if possible, give both of you a breath of fresh air—literally. Put the baby in a front pack and go outside for some exercise. Going for a walk may soothe your baby, and do the same for you. If the weather isn't cooperating, stay inside and dance, holding your baby close, supporting her head (music is optional).

The Basics

Here are some of the basics of soothing your crying baby:

- **Keep it moving:** Rock away in your glider or rocking chair, or just rock back and forth wherever you are, sitting or standing. Dance slowly around the room.
- **Go for a walk:** Walk her in the stroller inside, outside, wherever.
- **Sing or chant:** Soft, rhythmic coos may take your baby's mind off whatever is bothering her. You don't need to have a great voice or know the words, just hum something. If you really hate to sing, turn on the vacuum cleaner. It may not sound like much to you, but that annoying hum is music to some babies' ears.
- **Change the temperature:** If your house seems overly warm and you can't go outside because of the weather, stand in front of the open fridge for a minute or two.

- **Change the scenery:** Give your baby something interesting to look at. A plant, a mobile, or even a brightly patterned tablecloth will be interesting enough to distract her. Describe what you're looking at, and keep talking softly. She'll start to realize that she can't listen and scream at the same time.
- **Get naked:** Babies like skin-to-skin contact—and Dad's warm skin works just as well as Mom's. Kangaroo care, or skin-to-skin contact, is especially helpful for premature babies. It can help stabilize the preterm infant's heartbeat, temperature, and breathing. Lay the baby down on your chest with your arms wrapped around her. Or, if she likes water, take a warm bath together.
- **Get quiet:** Some babies may just need peace and quiet, without toys or distractions. Leave her alone. Put her in a comfortable position in her crib or on a blanket on the floor, turn down the lights, and keep the noise down.

More Soothing Options

You've picked your baby up, offered to feed him, burped him, changed his diaper, wrapped him in a blanket, and taken the blanket off again—and he's still crying. You can't figure out why, and he may have forgotten why. When you just want him to stop, it's time to try these all-purpose soothers.

Rock-a-Bye Baby

As old-fashioned as it sounds, a rocker or glider can be your best friend when trying to soothe a crying baby. The gentle rhythmic movement mimics the sensations your baby experienced in the womb. Your scent and warmth combined with the connection you share as you hold your baby and rock are calming and soothing. For parents, it's simply a relief to get off your feet and sit down.

Rockers have been around for centuries and rock on curved runners. The more modern rocker-glider has wooden arms under the seat that pivot front-to-back on steel ball bearings (which makes for an effortless, smooth, noiseless, horizontal gliding motion). Often you can purchase a matching ottoman.

Pacify Me

Babies like to suck and are calmed and comforted by sucking. You'll hear lots of pros and cons about pacifiers, called binkies by some parents. Almost every parent (and grandparent) has an opinion, but the American Academy of Pediatrics approves the use of pacifiers for baby's first year. Here are some points to remember before introducing a binky.

- Avoid introducing a pacifier during the first month of breastfeeding as it can lead to nipple confusion.
- Use a one-piece, dishwasher safe pacifier. Two-piece units pose a choking hazard.
- Buy extras of whatever kind your baby prefers, and replace a pacifier as soon as it begins to deteriorate.
- Don't overuse pacifiers. Try other means of soothing your baby (e.g., rocking or a new position).

Swaddling

In their first few weeks, some babies feel more secure, and are less likely to fuss, when wrapped snugly. Swaddling him will contain the flailing arms and legs, which may be startling the baby, and the heat from a slightly dryer-warmed blanket will calm him down. (Other babies hate this and will quickly let you know.) If your baby likes to be swaddled, see the following images to learn how to do it.

1. Position a square blanket like a diamond, and fold the top corner down.

Set-up

2. Lay your baby on his back on the blanket, the top corner just above his neck. Tuck one arm down and fold the blanket around his body and behind his back.

First wrap

3. Fold up the bottom part of the blanket, folding down any excess that would be covering his face.

Second wrap

4. Tuck the other arm down and fold the remaining corner of the blanket around his body and behind his back.

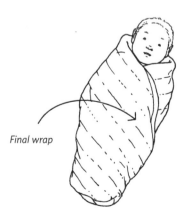

Final wrap

You can also buy pre-made swaddling gear such as Miracle Blanket (*www.miracleblanket.com*) and Aden + Anais muslin swaddling cloths (*www.adenandanais.com*).

COULD IT BE COLIC?

Then there are the cries that seem to have no rational cause and don't respond to soothing for very long. This may mean a baby is venting at the end of a long day, but if the crying goes on for hours every day, at roughly the same time, several days a week, then you can feel justified in calling it colic. Some pediatricians use the Rule of Three to diagnose colic: crying for no apparent physical reason for three hours a day, three days a week, for three weeks. By this definition, one out of five babies has colic.

···

Parenting Pointer

Get help if you have a colicky baby. Incessant screaming can be overwhelming; make sure you have some time for yourself—for everyone's sake.

···

In spite of trying for more than fifty years, doctors haven't pinpointed the cause of colic. Historically, it is believed to be some kind of abdominal pain (the word "colic" is derived from *kolon,* which is Greek for "large intestine"), but even that's not certain.

Colic may be caused by an immature digestive system that spasms rather than uses smooth muscle contractions. Or it may be that certain babies just notice the workings of their digestive system more. Some researchers have suggested that it may be an allergic reaction to something in the mother's diet—cow's milk in particular. This theory is controversial, as colicky babies don't have any symptoms of the stomach problems associated with such an allergy, like diarrhea or vomiting. Colic may be the reaction of a baby worn out by trying to make sense of a busy day. Or colic may simply be the ordinary crying of a particularly strong-willed and persistent baby.

Colic Remedies

Since no one really knows what colic is, no one really knows how to fix it. You can try laying him face-down with his stomach over a small roll of towels or a slightly warm (comfortable to the touch) hot-water bottle. Here are some other suggestions.

- **Motion:** Rocking, riding in a stroller or a car, swinging in a baby swing (or even a car seat swung back and forth), dancing, bicycling his legs.
- **Medication:** Simethicone is an over-the-counter remedy that is given to the baby in the form of drops and breaks down gas bubbles (brand names include Mylicon and Mylanta). While commonly used, evidence does not support its efficacy in treating colic.
- **Dietary changes:** Ask your doctor if you should eliminate dairy products from your diet if you're nursing, or switch to a soy formula if you're bottle-feeding. The connection between cow's milk and colic is anecdotal at best, but some mothers have had success with this.

Get Help!

In spite of reports that all of these strategies work for some babies some of the time, odds are if your baby is truly colicky none of this will help much and you'll just have to wait it out.

Colic is tough. When your baby first starts crying, you may be calm, soothingly saying, "Oh my poor sweetie, let's change your diaper and see if that helps." By the third hour you'll feel like shouting, "WHAT? WHAT IS IT? TELL ME WHAT'S WRONG SO I CAN FIX IT!"

The point is to keep trying (and enlisting your partner, your relatives, and your friends to help). Hold your baby, rock your baby, dance with your baby, or just sit and pat him—do anything that seems to help him calm down, even a little. It may seem pointless but you will know you're trying, and maybe your baby will know, too.

You may be surprised what works. One mother discovered it was the sound of the hairdryer that was the answer (sound, not heat). What works for one baby may not work for the next, but take the peace and quiet where you can get it.

PART 2

FEEDING

Chapter 5

BREAST AND BOTTLE FEEDING

According to the U.S. Centers for Disease Control and Prevention, 75 percent of new mothers gave breastfeeding a try in 2010, and 50 percent of babies were still breastfeeding at six months old. But breastfeeding isn't for everyone. Parenting is much more than any one decision, and bottle-fed babies thrive like their breastfed counterparts. This chapter gives you the information you need to successfully feed your baby, whether via breast or bottle.

BENEFITS FOR BABY AND MOM

Human milk is designed as the perfect food for infants. It contains elements that researchers are only beginning to discover. Over time, breastmilk changes from the colostrum produced in the first few days—which provides babies with antibodies to protect them from the germs they are encountering—to a blend of colostrum and milk, and eventually to pure milk. Milk then adjusts in subtle ways as the baby matures, even changing during the course of a feeding. A nursing baby first receives milk with a lower fat content; as she continues to feed, the fat content of the milk that follows increases.

The American Academy of Pediatrics recommends that:

- Mothers breastfeed for at least the first twelve months of life and as long after as is mutually desired.
- Babies breastfeed exclusively for the first six months of life.
- Newborns nurse whenever they show signs of hunger.
- No supplements—including water or formula—should be given to breastfeeding newborns unless there is a medical indication.

Breastmilk is powerful stuff. It can kill bacteria, viruses, and intestinal parasites, and can even stop the growth of cancer cells. Breastfed babies develop fewer allergies and have a lower risk of developing diabetes.

For the mom, breastfeeding releases oxytocin from your pituitary gland. This produces uterine contractions that help your uterus return to its nonpregnant size (thereby reducing the risk of postpartum hemorrhage). Nursing also burns calories, which will help you lose those pregnancy pounds. Prolactin, the hormone that produces milk, induces calm, so nursing may help you cope through the crazy first months of parenting. Finally, breastfeeding reduces your risk of developing breast, ovarian, cervical, and endometrial cancers.

You can probably still breastfeed even if you require certain prescription medications for your own health. Most medications enter breastmilk in small amounts that won't affect a nursing baby. But it is vitally important that you discuss with your doctor all drugs you currently take (including over-the-counter medications and herbal supplements) before you begin breastfeeding, as well as check on the safety of any new drug prescribed for you.

There are other good reasons to breastfeed your baby:

- **Breastfeeding is easy—for some moms.** Most mothers discover this after the initial awkwardness, while others may find the first few weeks of figuring out how to breastfeed correctly are a struggle. But, hey, it took you at least that long to learn to ride a bicycle, and aren't you glad you did? In the long run, breastfeeding will make your life much easier, just like that bicycle. When your breastfed baby is hungry, you pick him up, unsnap your nursing bra, and dinner is served. Once you get the hang of it, you'll probably manage to have a free hand—until it's time to unsnap the other side of your bra. You can read, dial a telephone, or even shop online while your baby nurses in a sling.
- **Breastfeeding keeps you free during feeding times.** When your bottle-fed baby is hungry, you have to check the refrigerator or the diaper bag and hope you find a prepared bottle, then warm it up while trying to distract your hungry and increasingly agitated baby. And bottle-feeding is a two-handed operation; you can't do much else while you're holding both the baby and the bottle.

- **Breastmilk is easier to digest than formula.** Breastfed babies rarely get diarrhea or constipation and their dirty diapers don't stink. There is an odor, but not a particularly bad one. In fact, the stuff looks and kind of smells like Dijon mustard.
- **Breastfeeding is significantly cheaper than formula.** In addition to the health and nutrition benefits of breastfeeding, there are also the perks of simplicity and cost savings. Breastfeeding babies are portable; you can take them anywhere for any amount of time without worrying about how long you can keep a bag of bottles cold or where you can find clean water to mix with powdered formula.
- **Breastfeeding is environmentally responsible.** You don't have packaging, cans, or containers to throw out.
- **If you're small-breasted, you may finally be able to wear clothes that require cleavage.** In addition to this temporary (and free!) bust enhancement, women with small breasts who choose to breastfeed have a special advantage. They can easily breastfeed with one hand (or no hands, after a little practice), since they don't have to support the breast or a bottle, just the baby.

THE FIRST FEEDING

If your baby is doing fine and you had a vaginal delivery, you can try to nurse him right away if you're up for it, but don't feel like you have to. Waiting until you both get your bearings is fine. Don't sweat it if you're ready and your baby isn't. There really is no rush. You'll both probably need a nap in the hours following the birth, after which you'll both wake up ready to tackle this new experience.

Get Organized

You'll probably want to start with the cradle hold or football hold (diagrammed shortly). Sit up in bed, rearrange your hospital gown, and settle a pillow on your lap. Make sure your back and elbows are supported; you may need more pillows.

Above all, get comfortable. If you have large breasts, tuck a rolled-up washcloth or towel under the breast you intend to nurse with to help support it. Then ask the nurse or your partner to hand you the baby.

Step-by-Step

Unwrap your baby and pull up his T-shirt, if he's wearing one. You want skin to touch skin. Rotate your baby to face your breast, supporting his head. Then, with the opposite hand, form a C with your thumb and forefinger and cup beneath your breast. Bring the baby close to your breast (don't lean down to the baby— that's a sure path to back pain), and lift up your nipple making sure that your hand doesn't cover the areola (the darker skin around the nipple). Tickle the baby's lips with the tip of your nipple. Wait until he opens really wide and then, bringing his head to your breast, shove your breast in as far as it will go. If you weren't quick enough, your baby may have only the nipple in his mouth. Use your finger to break the suction, take him off the breast, and try again.

Once he's on, check his position. His mouth should be covering at least a third of the areola and you should hear sucks and swallows. Don't fuss about whether his nose seems to be covered by the breast—he'll move if he can't breathe. Switch sides when you think your baby has drained the first breast; you won't hear swallowing anymore, or see his jaws or cheeks working. This may take as few as five minutes or more than twenty. Take a burp break when you switch breasts.

Breastfeeding Positions

Cradle hold

*Cross-cradle hold
(opposite arm)*

Football hold

Side-lying hold

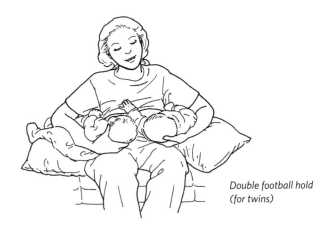

*Double football hold
(for twins)*

Burping

It is okay if your baby doesn't burp after each and every feeding, as long as it seems that she is otherwise doing well. However, if your baby seems more fussy or spits up more after feedings when she doesn't burp, you should keep trying.

The most common way to burp a baby is to simply place your baby against your shoulder and gently pat her back until she burps. Be sure to place a burp rag on your shoulder or you might get covered in spit-up. You could also try burping your baby as she sits on your lap. With this method, you lean the baby slightly forward and support the front of her chest, neck, and head with one hand while you pat her back with the other. If neither of these positions work for you, you could also burp her on your lap while she is lying on her stomach.

If you aren't able to get a burp, you might change positions and try again. You should also try to figure out if it works better to burp your baby at the end of the feeding, or to take a break to do it after several minutes of feeding.

Shoulder (high over the shoulder)

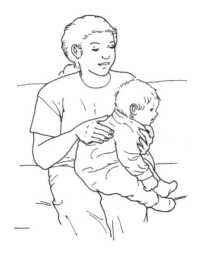

Lap (sitting upright)   *Knees (tummy down)*

Establishing a Good Milk Supply

At the first feeding, and over the next few days, your baby will be receiving colostrum, a yellowish fluid. Colostrum is full of antibodies and will protect your baby from a host of viruses and infections. It also acts as a laxative that flushes out the meconium—the black, tar-like waste accumulated in the baby's system before birth.

Nurse your baby on both breasts, and do a minimum of eight times a day for at least the first week. It will take a few days for your milk to come in, so don't worry if you don't seem to have any milk yet. Frequent nursing at this point is intended to establish a good milk supply.

TROUBLESHOOTING

Breastfeeding is not always easy. While you're both still learning, there are several things you can do to keep things going smoothly:

- Get comfortable.
- Bring the baby to your breast, instead of moving yourself to the baby.
- Make sure the baby is latched on correctly. She should have the areola in her mouth, not just the nipple. If it hurts, it's wrong.
- Make sure your baby's head is tipped slightly back and her chin is pressed into your breast. It is the movements of her chin and tongue that draw out the milk.
- Keep your wrist straight. Flexing the wrist supporting your baby's head may tip her down into a less efficient nursing position, and the strain on your wrist may cause inflammation and pain.
- Nurse at least eight times a day for the first few weeks—as often as once every two hours, or more if the baby is hungry.
- Don't watch the clock; let your baby tell you when she's done.
- Vary your nursing position. The baby will press on your breasts differently depending on how she is positioned.
- Use your finger to break the suction before taking your baby off your nipple. Pulling her off will hurt.
- Have a drink of milk, water, or juice. When your baby is drinking, you should be, too.
- Don't forget to burp your baby. Most babies swallow a little air along with the milk, and this trapped air can cause stomach pains. Try burping when you switch sides and after breastfeeding, but don't worry if your baby doesn't burp; some just don't.

Ask for Help

If you're feeling insecure, aren't sure if the baby is sucking correctly, or feel uncomfortable in any way, get some expert advice. The maternity nurses may be able to help you, as well as your child's pediatrician. You might also want to talk to a lactation consultant who is trained to help you learn how to breastfeed. Many hospitals have lactation consultants on staff (often OB/GYN nurses will also get this specialized training). If your hospital doesn't have a lactation consultant available, contact the La Leche League (*www.lalecheleague.org* or 1-800-laleche) for help or for a referral to a consultant in your area.

BREASTFEEDING POST-CESAREAN

Breastfeeding after a cesarean is more difficult, but well worth the effort. The postpartum benefits are the same as for the mother who delivered vaginally: early bonding with your baby and the release of oxytocin to help the uterus contract for the mother, and the immunological benefits of colostrum for the baby.

Depending upon what kind of anesthesia you had for your C-section, you may need a little extra time before you physically feel able to hold and nurse your baby. If you had an epidural you'll be awake and alert sooner than if you had general anesthesia. Once you are fully conscious and feel physically able to hold your baby, you can begin nursing. Ask your partner or a nurse to stay with you when you first start breastfeeding, in case you need help or get tired and need to hand the baby to someone else.

Your baby may be a little drowsier and lethargic, especially if you have had anesthetics for a prolonged period (e.g., you labored with an epidural for hours before the cesarean). You will need to encourage and stimulate him so he stays alert during breastfeeding. Rub his back, change his diaper, talk to him, and try to make eye contact. The anesthesia will be out of his system within a day or two.

Don't be a martyr about pain relief. You have had major surgery and will need some pain medication in the first few days. You will also probably be taking some antibiotics to avoid infection, so take only those medications prescribed by your doctor. While these drugs do pass in very small amounts into your milk, they will not harm your baby.

Finding a comfortable breastfeeding position after surgery is a little more difficult, but through trial and error you will find what works for you and your baby. The side-lying position is often preferred in the first few days after surgery. Turn slowly on your side and put a rolled-up towel next to your incision (in case the baby kicks). A nurse or your partner should place the baby on his side next to you, chest-to-chest, directly facing your breast. You will need help to roll over when you want the baby to nurse on the other breast. The football hold is less comfortable immediately after surgery, but is often preferred a few days later. Rest the baby on a pillow, over your incision, and hold him along the side. Whatever position you use, remember: Always be sure that the baby opens wide and latches on correctly to avoid sore nipples and ineffective milk transfer.

Some hospitals require, as a precaution, that all C-section babies be transferred for observation to the NICU immediately after birth. Healthy babies are usually reunited with their mothers within a few hours, if not sooner, and you can initiate breastfeeding then. Should your baby need to stay in the NICU longer for observation or treatment, ask about the availability of electric breast pumps and start pumping as soon as possible. This, along with pumping every couple of hours, will help stimulate your milk supply, prevent engorgement, and provide the valuable colostrum for your baby which can be fed to him in the nursery until he is able to breastfeed.

MILK'S HERE

When your milk comes in—two to four days after birth—and replaces the colostrum, you will know it. Your normally squishy breasts will get bigger than you ever imagined possible and may seem as hard as rocks. For some women, this transition from colostrum to milk can be rough, but at least it doesn't last long (typically just a day). You may feel like you are going from a size C to a size ZZ.

Fetch your baby and start nursing because the longer you wait, the more your breasts will hurt. If your breasts are too hard for your baby to latch on to, put a warm washcloth on them for a few minutes or take a shower. You can also massage your milk glands toward your nipple and squeeze out a little milk. If you are still uncomfortable after your baby nurses, put ice on your breasts for a few minutes, or tuck a cold cabbage leaf into your bra. While this may seem like odd advice, cabbage, possibly because of its sulfur content, draws out the excess fluid to reduce swelling and the cold feels good.

Baby Basics

Rest assured, your baby is eating enough if: he nurses eight to ten times a day; he has six to eight wet diapers a day after the first week; his poop resembles Dijon mustard mixed with cottage cheese by the fifth day; he seems healthy and alert; he gains weight after the first week; and your breasts feel full before each feeding and softer afterward.

Now when your baby begins to feed, you may feel a tingling or burning sensation a moment before milk begins to leak from your breasts. This is the let-down reflex, caused by the release of oxytocin, the hormone that triggers contractions in the muscles surrounding the milk-producing cells to squeeze the milk into the milk ducts. (You don't need to be feeding a baby to trigger this reflex. It can happen during sex, when you see a picture of a baby, if you hear a baby cry, and sometimes for no apparent reason.) If you don't feel it, you'll still know milk is flowing because your baby will start gulping. (He may also pull away for a moment if the milk is spraying too fast.)

GEARING UP

The nice thing about breastfeeding is you really don't need anything but your baby and your body. But it can be even nicer if you have:

- Lots of pillows to tuck around you.
- A nursing pillow. There are several types: a wedge that sits on your lap; a wide, partial ring for your waist (great for football holds or nursing twins); and the Brest Friend, which is a smaller ring with a back support.
- A nursing stool. This low stool lifts your legs just enough to ease the strain on your lower back.
- Cloth diapers, and lots of them, to catch messy burps and drool.
- An electric pump. The popular Medela Pump In Style is usually powerful enough, but rent a hospital-grade pump if you need more suction.
- A sling. Great for nursing while on the run.

BREASTFEEDING FASHIONS

Just because you are nursing doesn't mean that you can't look good. Breastfeeding fashions have moved into the twenty-first century. You can find sleek, comfortable clothes, including professional outfits for when you return to work but want to continue pumping. In the haze of those early weeks, look for comfort and easy access in whatever you wear.

- **Bras:** You will probably have more cleavage than usual, so you'll need comfortable nursing bras that offer good support. You may find the snap-front styles easier to manage than those with hooks. Avoid tight or underwire bras.
- **Casual wear:** Look for washable button-front shirts and T-shirts for easy nursing access. You can always drape a baby blanket for discreet breastfeeding in public.
- **A nursing dress:** You may eventually get sick of untucked shirts, so one official nursing dress, with its discreetly hidden slits, is nice to have.
- **Breast pads and shells:** To absorb milk leakage, tuck some cotton or flannel breast pads into your bra. Especially in the early weeks, when your milk lets down as your baby sucks on your breast, you'll want

something to absorb the leaking from the other breast. Breast shells are made from silicone and tuck into your bra and are especially helpful in the first weeks. They keep your nipples protruding which relieves engorgement and makes it easier for your baby to latch on. Any dripping milk collects in the shell, and you can freeze it for future use.

MAINTAINING YOUR MILK SUPPLY

You will have more success breastfeeding—barring a medical situation—if you get plenty of rest, surrender to your baby, and are surrounded by people who support you. Don't be discouraged by friends or relatives who are uncomfortable at the sight of you breastfeeding, or keep questioning your ability to feed your baby. If your baby wants to nurse every hour or two, let her. Her stomach will eventually get bigger, she'll become strong enough to feed more efficiently, and the time between feedings will increase.

If you are concerned about your milk supply, take more naps and make sure you are eating and drinking enough. Let your baby feed more frequently (if she's using a pacifier, you might want to take it away for a while) and consult your doctor or a lactation specialist.

BREASTFEEDING HILLS AND VALLEYS

Think back to when you first learned to ride a bike. You might have been riding along just fine for weeks, but then you varied your route and encountered your first hill. For breastfeeding moms, there are a few hills in the early weeks. Some, like the growth spurt and occasional leaking, will be faced by most. Others, like a breast infection, are rarer. Whatever the challenge, most can be mastered with determination and perseverance.

The Growth Spurt

It's almost noon. You've been up with your baby since 5 A.M., and you haven't yet taken a shower or gotten dressed because twenty minutes after he finished nursing, he wanted to nurse again. Clearly, you think, your baby is starving. You wonder if you should start supplemental bottles of formula. The answer is no, because this is a growth spurt.

Parenting Pointer

Growth spurts are typical at two weeks, six weeks, three months, and six months, but they can sneak up at any time. Your baby's seemingly endless appetite will let you know when another one has arrived.

Your baby has suddenly jumped up to a higher nutritional requirement level, and will nurse to increase your milk supply—which is exactly as nature intended. You may have a rough day or so, but very quickly your baby's hunger and your milk supply will be back in synch and feeding times will be back to normal.

Expect days when you do nothing but nurse. Console yourself with the fact that you are actually accomplishing a lot—building up your milk supply—and don't go running for a bottle.

Leaking

Leaking is most common in the early weeks of nursing, but can happen at any time, particularly when you're accustomed to nursing your baby at fairly regular intervals but get delayed. While leaking itself isn't a problem, the round wet spot on your shirt can be. To avoid or minimize this, wear print shirts, use breast pads or a thick cotton bra, and press against your breasts with your forearm when you begin to feel the tingle that signals a let-down.

Ouch! (Sore Nipples)

Sore nipples are typically caused by incorrect positioning or improper latch-on. To resolve a case of sore nipples, make sure your baby is latching properly. Then you can:

- Air-dry your nipples after each time you nurse. You can also make sure your nipples get air by using a breast shield. For a homemade solution, cut off the handles of two tea strainers (preferably plastic) and place them over your nipples, inside your bra.
- Catch some rays. Find a private sunny spot, or carefully use a sun lamp, and expose your nipples for three minutes several times a day.
- Express a little breastmilk and dab it on your nipples. Breastmilk has a number of healing properties—take advantage of them.
- Make a cup of tea, then save the tea bag. Place the tea bag (at room temperature) on your sore nipple for a few minutes.
- Soothe them with lotion. Rub on lanolin (check that it has been treated to remove any pesticide residues), olive oil, or aloe vera gel. Wash your nipples and pat dry before breastfeeding.
- Apply ice before nursing. Ice acts as a painkiller and helps bring out your nipples for a better latch-on.
- Take a break. Spend a day nursing on only one side to give the other nipple a chance to recover. Either hand express or pump the resting breast as often as you would nurse.

Clogged Milk Duct

A clogged milk duct is fairly obvious—you feel a small lump in your breast, and it can be painful. (The lump can be anywhere in the ducts, which run all over.) To treat it, put a warm washcloth over it for five minutes, then massage the lump gently, pushing the milk down toward your nipple. Then start nursing your baby, making sure the baby is positioned so she faces the clogged duct, and continue massaging. The more you nurse, the faster the clogged duct will drain.

Breast Infections (Mastitis)

Breast infections are serious. If you have flu-like symptoms, a low fever, red streaks or patches on the breast skin, pain in your breast, or a hard lump in your breast, you may have one. Check with your health care provider. She may prescribe antibiotics (which won't hurt your baby). She will also tell you to go to bed, drink lots of fluid, apply warm compresses on the infected side, and continue to nurse on the infected side.

Absolutely do not stop nursing as that will only make the infection worse. Do not delay treatment of a breast infection since untreated infections can abscess and require surgery.

Thrush

Also called a yeast infection, thrush may present with cracked nipples that burn the entire time your baby nurses. Your baby may also develop thrush in her mouth (white patches) and diaper area (rash). Talk to your health care provider for a definite diagnosis. To control thrush, make sure your nipples and everything that touches them are clean, use a nipple wash (one teaspoon of vinegar in one cup of water), or nystatin cream (a prescription drug) that stops yeast from reproducing.

No Let-Down Reflex

Some women have trouble breastfeeding at first because they aren't experiencing a let-down. In fact, some women who give up breastfeeding because they think they don't have enough milk actually have plenty of milk; they just don't have a let-down reflex. Without the let-down reflex the baby gets a trickle of milk, enough to sip but not gulp. Stress is the biggest inhibitor of the let-down reflex, so anything that can reduce stress helps, such as a warm bath or listening to music. There are also prescription medications that can jump-start a let-down, including Reglan, a prescription anti-nausea drug that can increase milk supply. It's vital that you discuss the issue with your doctor, as Reglan should not be taken by anyone with a history of depression.

Milk Flow That Is Too Fast

Milk coming too fast may make your baby gulp, choke, or pull away. You may want to express a little milk first. Try nursing from just one breast at each feeding (you may have to pump the other one between feedings if you're uncomfortable). Try leaning back in a recliner or on pillows while nursing, positioning your baby so the top of her head is above the top of your breast, so she can sip at the milk without it pouring down her throat.

Flat or Inverted Nipples

If your nipples don't protrude when you're aroused—or in a cold breeze—you may have what the breastfeeding books define as inverted nipples. To check, squeeze the areola at the bottom of the nipple and press it toward your chest. If your nipple doesn't protrude, it is flat. Truly inverted nipples can prevent successful breastfeeding, but most will respond to treatment—manually rolling your nipples several times a day, wearing a breast shield inside your bra that presses the areola and encourages the nipple to protrude, or pumping with a heavy-duty pump.

BABY'S BREASTFEEDING QUIRKS

Your baby will develop his own breastfeeding habits that may create problems for you. Here's how to handle these issues.

Breast Favoritism

Most babies will prefer one breast to the other. It may be because of the way you support the baby with your stronger arm, or the fact that one breast produces more milk, or that the baby simply prefers to lie on one side instead of the other. To avoid having the less-desired breast go completely into retirement (and make you look lopsided for the duration of breastfeeding), start each feeding with the breast that is out of favor. Your baby may be less likely to be picky when he's really hungry.

Rejection

You can feel pretty insulted when your baby pulls off and cries after nursing for a few minutes and refuses to latch on again. The key to ending rejection is finding the cause. The most common source of rejection is a flood of milk—too much for your baby to handle. If you suspect this is the problem, express or pump a little milk before you nurse. If that doesn't fix it, your baby may be teething, have a cold or earache, hate your new deodorant, or have found that something you ate changed the taste of the milk. It may be as simple as the weather—on a hot day your baby may not want to snuggle against your warm body—or a developmental spurt—your baby suddenly has noticed the world around him. If you can't figure out the cause, hang in there; hunger will eventually prevail. In the meantime, pump so that you maintain your milk supply.

Biting

Most breastfeeding moms get bitten at least once when the first teeth come in. They typically let out a yell, startle their baby into tears, and then feel horrible about scaring their child. The baby, however, doesn't try that again for quite a while. If you have a biter, use your finger to take the baby off of your breast, say "No" distinctly and calmly, and hold him off for a few seconds before letting him suck again. This usually works after a few bites.

CALL A DOCTOR IF . . .

Below are signs that you should check with your doctor about your baby or yourself. Remember: Check with your health care provider if you have a question, whether it's a sign on this list or not. Odds are that everything is fine, but trust your instincts and don't hesitate to ask.

- Your baby hasn't had a wet diaper in twenty-four hours.
- It is the fourth day after the birth and you see no evidence of white-colored milk (in leakage from your breast or spit from the baby).
- Your baby has no bowel movements on the fourth day after the birth.

- Your baby cannot latch on to a breast.
- Your baby is lethargic and is difficult to wake for feedings.
- Your baby latches on readily but feeds for only a minute or two and then appears to doze off.
- Your baby feeds endlessly, for an hour at a time, and doesn't seem satisfied, then sleeps for less than an hour before crying for another feeding.
- Your breasts are painfully hard and swollen (full and firm is fine, hard and painful is not).
- Your nipples hurt during the entire feeding, not just for a moment at latch-on, and you find yourself dreading feedings or shortening them because of the pain.

Parenting Pointer

If you need to nurse in public, know that mothers have a right to breastfeed wherever they have the right to be with their baby, whether or not there is specific legislation in a state. However, many states have passed legislation explicitly clarifying this right, and, in some cases, have set fines for people who try to interfere. Try to be proactive—don't wait until your baby is crying with hunger. Rather, pick your place and time before your baby is starving. Drape a lightweight baby blanket over your infant or use a nursing cover so you can have privacy while you get him latched on to your breast.

THE JOY OF PUMPING

Having a supply of pumped breastmilk on hand may be a good idea. Even if you rarely give your baby a bottle, at least he will recognize what's inside of it. However, if you don't have a reason to pump—for instance, no plan to go back to work or to attend an event to which you can't bring your baby—and you don't want to, then don't force it on yourself. You should, however, plan on bringing your baby with you whenever you go out for more than a few hours until he's eating solids, about six months old.

If you do decide to pump, get the most powerful pump you can. Some women with hair-trigger let-downs can use a hand pump or even express milk without a pump, but you'll have a better chance of success with a hospital-grade pump. Portable briefcase-style electric pumps aren't bad but are not quite as strong as the less stylish ones. You may want to rent a pump before investing in one.

Getting Started

Wait until your baby is at least four weeks old and, hopefully, settled into a regular nursing schedule. Pick a time at least an hour after he's nursed and an hour before you expect him to nurse again (or a time when there is something on TV that you like, since it's hard to pump and do much else but sit) and try to pump at the same time every day. If your baby for some reason cuts a feeding short, pump out the remainder. If you experience a let-down during a free moment, grab the pump and take advantage of it.

Use clean pump equipment and bottles (wash with hot soapy water and air-dry on a clean towel or run through the dishwasher). Wash your hands, get comfortable, and then do whatever best produces a let-down. This may be music, silence, or looking at a picture of your baby.

When you start to pump, unless your baby has just nursed, you'll probably get very little milk until your milk lets down. You should then pump until the milk flow stops. (For the first week don't expect to get much milk; your body has to adjust to producing extra for your pumping sessions.) Start on the minimum setting, and dial the pressure up until you're getting milk. If you're using a single pump, pump for five minutes on each side, alternating for as long as you are producing milk. Or use an adapter that lets you pump both breasts at once—after all, you really don't want a pumping session to last longer than it has to.

Storing Breastmilk

Store milk in breastmilk storage bags (available online and at major retailers) in 2-ounce and 4-ounce portions (single feeding amounts). The smaller portions are easier to defrost. Label the bags with the date and amount.

Breastmilk can be stored in the refrigerator for up to seventy-two hours. You can freeze breastmilk, but safe storage depends on the temperature of your freezer and where you store the milk. According to the La Leche League you can store breastmilk in:

- Freezers located inside a refrigerator: two weeks.
- Separate door refrigerator/freezer: three or four months (temperature varies because you open the door frequently).
- Separate deep freeze at constant -19°C (0°F): six months or longer.

Defrosted milk can be kept for up to twenty-four hours in the refrigerator (but should not be refrozen) and can be safely kept at room temperature for six to ten hours, depending on how cool your room is.

When you're ready to use the frozen milk, defrost it in warm running water. Don't use hot water, or you'll compromise the milk's immune-boosting effect. Shake it up, as the fat will have risen to the top. If you feed the baby unshaken milk, he'll get all cream, will get full, and may not get enough overall fluid.

BREASTFEEDING AFTER MOM GOES BACK TO WORK

You don't have to stop breastfeeding your baby when you return to work. You can continue to provide him with your milk by pumping and freezing it, so it can be defrosted and fed to him during your work hours. Start to build up a supply of breastmilk in your freezer a month before you return to work, and, if necessary, obtain equipment that you can use to pump at the office.

Workplace Logistics

Before you return to work (perhaps before you go on maternity leave), talk to your employer and your coworkers about your intention to breastfeed. If you have on-site daycare or your caregiver can bring the baby to you, try to schedule at least one nursing session. If that's not possible you'll want to pump when you would normally feed your baby. You need to know when, where, and how often you can pump. You may need to adapt your schedule so that you can include pumping sessions. With a good pump and practice, you will only need about fifteen minutes to pump both breasts.

Ideally, the room you use for pumping will have privacy, a chair, and electrical outlets. You'll also need a refrigerator for storing your milk (a small, bar-sized one will do). If there is no refrigerator available, many breast pump carrying cases also come with built-in, cooler-type compartments that stay cold enough to store your pumped milk until you can get home.

If you don't have a private office, ask if there is a conference room or another space you can use. Sitting on a toilet seat in the restroom is not a reasonable option. Point out to your employer that you will be able to pump more efficiently if you are in a space that is comfortable and private. Some mothers, when faced with no better option than a restroom, have chosen to pump in their cars during their breaks.

Pump It Up

To effectively return to work and pump several times a day, you'll need to invest in or rent an electric breast pump that expresses breastmilk from both breasts at once. These cost between $200 and $300, or can be rented for between $30 and $60 a month. You can also purchase car AC adapters, built-in milk coolers, travel cases, and hands-free kits. It may be worth the investment, especially if you plan to have more than one child.

BOTTLE FEEDING

When you begin bottle-feeding, you have a number of somewhat confusing options. Whether it's equipment or formulas, prepare yourself for a trial (and error) period as you figure out what you and your baby like best. If you have decided to bottle-feed your baby, ignore the comments and guilt that breastfeeding proponents will try and heap upon you. You've got enough on your plate that you don't need to waste time worrying about the breastfeeding police. Refuse to second-guess yourself. Your child will give you plenty of other things to stew about, so save your energy.

Choosing Equipment

You'll probably want to "test drive" some bottles and nipples to find the right ones for your baby. Here are some options.

Bottles

The three types of bottles (glass, plain plastic, and plastic with disposable liners) come in two sizes: small (four ounces) and large (eight or nine ounces).

That's where the simplicity ends. Since each manufacturer tries to distinguish itself from the others, there are hordes of variations within each category. You will find short, fat bottles and long, thin ones. There are bottles with a bend in the middle and bottles with handles.

The general idea behind all these bottle designs is to make it harder for air to get into the baby. Bottles with liners collapse as the baby sucks. The bottles with the bend are intended to be easier to hold at just the right air-bubble-preventing angle, but they're harder to clean. Except for your convenience and your baby's preference, the bottle you choose doesn't matter all that much.

Parenting Pointer

Buy more bottles and nipples than you think you need. You'll end up scrubbing bottles all day if you don't have enough.

Of greater concern is whether your bottle is manufactured with Bisphenol A (BPA), a chemical used to create the plastic called polycarbonate. BPA is an artificial estrogen and has been previously used by most major U.S. baby bottle manufacturers in their production. It's also found in many food storage containers and toys. There has been a growing dispute over the safety of BPA, with some studies showing that even low levels of BPA are harmful to animals and people and may increase your risk of cancer, diabetes, obesity, and early puberty.

To be safe, don't use bottles manufactured with BPA. There are plenty of BPA-free bottles on the market you can use. For an excellent overview of the issue, check out the Smart Plastics Guide at *www.iatp.org/documents/smart-plastics-guide-0* . For an update on which bottles (and sippy cups) are BPA-free, check *www.safemama.com*.

Nipples

Nipples differ in size, shape, and flexibility, but look for a nipple that most resembles the human breast. If you're bottle-feeding from the beginning, your options are open—a generic "breast" nipple is fine. If you are transitioning to bottle-feeding from breastfeeding, however, you need to be more selective. The nipple's shape should resemble yours. For example, if you have large breasts with fairly flat nipples, your baby may not be comfortable drinking from a long nipple on a small base. You may need to let your baby test a couple of shapes before you discover what works best. If your local supermarket doesn't have a wide variety, check the web.

When you're shopping for a nipple, you'll notice brownish nipples and clear nipples. The brown nipples are typically made of latex; the clear ones are silicone. If you can find a silicone nipple in the size and shape you need, choose it over the rubber one, which has a more noticeable flavor and gets sticky when it gets old. Because the rubber ones are opaque, it's also harder to be sure they're clean.

The other key variable is the hole in the nipple. Some nipples have multiple holes while others have one. Some holes are small, some large. Some have round openings and some are cut in an X shape. According to the manufacturers' labels, the small, slow-flow holes are for newborns while larger, faster-flow nipples are intended for older babies. The manufacturer doesn't always know best—your baby may have a different idea. If you're transitioning from breastfeeding and have a strong let-down, your baby may be used to gulping milk. A slow-flowing infant nipple might frustrate him. Try opening up the hole to permit a faster flow, or replace newborn nipples with faster-flowing ones.

Even with the right nipple, you may not always get the right flow of milk, or even the same flow you got the last time. Turn the bottle upside down and shake it a few times. You should see a spritz of milk followed by slow, steady drops. You can adjust the flow by loosening or tightening the bottle's ring. You also may find that some supposedly "fast-flowing" nipples are slower than those advertised as "slow-flowing"—check the flow rates for yourself. Be aware that nipple flow may change (typically, but not always, slowing down) with repeated washings.

Additional Paraphernalia

After you choose your bottles and nipples, you'll find that you need a few more gadgets to simplify preparing, cleaning, and traveling. The good news is that you won't need everything on this list. The better news is that most of the items will be useful long after your baby is beyond bottles.

- Bottles (If you're bottle-feeding exclusively, you'll need eight four-ounce bottles for a newborn and eight eight-ounce bottles for an older baby).

- A bottle brush.
- A graduated pitcher for mixing batches of formula.
- A basket designed to hold rings and nipples for the dishwasher (you'll use it later for all sorts of things).
- Bottle warmers (these pads heat up when activated by pinching, and can be recharged by boiling).
- Formula dispenser for traveling (a plastic case with several compartments for premeasured powdered formula; a two-chambered bottle—one chamber holds powdered formula, one holds water; or you can premeasure formula into bottle liners, twist-tie shut, and mix with premeasured water kept in a separate bottle).

CHOOSING A FORMULA

Next is the question of what goes in the bottle. If you're pumping and have a supply of breastmilk, you're all set. If not, you need to select a formula, one that is fortified with iron. There are milk-based and soy-based formulas. According to recent research, soy-based formulas do not lower the risk of allergies or colic, and may have problems of their own. According to the AAP, there are only three circumstances where a soy formula is preferred:

- The parents are strict vegans (who don't eat red meat, poultry, fish, or any products that come from animals like eggs or dairy products).
- The baby is diagnosed with lactose intolerance, which is rare among infants and more commonly found in older children and adults. This isn't just an allergy to cow's milk. Lactose intolerance is the inability to digest sugar lactose found in cow's milk and cow milk formula. Soy formula is lactose-free.
- The baby has congenital galactosemia, a rare disease in which the baby doesn't have the enzyme that converts galactose, one of the two sugars found in lactose, into glucose, a sugar the body can use. For these

children, consuming breastmilk, cow's milk, or other dairy products can result in a galactose build-up and eventual blindness, severe mental retardation, growth deficiency, and death.

Should your baby be unable to tolerate cow's milk formulas, your doctor may recommend a hypoallergenic formula over a soy-based formula. Hypoallergenic formulas, however, can cost up to three times more than standard cow's milk or soy formulas.

The bottom line is to always talk to your pediatrician about which formula to use at first and before you switch types. There may be other reasons why your baby is showing signs of discomfort.

You may have to try various formulas if your baby seems to reject one, vomits after most feedings, has constant diarrhea, or gets a rough red rash on her face or bottom. Any standard formula is fine as long as your baby likes it and seems to digest it well.

Formulas come packaged as a powder, concentrated liquid, or ready-to-serve liquid. Powder is the cheapest, most compact, and most portable, but it is slightly more difficult to blend than the concentrated liquid. Some researchers have expressed concern about liquid formula in cans, since most are lined with BPA. While formula manufacturers concede the presence of BPA in the cans, they insist that it is a trace amount that presents no danger to infants. To be safe, you may prefer to use powdered formula, prepared and served in BPA-free bottles.

There has been concern about trace amounts of melamine, an industrial chemical, that have been found in U.S. manufactured infant formula. The Food and Drug Administration (*www.fda.gov*) has issued a report that insists the formula sold in the United States is safe. According to Dr. Stephen Sundlof, director of the FDA's Center for Food Safety and Applied Nutrition, "The levels that we are detecting are extremely low," and do not pose a health risk to infants (even those who are fed formula exclusively for a year). Parents "should not be changing [their infant's] diet. If they've been feeding a particular product, they should continue to feed that product. That's in the best interest of the baby."

If you're not sure if your local water is fluoridated, check with your water department. At the age of six months, your child will begin needing fluoride in her diet to ensure the healthy development of her teeth. If your tap water doesn't contain fluoride, you can purchase fluoridated bottled water marketed for infants, have fluoridated spring water delivered, or ask your pediatrician to prescribe fluoride drops.

PREPARING FORMULA

Here are step-by-step instructions on how to prepare bottles of formula.

1. Boil the nipples and other bottle parts before the first use (this both sterilizes them and gets rid of the plastic flavor). You don't really have to sterilize them again after that, if you had a healthy, full-term infant, as long as you have a chlorinated water supply. (Well water can be a concern. Have your water tested for safety or boil the bottles in a pot for five minutes prior to each use.) For all subsequent washings, a run through the dishwasher or hand washing in hot, soapy water will get them sufficiently clean. You'll find it's best to wash or soak bottles soon after using as curdled milk can be difficult to scrub out.

2. Wash your hands, wipe off the top of the formula can, and mix the formula exactly according to the directions (unless you're using a ready-to-use formula). Too little water can cause dehydration while too much means your baby won't be getting enough calories. If you are concerned about the amount of chlorine in your tap water, use bottled water. It isn't necessary to boil the water unless the available water supply has known problems.

3. Pour the formula into the bottle. You probably think the next thing you need to do is to warm the bottle and then shake a few drops on your wrist to check the temperature, just like you've seen on TV. Wrong.

In fact, unless your baby is used to a warm bottle, he probably won't care if you serve it to him at room temperature or straight out of the refrigerator, although he may get used to (and come to prefer) the bottle temperature he gets most often. Think of the advantages of a baby who will drink a cold bottle. There's no struggling to warm a bottle while holding a hungry, crying, and increasingly agitated baby and no looking for hot water while on a trip. You can put a bottle in a cooler of ice right next to your bed for nighttime feedings.

If your gourmet child insists on warm bottles, go ahead and do that little wrist ritual—if the milk feels at all hot, it is too hot. If you've microwaved the bottle to heat it, shake it well so there are no hot spots. Most experts recommend against microwaving because of the danger of hot spots, but most formula-feeding mothers end up using the microwave. If you do microwave, however, stick to plain plastic bottles; bottle liners can explode and glass bottles can crack. Never microwave breastmilk because it contains too many fragile antibodies. Put a bottle of breastmilk in a cup of warm water if you want to warm it.

TOP TEN BOTTLE-FEEDING MISTAKES

Following are some things you should avoid while bottle feeding:

1. Boiling bottles to sterilize them is not really necessary. A trip through the dishwasher or a soap-and-hot-water wash is sufficient.
2. Don't change the proportion of water to formula (either because you think it's a hot day and your baby needs more water, or that extra formula will make him sleep better). You risk dehydrating or starving your baby.
3. Don't boil water to mix with powdered formula. Unless your water supply has known problems (in which case you may wish to use bottled water), water straight from the tap or filter is fine.
4. Don't leave the top on the bottle while heating in the microwave.
5. Don't microwave breastmilk (it kills the antibodies).

6. Don't forget to shake microwaved bottles well to eliminate hot spots.
7. Don't give your baby a bottle to hold in the crib. This can cause tooth decay and ear infections.
8. Be careful not to screw the nipple ring down too tightly. This cuts off the flow of milk and makes bottle-feeding frustrating for the baby.
9. Never prop up a bottle to feed your baby. If she is too young to hold a bottle, someone should be holding her. Propping a bottle to let a baby feed herself can cause choking.
10. Don't urge your baby to finish a bottle. Breastfed babies eat until they are full; bottle-fed babies should be allowed the same privilege.

FEEDING BABY A BOTTLE

Feeding your baby, whether it's from your breast or a bottle, is an opportunity for both moms and dads to bond with baby. Enjoy those close moments. A new dad can use bottle-feeding as a time to get to know his baby and her quirks—how she likes to be positioned to eat, exactly how to hold the bottle, when she needs to burp, and so on.

Settle into a comfortable chair with a nearby table on which to rest the bottle when you stop to reposition the baby. Ignore your smartphone and try to minimize other distractions. Hold your baby snuggled close, positioning his head in line with the rest of his body. He should be at about a 45-degree angle, so that his ears are higher than his mouth and his head tips back slightly. (Adjust the angle if your baby spits up during the feeding, but don't hold your baby completely flat. The milk can back up into the eustachian tube and cause an ear infection.) Pick up the bottle and then, with one finger on the hand holding the bottle, stroke the baby's cheek that is closest to your body. When he turns toward you, brush his lips with the nipple, and let him latch on himself; don't stuff it in. Make sure the tip of the nipple is in the back of his mouth. Hold the bottle firmly so it resists his suction; otherwise, he'll just be moving the bottle around instead of getting the milk out.

As he drinks, keep adjusting the angle of the bottle so that the nipple is always full of milk and not air. Don't tip the bottle up any more than you have to; the more you tip it up, the faster the flow, and a gulping baby is likely to swallow air. If the flow is too slow, however, your baby may get frustrated and fuss, or lose interest and doze off.

When your baby seems to fuss or pull away, stop for a burp, and then offer him the bottle again. If he's not interested, don't push him to finish the bottle. And don't obsess about how much your baby eats. Nursing mothers don't know how much their babies get, and breastfed babies do just fine. The amounts will vary from day to day, so just make sure that your baby is steadily gaining weight.

Parenting Pointer

If your baby doesn't finish a bottle of pumped breastmilk, you don't have to throw out the leftovers. Put it back in the refrigerator and bring it out for the next feeding, but don't do this more than twice.

TIMING THE INTRODUCTION OF A BOTTLE

If you're breastfeeding and intend to occasionally use a bottle or eventually switch to a bottle full-time, timing is everything: Do it after the third week and before the eighth week. If you start too early, you may permanently reduce your milk supply. If you start too late, your baby may not want to have anything to do with a bottle. After the third week, conduct bottle practice every day. You don't have to continue with daily bottles once your baby has demonstrated that she is willing and able to suck from a bottle's nipple, but do remind her at least several times a week that milk does, indeed, come in bottles. (Be prepared, though: At six or eight months, she may pull a fast one on you and begin refusing bottles no matter how successful she's been with them until that point.)

Another Chance

If you miss this introduction window, your baby may want nothing to do with a bottle and it may not be worth forcing the issue. You can just wait another month or two and then begin teaching her to drink from a cup. But if you must wean an unwilling baby to a bottle (because you have to be away from her or must take medication that would be dangerous for a baby, for example), it can be done.

First, make sure that you are holding the baby in a different position than the one in which you breastfeed—facing out, for example—or feed while walking around the room. Act thrilled and excited when you are getting ready to give your baby the bottle, as if you are just about to give her the most delightful treat. Don't act apologetic or worried. Expect your baby to reject your first attempts. Give up for a few moments and then try again, still acting as enthusiastic as you possibly can. Remember that even a few swallows taken from a bottle count as a win.

You can start by offering the bottle a few times a day when the baby is hungry, but take it away if she refuses. You might try offering a cup, or waiting a little while and then nursing her. If that doesn't work, try completely skipping a feeding, and then offer a bottle at the next feeding. The opposite method may work for some babies. That is, introduce the bottle when the baby is not frantically hungry, in the hopes that it will be perceived as something fun to play with, and then—what a bonus—the baby gets some milk, too. If this doesn't work, temporarily switch to a dropper or syringe; try anything that will get the milk into the baby's mouth from a source other than the breast.

If you're the nursing mother and are having no success with bottle-feeding, get yourself out of the picture. Let someone else struggle with this early introduction. Typically, most moms turn to the dads, but even better is an experienced bottle-feeder—her confidence will be communicated to the baby.

Chapter 6
START ON SOLIDS

By the time you're finally feeling comfortable about breast- or bottle-feeding, or whatever combination of the two you have worked out, people will start asking you whether your baby has started eating solids. Most parents wait until their baby is about six months old. Read on to learn all the ins and outs of solid food introduction.

TIME FOR MUSH

Currently, the AAP advises parents to wait until their infants are six months old before giving them any food except formula or breastmilk. Complementary feedings do not increase total caloric intake or growth rate, and lack the protective components of human milk.

Reasons for Waiting

By about six months, most babies are physically ready to swallow solid foods. The tongue extrusion reflex, in which most things that go into a baby's mouth are quickly pushed out by her tongue, fades away. An older baby's digestive enzymes have matured to the point where she can fairly efficiently break down solid foods. Her intestines have started secreting a protein called immunoglobulin A (IgA), which prevents allergens from passing into the bloodstream. It's important to wait for these capacities to develop, because a breastfed baby may lose some of her protection against infections and allergies once she starts solids.

Be Patient

Besides the health reasons for holding off on solids, there are a few practical ones. Solids will quickly transform the reasonably tolerable smell of a breastfed baby's poop into foul sludge. Cleaning up spit-up stains will become challenging. If you've got a trip planned, take it before you enter the solid food stage; a couple of days' worth of baby food can really weigh down your suitcase. (You'll also be happier if you can postpone the challenge of feeding a baby squirming on your lap in an airplane seat.)

. . . .

Parenting Pointer

Try not to pass your food hang-ups on to your children. You many think tofu is gross and avocados are slimy, but your child may love them if you feed them to him without comment.

. . . .

The only reason for jumping the gun on solids is if your baby is at least four months old and is acting like she's going to go ahead and start solids without you. Talk to your pediatrician before you do. She may be ready if she stares at you when you eat and grabs at your food, mouths all of her toys, can sit up (with support) fairly well, or nurses frequently or drinks huge amounts of formula but still seems hungry. Most importantly, she's ready if she doesn't immediately use her tongue to push out anything you put into her mouth.

But wait the six months—or a little longer—if you can. The window for the introduction of solid food is a lot wider than the window for the introduction of the bottle.

Babies can do without solids for as long as eight months without ill effect. Soon after eight months, however, your baby will begin to require the extra nutrients that come with solids. She ought to have a little experience with this new way of eating before that time comes, so starting daily eating practice sometime before eight or nine months is a good idea.

Your Baby Is Ready for Solids When . . .

- She's at least four to six months old.
- She's like a vulture when you're eating, ready to pounce on your food.
- She stops sticking her tongue out when her mouth is touched.
- She sits with support and controls her head well enough to lean forward when she wants more food.
- She's almost ready to sit up on her own.
- She indicates she's full when you are feeding her.
- She drinks more than 32 ounces of formula, or breastfeeds six or seven times a day and wants more.
- She's at least twice her birth weight or at least thirteen to fifteen pounds.

FIRST "REAL" FOOD

Rice cereal is easy to digest and unlikely to cause an allergic reaction. Alternatives, particularly if your baby has a tendency to be constipated, are barley and oat cereal. (Avoid wheat at first as wheat allergies and intolerances are fairly common.)

Instant, ready-to-mix rice cereal is widely available, and the standard brands are basically alike. To prepare instant rice cereal, mix about two teaspoons of the cereal with breastmilk or formula (if you're using a cereal that already includes powdered formula, all you need to add is water). Experiment with the texture to see what your baby prefers, but start out with the mixture a bit soupy (but not so thin it runs off of the spoon).

You can also make rice cereal from scratch, but the downside is that homemade cereals are not iron-fortified, and at six months your baby is ready for a boost of iron. The cereal-making process can be as simple (rice plus water cooked into a mush) or as elaborate as you choose. Talk to your doctor about whether your baby needs the extra iron fortification, especially if he's being fed with iron-fortified formula.

Let's Eat!

For your baby's first meal, pick a time when he's starting to seem hungry, but not frantically so. If your highchair isn't assembled, don't panic. You can also put your baby in an infant seat or on the lap of an available adult, making sure he is basically upright with his head tipped slightly back.

Do not put solid foods in a bottle or an infant feeder unless your doctor has told you to do so (which she will suggest only if your child has one of a very small list of medical conditions). It is easy to overfeed using a feeder, unlike a spoon that your baby can easily push away.

Scoop a tiny bit of cereal on an infant or demitasse spoon—or even your own finger—and put it just into the front of your baby's mouth. Don't shove it in; he needs to learn for himself how to get the food off of the spoon and far enough back into his mouth to swallow. Since you're introducing this at a stage when he is mouthing everything in sight, he'll probably open his mouth as soon as the spoon gets close.

Then let your baby do whatever he wants with the cereal. He may try to suck the spoon. He may push the cereal out with his tongue. Matter-of-factly scoop it off of his chin and back into his mouth. Eventually he may swallow and then open his mouth for another bite. Once he turns away he's had enough, even if it's only been a few spoonfuls. Respect his appetite and stop when he's full; don't try to coax in one last bite. Let your baby decide how much he wants to eat. The average baby eats the equivalent of one jar of baby food at each meal once he is eating confidently and has moved to three meals a day.

If he starts to get bored with this new game, wipe him off and put away the spoon and bowl, but bring it out again at around the same time the next day. If he balks completely—closes his mouth from the beginning, turns away from the spoon, or just starts screaming—try again tomorrow. If he balks several days in a row, give it up for a few weeks and try again; some babies just aren't ready when you think they should be.

Your baby may grab at the spoon—so give her one of her own to hold. She may want to smoosh the cereal with her fingers. Let her—she'll probably suck some off of her fingers as well. She may refuse to open her mouth. Try opening yours wide and take a bite yourself. It will be pretty bland, but make smacking noises like it's delicious.

GEARING UP

Following is a list of handy things to have when your baby is ready to try solid food:

- Infant feeding spoon or demitasse spoon
- Big bibs for baby; an apron for you
- Sturdy highchair with a safety strap or infant seat
- Topless plastic cups, preferably with handles; no-spill cups
- Food processor or blender; food grinder
- Washcloths
- A plastic mat, a towel, or a dog to catch spills
- For restaurants, disposable self-stick placemats for tables or highchair trays and a portable clip-on highchair are nice to have

LIFE AFTER RICE

Stick to rice cereal, once or twice a day, for two weeks or so—or even as long as a month. This food is easy to digest, unlikely to cause allergies, and can be prepared with a thicker consistency as your baby gets more proficient at eating.

Slowly introduce other foods to your baby's diet. "Slowly" is the key word here. Feed your baby a single new food, in tiny portions, for three to five days before moving on to another food, and watch for signs of allergic reaction. (Don't serve a mixed food until you've allergy-tested the ingredients first.) It is much easier to allergy-test at the food introduction stage than figure out what caused an allergy later. It's a good idea to keep a chart of what foods you've introduced, and what reaction, if any, you noticed.

While there is wide agreement that rice cereal is the perfect first food, there is less agreement on what the second food should be. One theory is that the next few foods should be vegetables, not fruits, so your baby doesn't get the idea that all food is sweet. The other theory holds the opposite: that fruits, because of their sweetness, are more likely to interest your baby and therefore should be introduced before vegetables.

Both theories make sense, so go with what seems to work for you and your baby. Every few weeks introduce a new type of cereal into the mix as well. In general, the order doesn't matter that much.

Top Ten First Foods

10.	Peas	**5.**	Bananas
9.	Sweet potatoes	**4.**	Applesauce
8.	Squash	**3.**	Barley cereal
7.	Pears	**2.**	Oat cereal
6.	Avocado	**1.**	Rice cereal

HOMEMADE BABY FOOD

Commercial baby food is easy and convenient, if relatively expensive. While it's easy enough to make your own, don't be guilted into preparing homemade baby foods if you have no time or interest. Buy the jarred food for the few months until your baby is eating table food.

Simple Food Made Simply

There's nothing complicated about making baby food. In fact, simplicity is the key. You can make a batch and freeze it to be defrosted as needed. Here are some simple steps to making baby meals:

- Buy the freshest vegetables and fruits and use them within a day or two.
- Peel, remove any seeds and cores, and then steam or boil until soft. Bananas don't need to be cooked—just mash with a fork.
- Puree the mixture well (in a blender, baby food grinder, or food processor).
- Freeze individual portions in ice-cube trays. Once frozen, you can take the cubes out of the trays and store them in bags in the freezer. Be sure to label and date the bags. Frozen fruit and vegetable purees are good for three months; pureed meat, fish, and chicken will last up to eight weeks.

Don't mix ingredients while you are still introducing them to your baby. You can mix two together—like carrots and sweet potatoes—once you know that your baby is not allergic to a particular fruit or vegetable.

Defrost in the microwave, but just until barely warm, and stir thoroughly to get rid of any hot spots. If necessary, add breastmilk, water, or formula to smooth or thin the puree. Avoid butter, oil, sugar, and salt.

Organic for Baby?

You may see some food labeled "natural," "free-range," and "hormone-free," but that doesn't guarantee that the food is organic. Only baby food labeled "USDA organic" has met standards set by the United States Department of Agriculture, and only those foods that have been certified to meet USDA standards can be legally labeled "organic."

In order to qualify as "USDA organic," the food must be at least 95 percent organic, meaning that all but 5 percent was produced without conventional fertilizers and pesticides. Organic food can't be irradiated, genetically modified, or produced with antibiotics or hormones. Any meat products must come from animals that have been fed organically grown feed.

While organic jarred baby food may be slightly more expensive, you can save if you shop at sales and buy in bulk.

If you are going to make your own baby food, look for fruits and vegetables that have been certified as USDA organic on their labels.

Parenting Pointer

Constipation is common in the early weeks of introducing solid food. You're giving your baby something a lot harder to digest than breastmilk or formula, and the most typical first foods—rice cereal, banana, and applesauce—are binding. Sometimes adding fluids (a bottle or cup of water a day) is enough to solve the problem. You can also feed your baby a little prune juice, or switch from rice cereal and applesauce to oat cereal and pureed pears.

Nitrate Alert

Fresh beets, turnips, carrots, collard greens, and spinach may contain nitrates, chemicals found in abundance in the soil from certain parts of the country. Nitrates can cause a type of anemia in infants up to six months of age. It's not a question of whether the vegetables are organic. To avoid this problem, the AAP recommends you buy commercially prepared forms of these vegetables. Baby food manufacturers screen the produce for nitrates.

BABY FOOD SAFETY TIPS

Take care to make sure that the food you feed your baby is safe and fresh.

- Don't feed your baby directly from the jar. Once saliva enzymes from the spoon touch the food, they break down nutrients and speed up spoilage. To avoid waste, spoon a meal's worth of food into a bowl. If you must feed from the jar, throw what's left away.
- Refrigerate unused food immediately.
- Don't keep a partially used, refrigerated jar of baby food longer than two days—even if it tastes fine to you, bacteria can make your baby sick.
- If you're giving your baby food from a can, either run the can opener through the dishwasher or use one reserved for this purpose (not the one you use to open the dog food).
- When making baby food yourself, make sure that you cook meats to the proper temperature. Use a meat thermometer to tell if the food has reached the proper temperature. Beef, veal, lamb, roasts, and chops all need to reach 145°F. Pork and ground meat (beef, veal, and lamb) need to reach 160°F. Poultry, such as chicken and turkey, needs to reach 165°F.
- Give your baby only pasteurized juices.

MEAT AND DAIRY

When your baby is around eight months you can, if you'd like, give him his first taste of meat. Don't panic if those little jarred meats never make it into your baby's mouth. Many babies never take to the taste of commercial baby food meats. You can try mixing meats with pureed vegetables or grinding up meat from your family's dinner, which at least smells better than the jarred meats. Or you can just wait until your baby is old enough to pick up a bit of chicken and chew it for himself. Meat is not necessary in the first year; your baby is getting all the protein he needs from formula or breastmilk.

Wait until your baby is at least twelve months old before feeding him dairy products. The protein in cow's milk can be difficult to break down.

BE ON THE LOOKOUT FOR ALLERGIC REACTIONS

Any of these symptoms indicate that your baby has reacted unfavorably to the new food you just tried:

- Skin reactions: Rashes on the face or trunk, severe diaper rash, hives, eczema
- Digestive problems: Vomiting, diarrhea, gas
- Swollen lips or eyelids
- Crankiness
- Stuffed nose
- Wheezing

Wheezing, though rare, is a reason to call your doctor immediately. Discuss with your doctor whether the wheezing was caused by the food and whether the food should be eliminated. Milder symptoms mean you should just put the food away for a while. Try it again in a couple of months, and odds are it'll be just fine.

Peanuts

Although high in protein, calories, and fat, neither peanuts nor peanut butter should be given to babies. About 1.5 million Americans have a severe allergy to peanuts. The symptoms can range from the mild—an itchy throat—to the serious—anaphylactic shock which can result in death. The AAP recommends that children at higher risk of developing a food allergy should not be given peanut butter until they are three years old. Your child is at higher risk if you or a family member has a food allergy, asthma, eczema, or hay fever. If you do serve your child peanut butter, remember that young children often swallow without chewing.

Label Literacy

You would think a jar of pureed plums would contain, simply, plums. But you can't assume that, so check the label. In the past, baby food companies would regularly add sugar and thickeners (like tapioca starch) to their products, reasoning that babies preferred sweeter, smoother foods. (This may be true, but may not be the preference to reinforce.) After a fuss in the press a few years ago, jarred baby foods, at least those designed as first foods, became purer. You should still check the label, however, in particular for foods labeled "fruit desserts" or "stage three" foods. Don't be fooled if the label says that the product includes fructose, dextrose, or maltodextrins—these are all different forms of sugars. Be on the lookout, too, for corn products, including corn syrup as a sweetener and cornstarch as a thickener. These can trigger allergies in a sensitive baby.

Also watch out for and avoid artificial flavors and colors (red #40, yellow #5, etc.). These can cause unpredictable allergic reactions and there is some unconfirmed evidence implicating them in neurological disorders.

ALL ABOUT THE CUP

You can begin teaching your baby to drink from a cup at about the same time you start solids, or even a little sooner.

Offer sips of breastmilk, formula, or water from a cup beginning at about five months—not for nutrition, but for practice. You can also let her have a drink from your glass of water by putting the cup to her lips and tipping it until a tiny sip pours out. Since most of it will trickle down her chin at first, try it when you're getting ready to change her clothes anyway. It's also a good idea to hold cup practice at bath time.

When your baby starts eating solids, she can also have small amounts of juice, preferably mixed with water. Keep the amount of juice small (less than four ounces a day), or she may fill up on juice and not get the other nutrients that she needs.

There are three basic kinds of infant cups, and you'll eventually want to get your baby used to all three of them. She should learn to drink from a cup without a top, controlling the flow with her lips. Like eating, this is a skill that has to be practiced. You will also want her to drink occasionally from a cup with a spouted lid. These cups allow the liquid to flow out in a small stream, and are perfect for when she's eating finger foods in her highchair and you want her to have a drink available, but don't want her to soak herself if you step away. The baby still has to control the flow herself, but the liquid pours out fairly slowly when the cup is tipped over.

You'll also want your baby to drink from a no-spill cup. These cups have valves inside their spouts and don't spill even if shaken. They're great for the stroller, the car, or even wandering around the house. The experience of drinking from them is closer to that of sucking from a bottle than it is drinking from a cup, so they shouldn't be your baby's only cups. Be sure to buy BPA-free sippy cups. Check *www.safemama.com* for a list of manufacturers that produce BPA-free cups.

FINGER FOODS

At eight or nine or ten months, most babies will be pretty proficient at slurping and swallowing, and you'll be used to the feeding routine. You've allergy-tested a number of foods and have a fairly long list of things your baby can and will eat. She's opening her mouth like a little bird whenever she sees the spoon, and you're getting a lot more of her food in her mouth than on her clothes. Daily menus are easy: a few bowls of cereal, a few servings of pureed fruits and vegetables, and you're set.

Then your baby pulls a fast one. "No more mush!" her pursed lips seem to say as she knocks the spoon out of your hand and pureed carrots spatter across the floor. Your baby is sick of goop. However, she has only a few teeth and is not nearly ready to handle a knife and fork.

One Lump or Two?

One option is moving to lumpier baby foods. The prepared versions are marked Stage Three or designated for older babies. If you are making them yourself, don't puree them as long and leave in some chunks. The change in texture and the more complex tastes of these foods may get your little bird opening her mouth again. Just in case, here are some other menus to try if your child starts to gag at the lumpier foods.

Cereal Strategies

Grab the Cheerios, or, to be brand neutral, oat cereal rings. Scatter a few on your baby's tray, and she'll try to pick them up and put them in her mouth. These may entertain her enough for you to slip in a few spoonfuls of mush between bites.

Cheerios are a popular food for nascent self-feeders for a number of reasons. First, they are made of oats rather than wheat, so allergies are unlikely to be an issue. Second, they are spit-soluble and quickly soften into easy-to-swallow mush. They are also difficult to choke on and more likely to stick to your baby's mouth than to be inhaled. Third, they give your baby great practice at picking things up with her thumb and forefinger. This pincer grasp is a developmental milestone (see the Appendix) that she is likely to be working on around the same time she becomes interested in self-feeding.

Another option is a teething biscuit. There are a number of varieties available, or you can make your own. Read the labels carefully, because some have a lot more sugar than others. Teething biscuits dissolve into mush as your baby gums them. (But don't leave your baby alone with one since large pieces can break off and pose a choking danger.)

Finger Food Buffet

There is no reason your self-feeder should have a boring diet. Provide her with a variety of foods to enhance nutrition and give her important experience with different tastes and textures. In addition to Cheerios, try (in baby-sized pieces): rice crackers; boiled, sliced carrots; cooked sweet potato sticks; thin slices of cheddar cheese sticks; plain yogurt; unsweetened applesauce.

If your baby is under twelve months, do not feed him: hot dogs, nuts and seeds; large chunks of meat or cheese; whole grapes; popcorn; chunks of peanut butter; raw vegetables; fruit chunks, such as apple chunks; and hard, gooey, or sticky candy.

Finger foods must be soft, break down into small pieces, and be easy to swallow. There are a host of fruits that meet those criteria, including cantaloupe, peaches, pears, plums, kiwis, avocados, and even apples, if they are first steamed or poached (slice them, add a spoonful of water, and cook them in the microwave). Just remove any peels and pits and cut into baby bite-sized pieces. For vegetables like broccoli, squash, and carrots, steam or boil them until reasonably soft.

Pasta makes a great early finger food as long as you pick small shapes and cook them soft. Serve it plain, with tomato sauce, or even with pesto.

Breakfast foods are also good finger foods for any time of the day. Whole grain waffles (purchased frozen and heated in the toaster), pancakes (use a whole-grain mix, make a batch, and freeze them; they are easily reheated in the microwave), and French toast (for babies under twelve months, make it with separated egg yolks mixed with formula or breastmilk). You can spread any of these with a fruit or vegetable puree to bump up the nutrition.

Whatever you're serving, give your baby only a few pieces at a time, and consider mealtime finished as soon as throwing the food on the floor becomes more interesting than putting it in his mouth.

The finger food stage can start as early as six months or not until several months later. It depends on your child's personality, for one. Babies with strong individual preferences and a lust for independence will move into this stage earlier than more easygoing babies. It also depends on the environment. If you don't mind a mess, your baby probably gets his hands into his cereal regularly, and that has already become his first finger-food experience. If neatness is important to you and you are quick to wipe up spills, your baby may have gotten the message that he should keep his hands out of the way at mealtime.

Either way, by twelve months your baby will probably do most of his feeding himself. Most of that will be with his fingers—although he may begin to experiment with using a spoon, he probably won't be very successful yet.

Parenting Pointer

These foods are the most likely to trigger allergic reactions in some babies. Be alert if you try any of them: citrus fruit, tomatoes, strawberries, wheat, corn, soy products, egg whites, cow's milk, shellfish, and peanuts.

Eggs

Doctors recommend that you wait until your baby is ten months old before introducing egg yolks into his diet. You should wait until your baby is at least a year old before offering him egg whites, as they often cause allergic reactions if introduced too early.

Honey

Honey is not recommended for infants under the age of twelve months as it may carry botulism spores that can be deadly for babies. Even baking may not destroy these spores. While not all honey contains botulism spores, there's no reason to take the risk since babies don't need honey.

Finger Food Options

Since a baby's airway is the size of the tip of his pinky, you should always serve finger foods under constant adult supervision. Only give finger foods to a child who is sitting up—not lying down or walking around. Be sure that all finger foods are soft and cut into small pieces.

Top Ten Finger Foods: Six to Eight Months

10. Graham crackers

9. Mashed potatoes

8. Peeled carrots (to gum on, before teeth emerge)

7. Arrowroot cookies

6. Teething biscuits

5. Bagels

4. Soft-cooked vegetables

3. Bananas

2. Zwieback

1. Cheerios

Top Ten Finger Foods: Nine to Twelve Months

10. Ripe peaches

9. Avocado slices

8. Small meatballs

7. Rice

6. Scrambled egg yolks

5. Tofu

4. Toast

3. Rice cakes

2. Egg noodles

1. Cheerios

Setting the Pace

Meals at the finger-feeding stage will be messy and may take a long time. Resist the temptation to step in and neatly tuck each bite of food into your baby's mouth. Eating isn't just about nutrition at this point—it's about learning. This is your baby's time to learn to like different tastes and textures; to learn to skillfully get food from the bowl to the mouth, gums, or throat; and to learn about when to eat and when to stop.

HOW MUCH FOOD SHOULD I OFFER MY CHILD?

Every baby is unique. Each child advances at his or her own pace and time. Pay attention to your child's developmental stages and feed according to those skills. The amounts of food to offer your child given in this chapter are just a guide; each baby is different and your child may eat more or less than these recommended servings. Your job as a parent is only to offer the foods to your child. Pay attention to your child's feeding cues to know if she is finished eating or wants to continue to eat. Here is a guide for feeding advancement for the first year through toddler eating.

Birth to Four Months

Babies at this age should only be taking breastmilk or iron-fortified infant formula. His schedule will be sporadic but overall his daily intake of breastmilk or iron-fortified infant formula should be 21 to 24 ounces. Your infant does not need any additional water or juice—these are not needed in the first year of life. Formula can provide all the hydration that your infant needs under age one.

Five Months

At this age, babies should be drinking only breastmilk or iron-fortified infant formula. She will begin to spread out her feeding and feed about four to six times per day. The overall goal amount of breastmilk or iron-fortified infant formula is about 24 to 34 ounces per day.

Six to Seven Months

Your infant should continue to drink 24 to 34 ounces of breastmilk or iron-fortified infant formula per day, but this is the appropriate time to introduce iron-fortified rice cereal in addition to breastmilk or formula. Your baby may eat about 4 tablespoons per day of cereal. Only introduce rice cereal with a spoon, as it is not appropriate to put rice cereal in a baby's bottle. You can also begin to introduce 4 tablespoons of vegetables and 4 tablespoons of fruits per day. Only introduce one new food at a time and wait three to five days between each new food to monitor your child for potential allergies.

Eight to Nine Months

Your baby is getting better at chewing so you can begin to move away from all-puréed foods to a more mashed food consistency. She should drink 24 to 34 ounces of breastmilk or iron-fortified infant formula per day. She can continue with the grain cereals, fruit, and vegetables and may take about $1/4$ to $1/2$ cup of each of these per day. It is now appropriate to begin to introduce some soft meat purées. If her pincer grasp is ready, go ahead and give her some soft finger foods such as soft crackers, toast, cereal O's, or teething biscuits.

Ten to Twelve Months

Time to work on independent feeding! Your baby can now begin to hold a cup and will be interested in playing with food and self-feeding. He should still continue to drink 24 to 34 ounces of breastmilk or iron-fortified infant formula per day. You can begin to offer small amounts of these in a sippy cup. Fruit juice can also be offered, but your child should only have 4 ounces of juice per day. Juice can contribute to overfeeding and obesity so be careful not to offer more than the recommended amount. Continue to expand the variety of cereals, fruits, vegetables, meats, soft breads, and finger foods. Babies will take about one-quarter cup to one-half cup servings of each of these per day at this age.

RECIPES TO TRY AT HOME

Following are some tasty first-food recipes that are great for early solid-food experimentation, starting at six months and up to a year or older. Watch for baby's readiness for certain textures and check with your pediatrician if you have questions about offering certain ingredients.

Baby's First Rice Cereal

Your baby should only receive rice cereal from a spoon. Do not put rice cereal in your child's bottle.

YIELDS 1 SERVING

1 tablespoon iron-fortified prepared rice cereal

4 to 5 tablespoons expressed breastmilk or formula

Mix above ingredients together. Consistency should be equal to or only slightly thicker than breastmilk or formula.

FIRST TASTE—GET YOUR CAMERA!

Your baby's first taste of infant rice cereal may be more exciting for you than for her! She may make funny faces, be disinterested, or dribble it all over herself. Or she may look at you like you have been holding out on her and gobble it all up. Enjoy this moment and each opportunity you have to feed your child. They are a gift.

Sweet Pea Purée

Sweet peas are often a child's first vegetable. If he does not like the first taste, continue to offer this periodically. It can take many tries for a child to accept new foods!

YIELDS 16 TABLESPOONS

1 cup sweet peas
1 to 2 tablespoons water

1. Steam the sweet peas in the water. Save water when done steaming.
2. Put peas in food processor or blender.
3. Process on and off until desired consistency reached (for ages 4 to 6 months, consistency should be equal to or only slightly thicker than breastmilk or formula). Use a small amount of the cooking liquid to thin the final product if necessary. If you plan to freeze the final product, do not thin with breastmilk or formula.
4. Work the pulp through a strong strainer to remove any fibrous material.

FREEZING TIPS

If you are planning on making a large batch of vegetables to freeze, use water to thin out the puree, if needed. Breastmilk and formula do not freeze well in purees so only use these to thin purees you are not going to be freezing.

Pumpkin Purée

For a shortcut, use a can of plain pumpkin—just open the can and serve. Make sure to buy plain pumpkin with no added spices, sugars, or dairy products.

YIELDS 16 TABLESPOONS

½ small "pie" pumpkin (approximately 8 ounces)

½ cup water

1. Peel, seed, and chop the pumpkin half.
2. Steam in steamer with water for 7 to 10 minutes.
3. Put pumpkin in food processor or blender.
4. Process on and off until desired consistency reached. Use a small amount of the cooking water to thin the final product if necessary. If you plan to freeze the final product, do not thin with breastmilk or formula.
5. Work the pulp through a strong strainer to remove any fibrous materials.

Squash Purée

Most babies love the sweet, smooth consistency of puréed squash. Acorn and butternut are two of the main varieties. Squash is a good source of calcium!

YIELDS 16 TABLESPOONS

16 tablespoons of squash (variety of your choice)

½ cup water

1. Peel, seed, and chop squash.
2. Steam in steamer with water for 7 to 10 minutes.
3. Put squash in food processor or blender.
4. Process on and off until desired consistency reached. Use a small amount of the cooking liquid to thin the final product if necessary. If you plan to freeze the final product, do not thin with breastmilk or formula.
5. Work the pulp through a strong strainer to remove any fibrous materials.

Sweet Potato Purée

Sweet potatoes are easy for most babies to digest, and are a favorite first food. They are also easy to keep on hand, because they last longer than fruit and other vegetables.

YIELDS 12 TABLESPOONS

1 medium sweet potato
3 cups of water

1. Peel and chop potato into small pieces that are all about the same size.
2. In a medium-sized pan, bring water to a boil. Place potato in water.
3. Cover and cook for about 10 minutes, until tender. Drain.
4. Place potato in a food processor or blender.
5. Process on and off until desired consistency reached. Use a small amount of the cooking liquid to thin the final product if necessary. If you plan to freeze the final product, do not thin with breastmilk or formula.

Apple Purée

Red Delicious, Braeburn, and Gala apples make particularly good apple purée, though almost any variety can be used.

YIELDS 12 TABLESPOONS

2 medium apples (variety of your choice)
1 to 2 tablespoons water

1. Peel fruit and chop apples into small pieces that are all about the same size.
2. In a medium-sized pan, combine the fruit and water.
3. Cover and cook for about 10 minutes until tender.
4. In food processor or blender, combine all ingredients.
5. Process on and off until desired consistency reached. If you plan to freeze the final product, do not thin with breastmilk or formula.

Avocado Mash

Avocado is a great first food. It's loaded with monosaturated fat (the good fat), folate, potassium, and fiber. Avocados do have more calories than other fruits and vegetables, so use in moderation.

YIELDS 6 TABLESPOONS

1 ripe avocado

1. Slice an avocado around the outside lengthwise.
2. Twist both sides off the seed of the avocado.
3. Scoop out flesh from one side of the avocado.
4. Mash until desired consistency reached.
5. Wrap remaining avocado with the seed in it with plastic wrap and store in the refrigerator.

Banana Mash

Bananas do not freeze well so only prepare the amount that you can use for 1 to 2 feedings. Bananas are an excellent source of potassium. In addition, each banana contains 4 grams of fiber and 2 grams of protein.

YIELDS 6 TABLESPOONS

½ ripe banana

1. Cut a banana in half and peel one half, removing any strings.
2. Place banana flesh in bowl. Mash with a fork until desired consistency is reached.

Pear Purée

Pears are very sweet, and most babies like them right away. Look for a ripe pear with a good fragrance that yields just slightly to the touch.

YIELDS 12 TABLESPOONS

2 medium pears

1 to 2 tablespoons water

1. Peel and chop fruit into small pieces that are all about the same size.
2. In a medium-sized pan, combine the fruit and water. Cover and cook for about 4 to 6 minutes, until tender.
3. Place the cooked mixture into a food processor or blender. Process on and off until desired consistency is reached. If you plan to freeze the final product, do not thin with breastmilk or formula.

Dried Plum Purée

Prunes contain 2 grams of fiber per ounce. Your child needs fiber to help maintain a healthy gastrointestinal tract and regular bowel movements. Adding prunes to your child's diet can help keep him or her regular.

YIELDS 8 TABLESPOONS

2/3 cup (4 ounces) pitted dried plums or prunes

3 tablespoons water

In food processor or blender, combine plums (or prunes) and water. Process on and off until desired consistency is reached. If the mixture is still too coarse, pass it through a fine strainer.

Papaya Purée

Papaya is a fruit that does not freeze well. It is recommended to only make what you can use fresh. It does keep for a few days nicely in the fridge and continues to soften over time.

YIELDS 12 TABLESPOONS

1/2 medium papaya
1 to 2 tablespoons formula or breastmilk

1. Cut a papaya in half lengthwise; scrape out the seeds and discard them.
2. Scoop out the flesh of 1/2 the papaya and put in bowl.
3. Add formula or breastmilk to papaya and mash with fork. Mash until desired consistency reached.

Peach Purée

If peaches are not in season, buy frozen unsweetened peaches, thaw, and use to purée for your baby. You can also make this recipe with fresh plums too! Just be sure to strain out any fibrous materials.

YIELDS 12 TABLESPOONS

2 medium peaches
1 to 2 tablespoons water

1. Cut peaches in half lengthwise and twist off of pit.
2. In food processor or blender, combine peaches and water. Process on and off until desired consistency is reached.

Pumpkin Pear Rice Cereal

Use whatever variety of pear is fresh at your grocery store or farmer's market for this dish. Good choices include Bartlett, D'Anjou, and Bosc.

YIELDS 6 TABLESPOONS

2 tablespoons prepared iron-fortified rice cereal (with either breastmilk or formula)

2 tablespoons Pumpkin Purée (recipe in this chapter)

2 tablespoons Pear Purée (recipe in this chapter)

Combine all ingredients.

Sweet Pea and Apple Purée

If your baby did not like plain sweet peas, try this mixture with apples. The sweet taste of the apples may help your baby to accept the peas in disguise.

YIELDS 4 TABLESPOONS

2 tablespoons Sweet Pea Purée (recipe in this chapter)

2 tablespoons Apple Purée (recipe in this chapter)

Combine all ingredients.

Peach and Avocado Mash

In the summer, many local nurseries allow you to go and pick your own peaches. Make this a fun family activity with your children as they grow.

YIELDS 4 TABLESPOONS

2 tablespoons Peach Purée (recipe in this chapter)

2 tablespoons Avocado Mash (recipe in this chapter)

Combine all ingredients and mash with a fork until desired consistency.

Brown Rice

Brown rice is a tender, delicious whole grain.

YIELDS 2 CUPS

1 cup brown rice

2 cups water

1. Combine brown rice and water in a small saucepan. Bring to a boil. Cover, reduce heat, and simmer 40 minutes or until water is absorbed.
2. Remove saucepan from heat, and let sit covered for 5 minutes. Fluff and serve.

Basic Barley

Barley is an easy and delicious grain that is as versatile as rice.

YIELDS 3½ CUPS

1 cup pearled barley

3 cups water

In a small saucepan, combine barley and water. Cover saucepan. Simmer 45 to 55 minutes, or until barley is tender.

Quinoa

Not only is quinoa high in protein, but it is also high in fiber and essential amino acids. Make sure your child tolerates rice, oatmeal, and barley before introducing quinoa.

YIELDS 2 CUPS

1 cup quinoa

2 cups water

1. Thoroughly rinse quinoa under running water. Combine quinoa and the 2 cups of water in a medium saucepan. Bring to a boil.
2. Reduce heat, cover, and simmer for 15 minutes or until the outer ring of each grain separates. Fluff before serving.

Oatmeal

Oatmeal is a high-protein, high-fiber whole grain.

YIELDS 2 CUPS

2 cups water
1 cup old-fashioned rolled oats

Bring water to a boil. Add oatmeal, reduce heat, and simmer, stirring occasionally, for 5 to 10 minutes or until water is absorbed and oats are tender.

Kasha (Roasted Buckwheat)

Kasha, most often found in Eastern European cooking, is a nutty grain with a fluffy texture.

YIELDS 2 CUPS

2 cups water
1 tablespoon butter or trans fat–free margarine
1 cup kasha

1. In a medium saucepan, bring water and butter or trans fat–free margarine to a boil.
2. Add kasha, cover, and reduce heat. Simmer for 10 minutes. Fluff before serving.

Lentils

Lentils feature prominently in cuisines from around the world, including the Middle East and India. If your baby needs a smoother texture, puree lentils before serving.

YIELDS 2 CUPS

1 cup lentils

4 cups water

1. Rinse lentils under running water, and pick over to remove any stones or debris.
2. Combine lentils and the 4 cups of water in medium saucepan and simmer gently with lid tilted for 30 to 45 minutes, or until lentils are tender.
3. Drain off excess water before serving.

Black Bean Mash

Dried beans are extremely affordable; canned beans are extremely convenient.

YIELDS 2 CUPS

1 cup dried black beans (or 1 (15-ounce) can of black beans)

3 to 4 cups water

1 tablespoon olive oil

1. Soak dried beans in water for 6 to 8 hours or overnight before cooking. Drain soaking water from beans and rinse.
2. In a medium saucepan combine dried beans with water, and bring to a simmer with the lid tilted. Cook 1 to 1½ hours or until tender.
3. Drain and rinse cooked beans (or drain and rinse canned beans, if using).
4. In a medium saucepan or sauté pan, heat olive oil over medium heat. Add beans and heat through for 1 to 2 minutes, or until desired temperature is reached.
5. Remove from heat and mash beans with a potato masher or fork.

Apple, Sweet Potato, and Cinnamon Purée

As your baby gets older, you can begin to experiment with slightly thicker mashes and adding spices. If your baby has trouble with the thickness, add more apple purée to thin. Try the thicker mash again in a week or two.

YIELDS 6 TABLESPOONS

2 tablespoons Apple Purée (recipe in this chapter)

4 tablespoons Sweet Potato Purée (recipe in this chapter)

1/8 teaspoon cinnamon

Combine all ingredients.

Two-Potato Mash

Because Yukon Gold potatoes are so flavorful, it is the perfect potato to use for this dish, which doesn't contain any added salt.

YIELDS 4 OUNCES

1 small Yukon Gold potato

1/8 cup water

1/2 teaspoon canola oil

4 tablespoons Sweet Potato Purée (recipe in this chapter)

1. Wash and peel potato and cut into small chunks.
2. In a small saucepan, bring potato and water to a boil. Cook until tender.
3. Transfer potato to a food processor or blender with oil. Purée. Combine both potato purées.

Chicken with Cherries and Brown Rice

Use your leftover chicken from dinner the night before. Cook a plain extra chicken breast when you cook dinner for your family to use in a purée for your infant.

YIELDS 2 CUPS

6 cups water

1 boneless, skinless chicken breast

½ cup pitted cherries

1 cup cooked brown rice

1. In a large pot bring the 6 cups of water to a boil.
2. Place chicken breast in pot and boil until done, approximately 10 minutes. Once done, cut into small pieces and allow to cool.
3. Blend chicken, cherries, and brown rice until desired consistency reached. Use broth from cooking the chicken, breastmilk, or iron-fortified formula to reach an age-appropriate consistency.
4. If consistency is too chunky, drain through a sieve and purée remaining mixture if necessary.

Chicken and Mango Purée

If fresh mangos are out of season, substitute frozen mango.

YIELDS 2 CUPS

6 cups water

1 boneless, skinless chicken breast

1 cup Mango Purée

1. In a large pot, bring 6 cups of water to a boil.
2. Place chicken breast in pot and boil until done, approximately 10 minutes. Once done, cut into small pieces and allow to cool.
3. Blend chicken and mango purée until desired consistency reached. Use broth from cooking the chicken, breastmilk, or iron-fortified formula to reach an age-appropriate consistency.
4. If consistency is too chunky, drain through a sieve and purée remaining mixture if necessary.

Beef Stew Mash

Most of your family stew recipes can be transformed into baby foods. Just limit the amount of spices and make sure the ingredients are age appropriate. You can purée just about any food for your child!

YIELDS 1 CUP

2 ounces ground beef

2 cups water

1 carrot, scrubbed and sliced

½ medium-sized russet potato, peeled and diced

1. In a medium-sized heavy saucepan, brown the beef.
2. In a small saucepan, bring 2 cups of water to a simmering boil. Add beef, cover, and cook 20 minutes. Add carrot and potato and cook another 15 minutes or until all ingredients are falling apart. Remove from heat and cool slightly.
3. Blend until desired consistency is reached. Use broth from cooking the beef to reach age-appropriate consistency.
4. If consistency is too chunky, drain through a sieve and purée remaining mixture if necessary.

Minced Pork Chop with Applesauce

Make this as a family dinner for your whole family. Once the pork is cooked, purée the pork with apple purée for your infant. This allows you to not make extra meals for your infant but use what you are preparing for the rest of the family.

YIELDS 2 CUPS

1 cooked pork chop
16 tablespoons Apple Purée (recipe in this chapter)

1. Cut pork chop into small pieces.
2. Blend pork and apple purée until desired consistency is reached. Use chicken or vegetable broth to reach an age-appropriate consistency.
3. If consistency is too chunky, drain through a sieve and purée remaining mixture if necessary.

Poached Fish and Carrots

Fish is a wonderful addition to healthful diets. Research the fish you are choosing for your family to make sure you are choosing low-mercury and environmentally friendly fish.

YIELDS 2 CUPS

¼ pound tilapia (U.S.-farmed)
16 tablespoons store-bought puréed carrots

1. Fill sauté pan with about 1" to 2" water and bring to a boil.
2. Add fish fillet, cover, turn heat down to low, and allow to poach for 5 to 10 minutes. Once done, drain fish, saving small amount of liquid, and chop. Ensure no bones remain in fish.
3. Blend fish and carrot purée until desired consistency is reached. Use broth from cooking the fish to reach an age-appropriate consistency.
4. If consistency is too chunky, drain through a sieve and purée remaining mixture if necessary.

Chapter 7

TODDLER FOODS

Your child has now been introduced to all the types of food groups. The goal is to continue to offer your child and your family a wide variety of textures, tastes, and food experiences. Playing with food is a normal and developmentally appropriate way to learn to accept new and different foods. Encourage playing with food.

TODDLER AND PRESCHOOL PATTERNS AND PORTIONS

Here are some guidelines on toddler eating portions, but keep in mind that every child is different. Notice that their serving sizes are much smaller than adult portions.

Grains and Breads: 6 servings per day

- Serving size: 1/4 to 1/2 slice bread or 1/2 cup grain
- *Example:* 1 to 2 slices of bread + 1 cup of cereal per day

Vegetables: 3 servings per day

- Serving size: 1/4 to 1/3 cup
- *Example:* 1/2 cup of cooked vegetables + 1/4 cup of beans

Fruit: 2 servings per day
- Serving size: $1/3$ cup
- *Example:* $1/3$ cup of apple + $1/2$ a banana

Milk: 2 servings per day
- Serving size: 8 ounces milk or 1 cup yogurt
- *Example:* 8 ounces of whole milk + 1 (8-ounce) yogurt

Most pediatricians advise parents to transition babies to whole milk at one year old. Toddlers should stay on whole milk until the age of two and then can be switched to a lower-fat milk. Toddlers need two servings of dairy per day, or about 16 ounces. If your child cannot tolerate dairy, he should eat two servings of calcium- and vitamin D–fortified dairy substitute.

Protein: 2 servings per day
- Serving size: 1 to 2 ounces meat, 1 egg, $1/2$ cup beans or tofu
- *Example:* 1 egg + 2 tablespoons of tofu at lunch + 2 tablespoons of meat at dinner

Children also need adequate amounts of zinc and protein in their diet. These nutrients can be obtained from two servings per day of meat, bean, or legume protein sources. Serving sizes for this age group are about 1 to 4 tablespoons of meat, and $1/2$ cup of beans or legumes.

....

Parenting Pointer

Children under the age of two need to get a high percentage of their calories from fat for adequate brain development. For this reason, you should not limit the fat your child consumes under the age of two. Choose healthy fats from avocados, olive oil, and canola oil. For children over the age of two, you can begin to lower fat in the diet, but children should never be on an extremely low-fat diet.

....

SPECIAL BODIES, SPECIAL NEEDS

Of course, no smorgasbord can meet the nutritional requirements of every child. Some children's bodies are unable to absorb proper amounts of iron, so they need a supplement. Also, many toddlers are allergic to certain foods or ingredients, or suffer from juvenile diabetes, and must therefore avoid certain ingredients. Make sure your toddler has regular medical checkups and discuss any special nutritional needs or concerns with your pediatrician.

Chewing and Chopping

Once toddlers sprout enough teeth to chop through a carrot, hard foods become more of a choking hazard, not less. Be sure to cut crunchy foods to the size of half a grape before serving. Some squishy foods can also pose problems, given the ease with which they can become lodged in youngster's throats. Foods like grapes should be cut in half, and hot dogs and other meats should be served in pieces small enough to be swallowed easily. Even very soft food can be a problem if toddlers stuff their mouths or try to talk while their mouth is full. Discourage them from doing either.

The Joy of Dipping

Some kids love sauces, salad dressings, and condiments like ketchup—either because of the taste or for the sheer joy of dipping. Many go through a phase of wanting to add ketchup to everything; they think it improves the taste of everything from turkey to cereal!

Adding sauces can encourage toddlers to do a better job on their veggies. But if they are just as happy to eat their foods *au naturel*, why encourage them to slather on extras that are typically high in salt, chemicals, and fat? Why suggest they add sugar to their grapefruit if they're happy to eat it plain? Salads don't need dressing; potatoes don't need salt; sandwiches don't need mayonnaise; and pasta doesn't need butter. Parents may be stuck with palates that prefer dishes that their own unwitting caregivers served decades ago. But rather than passing on unhealthy family traditions to the next generation, it's better to let them die out. So, before you resort to salad dressing, try a squeeze of lemon and pinch of herbs. Don't boil rice, pasta, or vegetables in salt. Add it after the food is on your toddler's plate, if necessary.

Leisurely Meals

If toddlers take ages to finish a meal, why rush them? The modern trend to race through life notwithstanding, nowhere is it written that food must be consumed within fifteen minutes. Toddlers need a long time to eat for several reasons. It is challenging for them to get food onto a spoon or fork and into their mouth. Furthermore, they don't have many teeth to chew with, and their poor ability to coordinate the muscles of their face and mouth makes chewing and swallowing difficult.

And of course, they must pause to enjoy the sensation of eggs sliding through their fingers and the sound of pickles being banged on a plate. Given that all that fingering and mouthing is good for their motor skills and cognitive development, they derive lots of benefit from the assorted activities they indulge in while satisfying their bird-sized appetites. Let them take their time. Otherwise, they may have difficulty consuming enough to keep them well nourished.

To end a marathon meal but still ensure they've had enough to eat, try the following tactics:

- Announce that since he's not eating, the meal is ending, and you're going to take away his plate.
- If he doesn't begin aiming the food toward his mouth on cue, he may not have understood. Demonstrate by removing the plate.
- If he fusses, assume he is still hungry and return his plate to him.
- If he resumes playing instead of eating, offer to feed him. (Until their fine motor skills develop, toddlers have trouble getting food into their mouths.)
- If he eats or allows himself to be fed, wait to remove the plate until the next time he begins playing. Then remove it for keeps.

- Offer water if he cries, and reassure him that he will be served again at snack time or the next meal.

HEALTHY APPETITES

It is all too easy to interfere with youngsters' ability to interpret the physical cravings that guide them to satisfy bona fide nutritional needs. So you don't confuse them, follow these dos and don'ts:

Do	Don't
Provide only healthy choices	Offer junk foods
Let children dawdle through their meals	Rush them
Offer to help feed them	Insist on helping
Serve previously refused foods early in a meal, when they're hungriest	Force them to eat things they don't like
Offer small portions, and let them know they are free to ask for more	Give large servings and coax them to eat
Make mealtime relaxed and enjoyable	Nag them about eating
Let them eat as little or as much as they want	Play "here comes the airplane" to induce them to open up and eat more

Up with Veggies

Sugar coatings work to get kids to eat cereal. Why shouldn't it work to get kids to eat veggies, too? As it turns out, it does. If you sprinkle a tiny bit of sugar on broccoli, peas, lettuce—or whatever—most children will gladly gobble the greens. Once they've developed a taste for the vegetables in question, reduce the amount of sugar added to subsequent servings until it is eliminated altogether. Of course, in acquiring a taste for carrots they may acquire a sweet tooth, too. If a child is already overindulging on junk, however, it's better to have it be junk that packs a good nutritional punch.

Cute Concoctions

Kids may resist the raw carrots, celery, alfalfa sprouts, and broccoli lying on their plates in traditional arrangements, which is to say in small piles. A glob of cottage cheese and smear of peanut butter on bread may not hold much appeal for finicky eaters. But turn those same ingredients into 3-D designs, and toddlers are apt to undergo a dramatic attitude change. Who can resist a figure made of carrot legs, celery arms, cottage cheese face, raisin eyes, tomato smile, and alfalfa sprout hair lounging amid broccoli trees growing in peanut butter sand anchored in cement—er, crackers? To entice kids to eat good foods, be creative! Here are a few other ideas you can try:

- Cut bread with cookie cutters to create interesting shapes before topping with cheese or vegetables. The leftover bread can be frozen and eventually used to stuff chicken or turkey.
- Arrange banana buttons or small clusters of blueberries onto half-cooked pancakes to create eyes, nose, and mouth. Continue cooking until done.
- Slice a banana lengthwise to make a boat; stand a piece of sliced cheese inside to make a sail; and float it in a pool of blueberry yogurt. You can even infest the water with shark fins made from salami slices. (If that combination doesn't sound appealing to you, remember that your child probably won't mind, and it all ends up in the same place, anyway!)
- Stuff celery with cream cheese or peanut butter and top with a row of raisins for an enticing dish of "ants on a log."

BROADENING CULINARY HORIZONS

The first and second times tots taste peas, broccoli, and any number of other foods parents consider healthy, it is common for toddlers to turn up their noses at them. After trying again and again, the best recourse, nutritionists say, is for parents to try yet again and again. It can take eight to ten exposures before a youngster develops a taste for a new food.

However, most tots are destined to dislike certain foods. Just as many adults never develop a taste for liver or cringe at the sight of Roquefort dressing, little ones have definite preferences. Other things being equal, one way to tell that a child is in a growth spurt is an increase in appetite. While her appetite is hefty, she may be more receptive to new and previously rejected foods. Offer them early in the meal, when she is hungry and less finicky.

Little Farmers

There is one (almost) guaranteed cure for kids who spurn leafy greens and assorted vegetables that parents consider healthy. When toddlers participate in growing them, their negative attitude is apt to undergo a dramatic transformation once it's time to eat the fruits (er, vegetables) of their labors. Homegrown tomatoes, carrots, and lettuce are so much more flavorful, it's much easier to get kids hooked on the taste.

Families don't need a garden; many vegetables have been developed that do well in patio pots. Herbs, of course, can be grown at any time of year; all they require is a sunny window. Help little ones pinch off chives, basil, parsley, cilantro, oregano, or other favorites to sprinkle on their salad or cooked vegetables.

Child Chefs

Involving little ones in food preparation creates the kind of pride of accomplishment that can bring about a willingness to eat their creations. Toddlers are so good at shredding important papers. Put that talent to work tearing the washed lettuce leaves into pieces and dropping them into the salad bowls. Pull up a chair or step stool so youngsters can join you at the counter. Enlist their help with a variety of food preparation chores by giving very young toddlers directions for one simple task at a time and giving a hands-on demonstration.

Until youngsters master a task and are old enough to remember how things were done in the past, they will need lots of feedback and repetition: "Put this bun on this plate." "Yes, that's right." "No, like this. Put the bun on the plate." Older toddlers should be able to handle more general single-step directions— "Put the buns on the plates"—although they may also need a demonstration. As they approach age three, they may be able to handle two-step directions—"Get the buns out of the refrigerator and put them on the plates."

Toddlers as young as fifteen months should be able to help with a number of chores such as:

- **Washing fruits and vegetables.** Since a brief rinse in water is all that's required, this is an easy one for toddlers.
- **Pouring water.** Let them pour water a cup at a time into the pot that will be used for boiling pasta, rice, eggs, vegetables, or cooked cereal. Keep them away from the stove, and let them work with cold to lukewarm water only!
- **Making salad.** They can place slices of tomatoes, carrots, celery, and cucumbers on the lettuce.
- **Spreading.** Let them use a plastic knife to spread peanut butter or cream cheese on celery sticks.
- **Chopping.** They can cut slices of bananas, cheese, hot dogs, grapes, or other soft foods with a plastic knife.
- **Making omelets.** Let them sprinkle shredded cheese onto the eggs; the eggs and pan must be cool.
- **Helping make hamburgers.** Toddlers can put one roll on each plate, or (if you're serving lunch family style) they can stack them all onto one plate.
- **Cutting cookies.** Put each ingredient for the cookie recipe into a separate bowl. Help toddlers pour them all into one bowl, stir, roll out the dough, and cut it with cookie cutters.
- **Stirring juices.** After you pour the thawed juice into the pitcher of water, have your toddler stir. Teach her to stir gently, but use a big pitcher so there's room to slosh!
- **Cleaning the counter.** Toddlers can wipe down the counter with a damp dishrag or sponge. (Not that you'll end up with a clean counter for the first year or two or even three. Focus on the participation, not the result.)

- **Setting the table.** Keep the directions simple! First instruct them to put a fork by each plate. When they are finished, they can do the spoons, and then the bread knives. They can also put out the butter, ketchup, salt, and pepper, and napkins, too, if they're given one item to do at a time.

Include toddlers in the decision-making, too. For instance, ask "Do you want to put green or black olives on the salads?" and let them dip their (washed) fingers into the jar to add some to the plates. At mealtime, be sure you gush your compliments to the chef! It may take an eighteen-month-old ten minutes to extricate a slice of cheese from its cellophane wrapper, and it may be pretty mangled by that point. Still, the parent can place a piece of bread on the child's plate, hand him the remaining cheese, and tell him to put it on his bread to finish making his sandwich.

It only takes a few minutes spent together in the kitchen each day—by the time youngsters are three, they will be able to make a substantial contribution. In the long run, parents will be paid back with interest for the time and extra work kiddie "help" costs them now. In the short term, the benefits include:

- The entertainment value of a fun activity
- The boosts to self-esteem that come from actively participating in family life
- The time spent interacting with parents and other family members
- Increased interest in eating what they've prepared
- A sense of accomplishment
- Increased autonomy
- A recognition of their worth as a contributing family member

FOOD STRUGGLES

It's easy for mealtimes to degenerate into food struggles when parents obsess about each pea on their child's plate, so it's not a good policy to spend mealtimes counting them. If you pay too much attention to exactly what a child consumes, it's easy for food struggles to develop—and they are notoriously difficult to win. Parents can lead a toddler to broccoli, but even if they tried to force it down her throat, they can't keep it in her stomach. Overall, the biggest impediment to a well-balanced diet is that bane of modern households: snacking.

"I'm Huuuuungry"

It's not time for dinner, but your toddler is hungry. Should she have to wait? If the answer is "yes," you risk sending the message that the clock is more important in determining her need to eat than the signals her tummy is sending. The goal, some nutritionists suggest, should be for toddlers to learn to tune in to their internal hunger cues, not ignore them.

By offering part of the regular meal in advance, like the salad or vegetables, the child gets a nutritious snack and a head start on dinner, and the cook isn't saddled with the chore of preparing extra dishes. A child may turn up her nose at the chance to start on her soup before the rest of the family. But if she's hungry, she'll eat it. The trouble begins when the cook prepares special between-meal snacks to satisfy kiddie culinary whims. That can make snacking more pleasant than eating the standard fare served at mealtimes and create the kind of extra work that parents resent.

Eating Jags

The predictability of an unvarying menu can help anxious youngsters feel more secure. Refusing to eat anything except a few special dishes can also be a way of establishing personal control. There are two distinctly opposite, but equally valid, ways of approaching this problem.

The first way is to eliminate all food struggles by serving what your child wants. If a war for control is driving the resistance, catering to toddler demands eliminates the toddler's need to battle over food. Supplement his diet with vitamin tablets, milk, and fruit juice to maintain nutrition. Continue to make other foods available by placing them on his plate if he'll allow them to be there, or place them on a separate plate nearby. If both of those create upset, simply follow your normal serving procedures for the rest of the family. If your toddler does request something additional, dish out a serving. Studiously avoid questions about whether he likes it and comments about being glad that he's eaten something besides the usual. The goal is to not draw attention to his eating or make an issue of it, thereby preventing a basis for renewed resistance.

The second way is to ignore the child's demands, serve what you will, and wait until hunger motivates him to eat. The refusal to eat a well-balanced meal often stems from snacking. Some toddlers constrict their diets to the point that it seems that if it were up to them, they'd only eat one or two things—such as grilled cheese sandwiches, hamburgers, or a particular type of cereal—three meals a day, every day. "If I don't fix what he wants, he wouldn't eat anything," their parents claim.

But how true is that, really? The bottom line is that many youngsters consume far more between meals than during them, so when breakfast, lunch, and dinner arrive, they can afford to be choosy. The surefire way to end eating jags and get the vast majority of toddlers to eat what they're served at meals is to stop fulfilling their desire for off-the-menu items and junk-food snacks.

Test of Wills

Many parents find that eliminating unscheduled snacking is easier said than done, however. Children's refusal to eat dinner means that they will be hungry soon after. If parents hold firm on their "nothing until the next regularly scheduled meal or snack" policy, they soon have a very cranky youngster on their hands. If they hold firm through the crankiness, they have a truly hungry child on their hands, and the "I hungry" wails can be wrenching enough to thaw the firmest parental resolve.

Children will not die of hunger from being put to bed without their dinner. Unless they are suffering from diabetes or another disorder, they won't end up nutritionally deficient, either. So if parents don't back down, the problem will be solved when the child sits down to breakfast with bona fide hunger pangs.

Well, we hope. Some toddlers crawl out of bed, make their way to the kitchen, and help themselves to a midnight snack. A few will be outraged enough that their determination not to give in by eating what is served for breakfast the next morning prevails over their hunger. Consult your pediatrician if you are worried that your child will be nutritionally deprived if you hold firm.

Children with autism often have very persistent food obsessions, but although this is rare, it is possible for any exceptionally strong-willed toddler to dig in his heels and reject food despite intense hunger. More often, it is the parents' fear that the child will die of malnutrition before deigning to eat a well-balanced meal that drives them to allow continuing between-meal snacks.

Passing on the Problems

A 2001 study in *Journal of the American Academy of Child and Adolescent Psychiatry* that mothers with eating disorders were more intrusive with their infants during mealtimes (and during play, too). Toddler weight was found to be related to both the amount of conflict during mealtimes and the mother's preoccupation with her own weight—with lower toddler poundage associated with more conflict and more personal maternal weight worries.

Further, toddlers must be simultaneously nurtured (by being fed) and given firm limits (by restraining them in a highchair and keeping them from throwing food). Balancing the two is a heady emotional experience, and research shows that parents who had highly conflicted relationships with their own parents have a harder time filling both roles.

All the emphasis on food can make the toddler years particularly trying for adults with eating disorders. This is a good time to enter counseling or therapy, or to join an Eaters Anonymous support group to get some real dietary help.

Baby Basics

Toddlers, like adults, will eat out of boredom. If the parent responds to requests for a snack by offering several healthy alternatives but the child refuses anything but a cookie, she's probably not hungry. An appealing activity or nap may do a better job of eliminating the crankiness.

Big-People Diets

Whether toddlers with disturbed eating patterns are mimicking their parents' behaviors or have inherited them is unknown. But research shows that if parents have difficulties controlling their food intake, their children are apt to have problems, too. It would seem important for parents to clean up their dietary act if they can and to insist that their offspring eat appropriately even if they cannot. Eating habits established during these formative years are apt to last a lifetime. Someday your child will be grown and craving the comfort foods that tasted so good during childhood, so make sure those mouth-watering dishes are wholesome!

No Sweets!

Some parents are determined never to allow candy to pass their children's lips so they won't develop a taste for sweets. Unfortunately, this strategy can backfire by imbuing creamy, crunchy, gooey, sugary foods with the heady mystique of the forbidden.

Although palates differ, anthropologists believe that the human love of sweets is inborn. Apparently our taste buds were designed to guide primitive humans toward edible, calorie-rich plants (typically sweet) and away from poisonous ones (generally bitter). Unless children are being raised on a desert island, sooner or later they will discover the wonders of cakes, candy bars, cookies, and pies. And if they have a normal set of taste buds, they will probably love them.

If a bank teller or doctor's receptionist offers your toddler a lollipop, jumping in to forbid the gift in the absence of a compelling reason may be exerting the kind of control that causes youngsters to work overtime to satisfy their inborn sweet tooth. (A compelling reason to step in would be if the child has a medical problem, such as diabetes or an allergy.) Certainly it is reasonable to insist toddlers wait to consume their gift until later. In doing so, parents may teach the most important lesson: It's okay to eat sweets at certain times. It's when they're consumed just "whenever" that they become a problem.

At least, that is the generally accepted wisdom from experts in the toddler nutrition field: Monitor the consumption of "junk foods" at home and accept that standards will be lower outside of it. However, there may be merit to a stricter approach, given the exceptionally poor diets of most Americans, the rise in obesity and cholesterol in children, and the omnipresence of less-than-optimal food that subjects youngsters to continuing temptation.

Intercepting the lollipop the child is being offered and handing it back to the gift-giver, and saying something like "Haven't you heard? That kind of food isn't good for kids. But thank you anyway," may not win you points in a popularity contest. (But who knows? Maybe she'll consider filling her candy bowl with tiny packages of raisins instead.) Even so, standing up to her will be an impressive demonstration of how to "just say no" to junk food. As you walk smugly into the parking lot dragging your irate youngster, you can drive home another message to help ward off the other great source of bad-diet pressure by thinking out loud, "I don't know what's wrong with her. She must watch too many TV commercials or something."

WHEN TO WEAN FROM BREASTFEEDING

It is unusual to see toddlers nursing, because most parents struggle in earnest to wean them from the bottle or breast early in the second year of life. This is unfortunate. Children continue to receive protection against illness as long as they nurse. In societies where nature is allowed to take its course, self-weaning occurs between ages 3 and 4; the *minimum* age is 2½. When they are ready to stop nursing, they simply taper off and lose interest.

....

Parenting Pointer

The American Association of Pediatrics now recommends that breastfeeding continue for at least twelve months, and "thereafter for as long as mutually desired." The World Health Organization recommends "two years of age or beyond." Weaning at eighteen to twenty-four months is associated with higher IQ; virtually no research is available on youngsters weaned at older ages.

....

If you need to wean a toddler before he's ready, it will probably be difficult. Remember that you are severing a powerful emotional attachment. You can soften the blow by trying the following:

- Choose a time when the youngster isn't coping with other major stresses.

- Tell your child you are going to wean him.
- Provide milk in a cup with meals.
- Nurse after meals, when the child has less of an appetite.
- Eliminate one bottle or nursing session at a time, beginning with the one the child is least attached to, typically in the middle of the day.
- Avoid the cues that trigger the desire to be nursed by staying busy and sitting in a different chair.
- Spend the time you would have devoted to nursing reading a story, reciting nursery rhymes, or playing together.
- Offer bottle-fed babies a bottle of water.
- Wait five days before eliminating a second bottle or nursing session.
- Eliminate bedtime feedings last. (Provide other kinds of comfort until the child learns to fall asleep without being nursed. If possible, have Dad handle bedtime.)

Parenting Pointer

For relief from full breasts, try expressing enough milk to relieve discomfort. You can also cover the breast with a cold cabbage leaf for two hours or until the leaf wilts. Cold cabbage compresses reduce milk supply by suppressing lactation. To reduce swelling, apply ice for about twenty minutes between feedings.

RECIPES FOR TODDLERS

Following are recipes to try for children older than a year who display readiness for these ingredients and textures.

Vegetable Rice Soup

This soup cooks up pretty thick so it's easy to keep on the spoon for feeding. It also works well for an older baby who is learning self-feeding skills. If you don't have brown rice, substitute white rice, orzo, barley, or quinoa.

YIELDS 10 CUPS

1 carrot

1 celery stalk

1 potato

½ small onion

1 small sweet potato

1 cup chopped spinach

1 cup brown rice

8 cups water

1 (15-ounce) can diced tomatoes

½ teaspoon dried oregano

½ teaspoon dried basil

½ teaspoon dried thyme

1. Finely chop all vegetables.
2. Combine all ingredients in a large stock pot. Bring to a boil. Reduce heat, cover, and simmer for 45 minutes or until rice is soft.

Chicken Noodle Soup

Chicken noodle soup is a great method to introduce chicken to your child. Cut pieces of chicken very tiny to avoid choking. Boiling the chicken in this soup gets the meat perfectly tender for your toddler.

YIELDS 8 CUPS

1 pound boneless chicken breasts cut into 1/4" pieces

1/2 red onion, diced

2 celery ribs, sliced

1 medium carrot, sliced

1/4 red bell pepper, diced

3 garlic cloves, minced

2 tablespoons butter or stick trans fat–free margarine

2 tablespoons olive or canola oil

1/4 cup all-purpose flour

1 teaspoon dried basil

1/2 teaspoon dried oregano

1/8 teaspoon pepper

3 (14 1/2-ounce) cans chicken broth

1 (14 1/2-ounce) can diced tomatoes, undrained

1/2 summer squash or zucchini, sliced

6 ounces uncooked whole-wheat spiral pasta

5 ounces fresh spinach, chopped

1. In a large saucepan, sauté the chicken, onion, celery, carrot, red pepper, and garlic in butter and oil for 5 minutes.
2. Stir in the flour, basil, oregano, and pepper until blended.
3. Slowly add chicken broth, tomatoes, and zucchini. Bring to a boil. Reduce heat; cover and simmer for 1 hour.
4. Return to a boil; stir in the pasta and spinach. Reduce heat; simmer, uncovered, for 12 to 15 minutes or until pasta is tender.

Blueberry Mini Muffins

Fresh or frozen blueberries work well in this recipe. If you are using frozen, the batter will take on a purple hue unless you thaw them first. Flaxseeds are a great source of omega-3 fatty acids and a good source of dietary fiber. In addition to incorporating this nutritional powerhouse into baked goods, ground flaxseed can also be sprinkled on cereal or yogurt.

YIELDS 42 MINI MUFFINS

2 cups white whole-wheat flour

1½ teaspoons baking powder, divided

½ teaspoon salt

½ cup applesauce

½ cup flaxseed meal

¼ cup canola oil

½ teaspoon vanilla

¾ cup apple juice concentrate

¼ cup plain yogurt (dairy or soy)

¼ cup milk (dairy or soy)

1½ cups blueberries

1. Preheat oven to 350°F.
2. In a medium bowl, combine flour, 1 teaspoon baking powder, and salt.
3. In a large bowl, combine applesauce with ½ teaspoon baking powder. Add flaxseed meal, oil, vanilla, apple juice concentrate, yogurt, and milk. Combine well.
4. Slowly add dry ingredients to wet. Add blueberries.
5. Spoon batter into lightly oiled mini muffin pans. Bake 25 to 30 minutes, or until a toothpick inserted into the center of a muffin comes out clean.

Banana Bread

This banana bread has a great texture and a not-too-sweet banana flavor.

YIELDS 1 LOAF

2 cups white whole-wheat flour

1 tablespoon plus ½ teaspoon baking powder, divided

1 teaspoon baking soda

¾ teaspoon salt

½ cup applesauce

½ cup butter or trans-fat-free margarine, softened

2 tablespoons apple juice concentrate

⅓ cup agave nectar

1 teaspoon vanilla

4 ripe bananas

1. Preheat oven to 350°F.
2. In a medium bowl combine flour, 1 tablespoon baking powder, baking soda, and salt.
3. In a large bowl, combine applesauce with ½ teaspoon baking powder. Thoroughly mix in butter or margarine, apple juice concentrate, agave nectar, and vanilla.
4. Mash bananas. Mix bananas into wet ingredients.
5. Slowly mix dry ingredients into wet.
6. Pour batter into a lightly oiled standard loaf pan. Bake 1 hour or until a toothpick inserted into the center of the loaf comes out clean.
7. Cool 10 minutes in pan, then cool completely on cooling rack.

Tofu Bites

Who needs highly processed chicken nuggets when these tasty, high-protein treats are so easy to make?

YIELDS 24 BITES

1 pound tofu (firm or extra-firm)

¼ cup whole-wheat flour

1 teaspoon garlic pepper

2 teaspoons olive oil

1. Preheat oven to 425°F.
2. Drain tofu and cut into 24 rectangle-shaped bites.
3. Combine flour and garlic pepper in a shallow bowl. Dredge each tofu piece through the flour mixture.
4. Spread olive oil on a cookie sheet. Place coated triangles on oiled cookie sheet.
5. Bake 10 minutes or until golden brown.

Tomato and Orzo Soup

This is an easy way to turn a few cans of soup into a family meal.

YIELDS 6 CUPS

4 cups roasted red pepper and tomato soup

1 cup black beans, drained

2 cups cooked orzo pasta

6 tablespoons whole-milk plain yogurt

1. Put roasted red pepper and tomato soup in a medium saucepan. Add beans to the soup. Combine soup and beans with pasta.
2. Top each serving with 1 tablespoon of the yogurt.

Farmer's Pie

Serve this tender casserole with applesauce for an autumnal feast.

YIELDS A 3-QUART CASSEROLE

2 large sweet potatoes

Water to cover

1 tablespoon olive oil

2 cloves garlic, minced

1/4 cup grated onion

1/4 cup grated zucchini

1/4 cup grated carrot

3 cups veggie burger crumbles

1/2 cup plain yogurt (dairy or soy)

1/2 teaspoon salt

1. Preheat oven to 350°F.
2. Peel and dice sweet potatoes. In a large saucepan, cover sweet potatoes with water. Bring to a boil; boil uncovered until tender, approximately 10 minutes.
3. While potatoes are cooking, heat olive oil in a medium skillet. Add garlic and vegetables. Sauté until soft, approximately 5 minutes. Add veggie burger crumbles and heat through.
4. When sweet potatoes are tender, drain and return them to the pot. Mash the sweet potatoes with yogurt and salt using a potato masher or fork.
5. Scrape the burger mixture into a 3-quart casserole. Spread the sweet potatoes on top. Bake uncovered for 40 minutes.

Turkey Chili

If this chili is not spicy enough for the adults, add extra chili powder, green chilis, or serrano peppers to the adult portion and heat through.

YIELDS 12 CUPS

2 tablespoons canola oil

1 red onion, chopped

1 clove garlic, minced

1 pound ground turkey breast

1 pound butternut squash, peeled, seeded, and cut into 1" cubes

$\frac{1}{2}$ cup vegetable broth

2 (14$\frac{1}{2}$-ounce) cans petite diced tomatoes

1 (15-ounce) can black beans with liquid

1 (15$\frac{1}{2}$-ounce) can white hominy, drained

1 (8-ounce) can tomato sauce

2 teaspoons chili powder

1 tablespoon ground cumin

$\frac{1}{8}$ teaspoon cinnamon

8-ounce container of plain yogurt

1. In a large pot, heat the canola oil over medium heat. Add onion and garlic; cook and stir for 3 minutes until clear.
2. Add ground turkey. Stir until crumbly and no longer pink.
3. Add the butternut squash, broth, tomatoes, black beans, hominy, and tomato sauce; season with chili powder, cumin, and cinnamon.
4. Bring to a simmer, then reduce heat to medium-low, cover, and simmer until the squash is tender, about 20 minutes.
5. Top each bowl with 1 to 2 tablespoons of yogurt to serve.

Whole-Wheat Rotini with Bolognese Sauce

In Italy, bowls of pasta are layered differently. The sauce is the most important part of the meal so the pasta is added to the sauce, instead of the sauce being added on top of the pasta.

YIELDS 2 CUPS OF SAUCE

2 tablespoons olive oil

2 tablespoons butter or trans fat–free margarine

½ Vidalia onion, diced

½ celery stalk, diced

½ carrot diced

1 pound ground beef

15 ounces tomato sauce

2 tablespoons tomato paste

Whole-wheat rotini, cooked

Parmesan cheese, grated

1. In a large pot, heat olive oil and butter over medium heat. Add onion, celery, and carrot and sauté until onion is clear. Add ground beef and cook thoroughly. Add tomato sauce and paste and heat through.
2. Mix whole-wheat rotini and sauce, top with parmesan cheese, and serve.

Blackberry Frozen Yogurt

Blueberries, raspberries, or strawberries can be substituted for blackberries in this recipe.

YIELDS 1½ CUPS

½ cup frozen blackberries

1 tablespoon apple juice concentrate

8 ounces of vanilla yogurt (dairy or soy)

1. Blend all ingredients in a food processor or blender.
2. Transfer to a freezer-safe container. Freeze for 1 hour. Remove from freezer and fluff with a fork.
3. Return to freezer, repeating process until ready to serve.

Hummus

This creamy, mild hummus is just right for younger taste buds.

YIELDS 2 CUPS

2 cups cooked garbanzo beans (homemade or canned)

2 teaspoons lemon juice

3 tablespoons olive oil

1 clove garlic

¼ teaspoon cumin

⅛ teaspoon salt

If using canned garbanzo beans, drain and rinse beans. Process all ingredients in a food processor or blender until smooth.

Happy Birthday Vanilla Cake

This birthday cake gets its sweetness from apple juice and maple syrup instead of from refined sugar.

YIELDS 1 (8" OR 9") CAKE

1 cup white, all-purpose flour

1/2 cup oat flour

2 1/4 teaspoons baking powder, divided

1/4 teaspoon salt

1/4 cup applesauce

1/2 cup apple juice concentrate

1/2 cup milk (dairy or soy)

1/4 cup canola oil

1/4 cup maple syrup

1 1/2 teaspoons vanilla

1. Preheat oven to 375°F. Lightly oil an 8" or 9" square or round cake pan.
2. In a medium mixing bowl, combine flours, 2 teaspoons baking powder, and salt.
3. In a large mixing bowl, combine applesauce with 1/4 teaspoon baking powder. Add apple juice concentrate, milk, oil, syrup, and vanilla to the applesauce.
4. Mix dry ingredients into wet, one half at a time.
5. Scrape batter into pan. Bake 25 minutes, or until a toothpick inserted into the middle comes out clean.

Spinach Tomato Scramble

You can try to substitute chopped collard greens, kale, or other greens in this recipe to give your child's diet a greater variety of green vegetables.

YIELDS 6 SERVINGS

3 whole omega-3 fortified eggs

6 omega-3 fortified egg whites

¼ cup whole milk (dairy or soy)

1 teaspoon olive oil

½ cup spinach, chopped in food processor very fine

½ cup chopped tomatoes or mild salsa

½ cup shredded Swiss cheese (optional)

1. Blend eggs, egg whites, and milk using a whisk.
2. Add 1 teaspoon olive oil to a medium skillet and heat on medium. Once heated, pour egg mixture into pan and stir with spatula. Mix in spinach and tomatoes or salsa. Sprinkle with cheese, if desired.
3. Continue to stir and scramble until done. Remove from heat and serve.

Chicken Pot Pie Muffins

Timesaver tip: Purchase a rotisserie chicken at your grocery store to use for the shredded chicken. This makes assembling this dish a snap.

YIELDS 12 MUFFINS

1¾ cups chicken broth

¼ cup butter

4 cups whole-wheat croutons with garlic

1 packet dry ranch seasoning dip

1½ cups shredded chicken, cooked

1 cup frozen mixed vegetables (peas, carrots, green beans)

1 (8-ounce) can white corn, drained

1 tablespoon wheat germ

1 tablespoon ground flaxseed meal

3 tablespoons water

3 eggs

1½ cups shredded Cheddar cheese

1. Preheat oven to 375°F.
2. In a small saucepan, combine broth and butter and heat over medium heat until butter is melted.
3. In large mixing bowl, combine croutons and dry ranch packet. Then add chicken, mixed vegetables, corn, and wheat germ to bowl and mix well.
4. In a small bowl, mix flaxseed meal and water and allow to sit for 2 to 3 minutes. Add 3 eggs and whisk with fork. Pour this mixture into the large mixing bowl and mix.
5. Pour butter and broth mixture into the large mixing bowl and mix ingredients together well.
6. Scoop mixture out into lightly oiled muffin tins. Top each muffin with Cheddar cheese. Bake for 18 to 20 minutes until done.

Arrounce Verde con Frijoles Negro

For a fun twist, serve this dish with warmed whole-grain tortillas instead of forks.

YIELDS 6 CUPS

5 cups vegetable broth, divided

1 bay leaf

2 cups short-grain brown rice

1 bunch spinach

2 tablespoons lemon juice

2 garlic cloves

2 cups cooked black beans

Pepper to taste

1. In a large saucepan, bring 4½ cups vegetable broth, bay leaf, and rice to a boil. Reduce heat, cover, and simmer 40 minutes.
2. While rice is cooking, thoroughly wash spinach and remove stems. Combine spinach, lemon juice, and garlic in food processor. Process into a paste, adding extra vegetable broth when necessary.
3. Remove bay leaf from rice, fluff with a fork, stir in drained and rinsed beans and spinach mixture. Add pepper to taste.

Thumbprint Cookies

These cookies get all of their sweetness from fruit. Experiment with different flavors of fruit spread (e.g., strawberry, apricot, blueberry, or plum).

YIELDS 30 COOKIES

2 cups white whole-wheat flour

1/4 teaspoon salt

1/4 cup applesauce

1/4 teaspoon baking powder

1/3 cup apple juice concentrate

2 tablespoons milk (dairy or soy)

2/3 cup butter or trans fat-free margarine, softened

1 teaspoon vanilla

1/2 cup all-fruit spread

1. Preheat oven to 350°F.
2. In a medium bowl, combine flour and salt.
3. In a large bowl, combine applesauce with baking powder. Add apple juice concentrate, milk, butter or trans fat–free margarine, and vanilla to the applesauce mixture. Mix well.
4. Slowly add dry ingredients to wet. Stir to combine.
5. Form batter into 1" balls. Make a depression in the middle of each ball with thumb or back of a spoon.
6. Fill depressions with fruit spread. Bake for 10 to 12 minutes.

Happy Second Birthday Carrot Cake

This extra-moist cake gets all of its sweetness from pineapple and maple syrup, rather than refined sugar.

YIELDS 1 8" CAKE

1½ cups white whole-wheat flour

½ cup oat flour

2 teaspoons baking powder, divided

1 teaspoon baking soda

¼ teaspoon salt

1 cup canned crushed pineapple

¼ cup softened butter or trans-fat free margarine

½ cup maple syrup

1 teaspoon vanilla

2 medium carrots, peeled and grated

1. Preheat oven to 350°F.
2. In a medium bowl, combine flours, 1½ teaspoons baking powder, baking soda, and salt.
3. In a large bowl, combine crushed pineapple with ½ teaspoon baking powder. Add butter or margarine, maple syrup, and vanilla. Mix well with a wooden spoon.
4. Slowly mix dry ingredients into wet. Mix in grated carrots.
5. Scrape batter into a lightly oiled 8" baking pan. Bake 45 to 50 minutes, or until a toothpick inserted into the middle of the cake comes out clean.

Cream Cheese Frosting

This no-sugar-added frosting pairs very nicely with Happy Second Birthday Carrot Cake.

YIELDS 1 ⅓ CUPS

1 cup cream cheese (dairy or soy)

⅓ cup pineapple purée or canned crushed pineapple

2 tablespoons apple juice concentrate

Using a blender or electric mixer, combine all ingredients.

PART 3

SLEEP TRAINING

Chapter 8
SLEEP LIKE A BABY

With all the other things to be concerned about during your baby's first year—including her overall health, safety, growth, and development—whether she is sleeping well may seem like a small problem. However, the parent who is getting by on little or no sleep each night will understand how important it can be to have a baby who is sleeping well.

SLEEP BASICS

Your baby will sleep a lot during her first year. This starts with about sixteen or seventeen hours a day during her first month, and gradually decreases to about fourteen hours by her first birthday. So even when she is a year old, your baby will likely be spending more than half of each day sleeping.

Not all of that sleeping will be at night, though. Early on, instead of long stretches of sleep, your newborn will probably have regular cycles of eating, sleeping, and waking each day. Although there may be one longer stretch of four or five hours, most of these cycles will be just two or three hours. Over the next three or four months, your baby's sleep patterns should become more organized. She will still be sleeping a lot (about fifteen hours at four months) but there will be more sleep at night, longer periods of wakefulness during the day, and more regular nap times.

Parenting Pointer

Parents often over- and underestimate how much their baby is sleeping. To get a better idea of how much sleep your baby is getting, keep a diary or log of your baby's naps and overnight sleep times. That can also help you to find your baby's natural sleep schedule.

Just as your baby's sleep patterns change over this first year, sleep advice also changes. It is important to realize that much of the advice for older children—letting them fall asleep on their own, not letting them fall asleep while feeding, and perhaps letting them cry it out—doesn't apply to your newborn or younger infant. Your newborn probably will fall asleep breastfeeding or drinking a bottle or may need to be rocked to sleep. Helping your child get to sleep in these first few months doesn't mean that you are creating problems for later.

As your baby gets older, you may have to work a little more at preventing and fixing sleep problems that develop so that all family members can get a healthful amount of sleep. However, for many babies, whether or not they sleep well is just part of who they are naturally. It is possible to create good and bad sleepers, but sometimes you just have to wait and adjust to your child's natural sleep schedule until things work themselves out as the child gets older.

NIGHT FEEDINGS

In early infancy, nighttime feedings are to be expected. Your newborn will likely continue to eat every two to three hours at night, just as she does during the day. She may go for one long stretch of four to five hours without eating, but in general, she will eat two or three times at night, during the time when you would usually be asleep.

Once she is gaining weight adequately, it is fine if your baby wants to go even longer between feedings at night. Still, you usually shouldn't expect your baby to go all night without waking up for a feeding until she is four to six months old. Talk to your pediatrician if you think your baby is going too long at night without eating.

Also, six months is not a magic age at which all children stop needing to eat at night. Some older infants still need one or two feedings at night, although others aren't really hungry and are just used to eating to help them fall asleep. If you think that's the case, you can gradually decrease the length of each nighttime feeding or put less formula in her bottle. You may have to go back to her customary feedings if she isn't satisfied with the decreased feedings or seems to wake up more afterward.

WHERE WILL YOUR BABY SLEEP?

Even if you have a well-designed nursery and a beautiful crib, it can be tough to decide where your baby will sleep. Should you put him in his crib right away or use a bassinet or bedside sleeper to keep him close? Or do you plan on letting your baby sleep with you in your bed? Although you will have to decide what is best for your baby, you should avoid letting your baby get used to sleeping in a bouncy chair, moving swing, or car seat. Although all of these can be acceptable options, especially if it is hard to get him to sleep any other way, your baby may become dependent on them, and have a hard time moving to a crib later on.

Bassinet or Crib?

Your baby can start off in a crib, or you can first use a bassinet and then have him graduate to a crib once he outgrows his bassinet or is sleeping for longer stretches at a time. In the first few weeks and months it can be easiest to keep your baby nearby in a bassinet, because he frequently wakes up to eat. That way, you can wake up, feed him, and then put him right back to sleep. Even if your baby wakes up frequently, this can help everyone quickly get back to sleep and still get some rest through the night.

A bassinet is also a lot cozier than a crib will be for your newborn baby. On the other hand, starting him off in a crib does save you the expense of buying a bassinet, and if swaddled, he will likely feel just as cozy and comfortable in a crib.

The main downside to having your baby nearby is that it may cause you to wake up every time that he stirs or wakes up briefly, even if it isn't a full awakening that requires your attention. That closeness does offer some reassurance, though, for many parents who worry about their younger baby through the night. In fact, the AAP now recommends that babies share a room with their parents until they are at least six months old, in a separate but close crib, bassinet, or cradle.

The Family Bed

Having your baby sleep in bed with you is a controversial way to put your baby to sleep. Although advocates praise the benefits of a family bed, other people question how safe it is and say that it may increase the risk of SIDS. While the American Academy of Pediatrics (AAP) and the Consumer Product Safety Commission (CPSC) are against co-sleeping, there are many other experts who highly recommend the practice. Most notable of these experts is the respected pediatrician and author Dr. William Sears. A bedside sleeper or co-sleeper right next to your bed can be a safe way to get all of the benefits of having your baby sleep very close to you.

SLEEPING THROUGH THE NIGHT

For most parents, the ultimate goal is having a baby who sleeps all night long. After all, if your baby is sleeping well, then that probably means you are sleeping well too. If you are expecting your baby to come home from the hospital and immediately be able to sleep through the night, though, you are in for a big disappointment.

So when will your baby start sleeping through the night? That really depends on what you mean by "sleeping through the night." Some parents consider that to mean a good ten- or eleven-hour stretch without waking up. Most other parents are satisfied with six or eight hours and consider that to be sleeping through the night, because that means that they are getting a nice long stretch of uninterrupted sleep.

When to Expect It

Although you sometimes hear of infants sleeping through the night at two months, the average infant doesn't begin to sleep all night until four to six months. It doesn't necessarily mean that you are doing something wrong if your younger infant isn't sleeping well, or that other parents have a magic way to put their baby to sleep. Again, some babies are just naturally better sleepers than others.

....

Parenting Pointer

It can be hard to live in a sleep-deprived state for much of your infant's first few months. In addition to mom and dad taking turns caring for their baby at night, you can consider hiring a night nanny. Although not inexpensive, they can provide total care overnight or simply bring your baby to mom for breastfeedings, allowing parents to get a good night's rest.

....

If your baby isn't sleeping well by four to six months, or is waking up very frequently before that, you should look for things that may be interfering with her sleep. Is she falling asleep while feeding or being rocked, then waking up every hour, and needing that same routine to get back to sleep? Then you may have created poor sleep associations and need to adjust your bedtime routine to help her fall asleep on her own.

Another common issue is the baby who was previously sleeping all night and then begins waking up a lot when he gets older. This can occur when your child is sick, after she has just gotten over an illness, or as she goes through a new developmental stage. With the onset of separation anxiety at about nine months, or when your child learns a new skill, such as sitting up or crawling, infants may begin waking up more. If you stick to your usual sleep routines, your baby should quickly begin to sleep well again. Try not to create any new sleep habits during these times, and see your pediatrician if the poor sleep lingers more than a few nights or your child is also fussier than usual or seems sick.

Bedtime Routines

Once your baby is two to three months old, you can begin to work on a regular bedtime routine to help him sleep through the night. That usually means putting him to sleep while he is drowsy, but still awake, so that he learns to fall asleep on his own. You can still get him ready for bed, perhaps give him a bath, read a story, or sing a lullaby. A last feeding will also be a part of his bedtime routine, but you should try to not let him fall asleep while eating as he gets older. Also, your baby will not learn to fall asleep on his own if he falls asleep watching a moving mobile or listening to music.

If your baby cries after you try putting him down while still awake, you should check on him after a few minutes and try to soothe him to sleep. The eventual goal will be for him to fall asleep without much fussing after you put him down.

The idea behind teaching your baby to fall asleep by himself is that if he later wakes up, then he will be able to put himself back to sleep. Everyone goes through brief periods of light sleep as they drift through different sleep stages. Infants who don't know how to go to sleep on their own often wake up during these light sleep stages, while those who do and have good sleep associations might continue to sleep.

BACK TO SLEEP

You most likely already know this, but it's important to repeat that the AAP recommends healthy infants be placed on their backs to sleep. Recent studies have shown that in the twenty years since back sleeping was first recommended, the incidence of Sudden Infant Death Syndrome (SIDS) has been reduced by 50 percent. Without question you should put your baby down to sleep on her back, as tummy and side sleeping positions are not as safe.

Parenting Pointer

SIDS is responsible for more deaths than any other cause for babies one month to one year of age.

Here are the National Institute of Child Health and Development recommendations to keep your baby safe while she is sleeping and reduce the risk of SIDS:

- The back sleep position is the safest, and every sleep time counts.
- Place your baby on a firm sleep surface, such as on a safety-approved crib mattress covered by a fitted sheet. Never place your baby to sleep on pillows, quilts, sheepskins, or other soft surfaces.
- Keep soft objects, toys, and loose bedding out of your baby's sleep area. Don't use pillows, blankets, quilts, sheepskins, and pillow-like crib bumpers in your baby's sleep area, and keep any other items away from your baby's face.
- Do not allow smoking around your baby. Don't smoke before or after the birth of your baby, and don't let others smoke around your baby.
- Keep your young infant's sleep area close to, but separate from, where you and others sleep. Your baby should not sleep on a couch or armchair with adults or other children, but she can sleep in the same room as you. If you bring the baby into bed with you to breastfeed, put her back in a separate sleep area when finished.
- Think about using a clean, dry pacifier when placing the infant down to sleep, but don't force the baby to take it. If you are breastfeeding, wait until your child is one month old or is used to breastfeeding before using a pacifier.

- Do not let your baby overheat during sleep. Dress your baby in light sleep clothing, and keep the room at a temperature that is comfortable for an adult.

THE DAY-NIGHT TRANSITION

You can begin to teach your baby that it's much more fun to be awake during the daytime than it is at night. If your baby was in the nursery at the hospital, day differed little from night. There were lights on, babies crying, and people moving about twenty-four hours a day. At home, though, you can make day and night distinct. Try waking your baby up every two hours in the daytime, and make these fun times. Talk to him, get out those baby toys, take him outside to listen to the birds, and introduce him to visitors.

At night, don't talk to him much, don't turn on anything more than a nightlight, don't play with him—don't even change his diaper unless it's dirty or soaking through. In time, most babies will welcome nighttime with their longest chunk of sleep—as much as four or five hours. (Realistically, though, you probably won't go to bed the minute your baby does, so you still won't be getting nearly as much sleep as you need.)

Between six and twelve weeks, your baby should begin sleeping for five to six hours at night. (But still not, unfortunately, in long enough stretches to make you feel like you've really slept.) In addition, by three months your baby will probably be taking two one- to two-hour naps during the day. But like all other statistics, these are inexact: Lots of babies sleep less; some sleep more. Talk to your health care provider about your baby's sleep patterns.

SLEEP STRATEGIES

There are plenty of programs to help you get your baby to sleep just a little longer; some may work for your new baby but won't work for your next one. Some may seem remarkably sensible to you, but to someone else they may seem crazy.

Before exploring the different programs described in Chapter 9, let's look at the relative importance of sleep issues. You may read that it is important for your baby to learn to fall asleep by herself because learning this will make her self-reliant. You may also read that babies will sleep more soundly if alone in a crib.

Whatever the program or strategy, you've got to decide what works best for you and your baby. No one practice will work for every baby. Rather, it's what works best with this specific child. Don't be intimidated just because a program is very popular. If a program makes you uncomfortable, try something different.

Tried and True

In addition to structured sleep methods, there are some simple practices that, while they won't work for all babies, should prove helpful and work for yours. When your baby is a newborn, let her fall asleep in your arms, then gently put her down (on her back) in the crib, keeping one hand on her chest the whole time. Place both hands on her for a moment after she's down, and then lift them very slowly.

Keeping your baby awake when she's tired during the day will not make her sleep better at night—it will just make her crankier. Nap timing does have an effect, however, and you'll be much better off if your baby takes an afternoon nap than if she stays awake all afternoon and falls asleep at 5 P.M. Don't worry about building a bad habit in a baby who's less than three months old—if it works for tonight, it's good enough!

You don't have to turn your house into a library when your baby is sleeping—let the radio play, the dishes clatter, and the doorbell ring. She'll quickly learn to sleep through the noise, and you'll be able to relax instead of tiptoeing around.

The Real World

In the real world, mothers are reading stacks of books about sleep, talking about it with their friends, and doing whatever works for them. Sometimes, of course, they don't tell anybody about it, feeling guilty that they aren't following the rules. "Sure my baby is sleeping through the night," a mom you meet at the park will tell you, not bothering to mention that her definition of "through the night" is midnight to 4 A.M. Some mothers are better with hype than others.

SLEEP PROGRAMS

In the following pages you'll find summaries of a variety of techniques designed to help your child learn to sleep through the night. If one works for you, bravo! If it doesn't, use trial and error to develop a system that you and your baby can live with. Don't be afraid to modify the experts' suggestions. Don't worry that you must stay with whatever strategy you choose. You may find that the method you used for your first child is completely ineffective for your second.

There are a few rules that many—but not all—of these programs share. If you don't want to go all the way with any one approach, you might start with these elements as you work out a system of your own:

- Try to put your baby down to sleep when she is drowsy but awake. This may teach her to put herself back to sleep when she wakes up.
- Establish a pre-bed ritual and don't vary from it. For example, you might have bath time, then read a book(s), and sing a few songs or lullabies. Whatever the ritual, your child will associate these steps with bedtime.
- When baby is old enough, introduce a "lovey," also known as a "transitional object." The idea here is that the baby will look for the lovey when she wants to calm down. Some people question whether you want your baby to bond with you or with a stuffed yellow duck. The truth is that children understand the difference between their parents and a toy, and loveys are a reminder of the reassurance and love that you provide.
- Don't rush in at the first sound your baby makes. Often she will fall back asleep on her own.

And there is always one other option: Don't do anything. Your baby will eventually sleep through the night—at least some time before she's a teenager, at which point your problem will be dragging her out of bed before noon.

American Academy of Pediatrics' Method

All humans, adults and children, go through sleep cycles that include arousals and wakings. For that reason, the AAP's *Guide to Your Child's Sleep* encourages parents to help infants over three months old learn how to soothe themselves so that they can quickly fall back asleep between one of those cycles.

The key once again is to have a routine for naps and bedtimes. Starting when the baby is about six weeks old, you should go through your pre-bed routine of singing song(s), reading a book, rocking, etc., but keep the baby awake until he is in the crib. The nursery should be dim and quiet. Offer him a "lovey" if it helps.

If the baby wakes up in the middle of the night, don't rush into the room as soon as he cries as he may fall back asleep on his own. If he doesn't, go in to comfort him, but don't pick him up. Pat him gently, speak in a low voice, and leave once he calms down.

Ferberizing

This program was proposed by Dr. Richard Ferber in his 1985 book *Solve Your Child's Sleep Problems*. Recently updated and expanded, it's intended for babies six months or older—not newborns. Dubbed "Ferberizing" by moms, the goal is for the baby to learn to put himself to sleep alone in a crib, and then to put himself back to sleep without a fuss when he wakes up during the night. This is meant to be a positive experience that gradually teaches the child to fall back on his own resources for comfort.

Ferber likens the process to what an adult would have to go through should she be forbidden to sleep with a pillow. At first she'd have trouble falling asleep and would wake repeatedly, but after a few nights she'd get used to it and sleep just fine.

Ferber's system, like many others, starts with a bedtime ritual (a bath, perhaps, followed by a book or a song). You or your partner then put your baby to bed while he is still awake. The parent leaves the room, and the baby cries. On the first night, the parent returns in five, then ten, then fifteen minutes, and at subsequent fifteen minute intervals to reassure the baby that he has not been abandoned. The parent does not stay in the room, rock the baby, or give him any "crutches" (like a bottle or a pacifier). Instead, you let the baby hear your voice, you rub him, and you stay only two or three minutes each time you go in to offer comfort. No matter what, the parent does not take the baby out of the crib. This is repeated every time the baby wakes during the night. Starting on the second night, each interval is extended by five minutes.

While Ferber offers gradual alternatives (sitting next to the crib in a chair, for example, and moving the chair farther away every night), the approach of leaving for timed intervals is the one he most recommends.

Ferberizing may go on for hours a night, for days, or even weeks and eventually works. The big question is whether you are able to make it to the "eventually." (In most cases dads have an easier time sticking to this program; the hormones released in nursing mothers when listening to a screaming baby for an extended period of time do not make things any easier.)

Since Ferber's book came out, a number of similar but slightly modified plans have been published. Maybe the best news is that recent research has shown that you may not need to repeat the Ferber process each time the baby wakes up during the night. Do it once at the beginning of the night, and then go ahead and rock him to sleep when he wakes up. In most cases this won't delay the baby from consistently sleeping through the night.

Dr. Sears and the Family Bed

Parents, babies, and young siblings sleeping together in the family bed is the way babies have slept throughout most of history—and still do in much of the world. In the United States today, it has been repopularized by Dr. William Sears as one of the tenets of a child-rearing philosophy called "attachment parenting." In his books *Nighttime Parenting* and *The Baby Book*, Sears wrote that babies sleep differently than adults, with more waking periods and longer periods of light sleep, for a reason—they need to be able to wake easily when they are hungry, cold, or their breathing is compromised. He stresses that it's more important that a baby feel reassured and has a sense of intimacy than that he learns independent sleep habits.

The family bed has several benefits beyond the closeness and awareness it fosters between you and your baby. You may find it easier to get your baby to sleep, and your sleep cycles will become synchronized. When you do wake up, it will be out of a light sleep rather than a deep one, and soothing or feeding him will be that much easier.

Putting your baby in a crib has its own benefits. You may find that you sleep better with more room and without a squirming, kicking bundle beside you. If you can't sleep for fear of squashing the baby, or if you have a panic attack every time he makes a noise, you won't sleep at all or function well when you're supposed to be awake.

Sears suggests nursing or rocking the baby into a sound sleep before putting him down, either in a cradle or the parents' bed. You should get to the baby quickly whenever the baby wakes up, he says, since you'll probably have an easier time getting him back to sleep if he doesn't scream himself into hysteria first. Here's where having the baby in bed with you is an advantage—you can often soothe, or even breastfeed, your baby without fully coming awake yourself.

The family bed became controversial in 1999, when the CPSC issued a warning against adults sleeping with babies in adult beds. This warning was based on information obtained when the Commission used death certificate data in a study that attempted to identify products associated with infant suffocation. The study was criticized for its methodology, most significantly for not taking into account other risk factors such as parents under the influence of drugs and alcohol; the number of babies sleeping on sofas or waterbeds; and the number of mothers who smoked during pregnancy or at the time of the baby's death. Despite the criticism, there has been no better study since.

Dr. Sears supports the CPSC's continuing research on the safety of the family bed and suggests using an Arm's Reach Co-Sleeper Bassinet as an alternative. This crib-like bed fits safely and snugly adjacent to the parent's bed. The co-sleeper arrangement gives parents and baby their own separate sleeping spaces, yet keeps baby within arm's reach for easy nighttime care.

Alternatively, you may get many of the same benefits of a family bed by room-sharing, or putting your baby's crib in your bedroom. One British study found room-sharing lowered a baby's risk of SIDS.

Dr. Weissbluth and Sleep Training

Dr. Marc Weissbluth, a sleep disorders specialist at Children's Memorial Hospital in Chicago and the author of *Healthy Sleep Habits, Happy Child*, believes that establishing healthy sleep habits in infants is critical to a child's long-term overall health. Dr. Weissbluth insists that parents need to establish consistent naps and early bedtimes to avoid the baby becoming overtired. In that state, he maintains, it's more difficult for the child to fall asleep. He warns against keeping a baby up late in order to accommodate a parent's schedule. The price, he cautions, is a sleep-deprived child.

When the baby is very young, Weissbluth advocates putting her to sleep after two hours of wakefulness, and doing whatever it takes to achieve this (rocking, singing, etc.). Your baby may cry in protest. Allow the crying to continue from five to twenty minutes, then pick her up and try again. From four to twelve months, Weissbluth recommends your baby take two naps a day (never in the car or stroller) and then enforcing an early bedtime. If the baby cries at bedtime, says Weissbluth, do not go in her nursery at all, because "down is down."

The No-Cry Sleep Solution

Elizabeth Pantley, author of nine parenting books, offers a series of steps to help parents tailor a sleep program for their child. Her book *The No-Cry Sleep Solution* is a thoughtful, practical guide that has become a bestseller by offering useful advice in a gentle, reassuring manner. She believes no baby should cry himself to sleep and urges parents to be realistic about what constitutes "sleeping through the night" (usually about five hours straight for a young baby). Her ten-step program will lead you through the process of helping your baby sleep. Pantley's plan involves discovering the stumbling blocks that are keeping your baby from sleeping; developing a sleep log so you can analyze his sleep patterns; working with his biological sleep rhythms; and offering a variety of sleep solutions that match your parenting style.

Focal Feedings

This modified "cry it out" approach is advocated by Joanne Cuthbertson and Susie Schevill, authors of *Helping Your Child Sleep Through the Night*. Their program varies slightly with the age of the child, but in essence includes waking up your baby at 11 or 11:30 P.M.—or just before you are ready to go to bed—and feeding him. This will theoretically prevent him from waking up an hour or two later and interrupting your deepest sleep.

If you are breastfeeding and the baby wakes up before the scheduled feeding, have your partner try to settle him in his crib without picking him up. If the baby doesn't fall asleep within ten to twenty minutes, your partner should pick him up, walk him around—anything to distract him for another hour or so before the next feeding. The idea is to get the baby adjusted to longer periods of sleep between awakenings. An alternative is to limit the amount of time the baby nurses In the middle of the night (which can be easier on both of you than not feeding him at all).

Scheduled Wakings

In this program, you try to take control of your baby's night wakings. Note which times your child typically wakes up, then set an alarm clock to wake you up before he does. Wake him up, feed him, and put him back to sleep. After he's used to this, start waking him up later and later, so he'll eventually forget to wake up on his own.

DAYTIME NAPS

Because babies need a lot of sleep and they don't get all of their sleep at night, regular naps are an important part of your baby's sleep schedule. In the first few weeks and months, as your baby is still in a regular sleeping, waking, and eating cycle, you don't have to think of daytime sleep as naps. They are just another part of your baby's overall need for sleep.

Later on, by three to four months, your baby's sleep will become more organized. You can then expect her to sleep more at night, and have three regular naps during the day. Although the length of naps varies, they are usually about one and a half hours each.

By six months, most infants only require two daytime naps and they are sleeping even longer at night. This routine of an early morning and early afternoon nap will probably continue until your child is well into her toddler years. If your baby doesn't nap well, make sure that you are not waiting until she is overtired before putting her down, and that you have a regular and strict routine for naps. Your infant is less likely to take good naps if she sometimes takes a nap at home, sometimes in the car, and falls asleep in her stroller other times. Try to organize your daytime schedule around your baby's naps.

AVOIDING COMMON SLEEP PROBLEMS

In addition to frequently waking up, common sleep problems include having trouble falling asleep and simply not sleeping enough. They all can contribute to both you and your baby not getting enough sleep, leading to fussy and irritable babies and parents. The most common sleep problems include:

- Taking a long time to fall asleep
- Frequently waking up
- Waking up too early in the morning

- Not taking regular, long naps during the day
- Having a backward sleep schedule, sleeping a lot during the day and staying up most of the night

Most of these problems can be resolved by avoiding the bad habits mentioned earlier, sticking to a regular routine for naps and bedtime, and teaching your infant to fall asleep on his own with a good bedtime routine.

....

Parenting Pointer

Swaddling in a blanket is a popular way to help newborn babies sleep well. Being wrapped firmly in a blanket can help to prevent her from making jerking movements that can wake her up and will help her to sleep cozy and secure. You should stop swaddling your baby as she gets older, especially once she is able to roll over.

....

Is It a Problem?

Before you begin to look for advice on "fixing" a sleep problem, you first have to decide whether you or your baby even has a problem. If your nine- or twelve-month-old is sleeping for four or five hours at a time, wakes up once or twice at night to feed, and you both quickly go back to sleep, then there may not be a problem. Especially if everyone is well rested the next day, you may not want to adjust anything to eliminate those feedings or awakenings, although many others would expect this older infant to sleep through the night without needing to eat.

What if your older infant continues to fall asleep breastfeeding or with a bottle or pacifier? Isn't that a problem? It can be if he hasn't learned to fall asleep on his own and is frequently waking up after falling asleep like that. However, if your bedtime routine works for you and your baby is sleeping well, then it isn't really a problem that needs to be fixed.

Mistakes and Misunderstandings

Many sleep problems can be avoided if you have realistic expectations and know the bad habits to avoid. If you expect your baby to sleep through the night at two or three weeks of age and you let him cry it out all night, then you will quickly have a very sick baby. Likewise, thinking that it is normal for a nine-month-old to feed every hour through the night will probably leave you both sleep deprived. Some of the most common mistakes and misunderstandings include the following:

- Don't let your newborn skip meals because he is sleeping a lot. Although you don't have to wake up an older baby who is feeding and gaining weight well, in the first few weeks you should wake up your baby if he has gone more than four to six hours without eating.
- Don't start solid foods like cereal early in order to help your baby sleep longer—this probably won't work anyway.
- Don't wait until your baby is overtired to put him to sleep.
- Be careful not to skip naps because you are out and about and busy. Try to adjust your daily routine to your child's nap schedule.
- Don't put your younger infant to sleep with a security object, like a large stuffed animal or blanket, as it may raise the risk of SIDS.

One of the most important sleep habits to avoid is putting your baby to sleep on his stomach, even if you think it helps him to sleep better. The extra risk of SIDS isn't worth a little more sleep at night.

JUST FOR DADS: YOUR ROLE IN BABY'S SLEEP

As in all other aspects of parenting, a father should have an equal role with his partner when it comes to caring for their baby at night. This usually means taking turns attending to the baby each night or each time she wakes up. That way, both parents can get some sleep, especially during the first few months when nighttime awakenings are the most common.

A father can help with nighttime feedings even if his baby is exclusively breastfed. He can feed a bottle of pumped breastmilk or even simply bring the baby to mom to breastfeed and then return the baby to the bassinet or crib.

If you decide that one parent will take on the sole role of caring for the baby at night, then the other can make up for it by doing more at other times. This is a good compromise if, for example, one parent has a very hard time getting back to sleep after waking up at night. Good ways to make up for not getting up in the middle of the night can include taking over the first and last feedings of the day, so that your partner can go to sleep a little earlier and sleep in the next morning.

Chapter 9
HELPING TODDLERS SLEEP

Minding a toddler is an every-waking-moment job. It's no wonder that caregivers look forward to toddlers' sleep time like thirsty desert wanderers crawling toward an oasis. Many parents can recover and regroup, work on a personal project for more than ten minutes, or have an adult conversation only when their youngster's eyelids drift closed.

COUNTING THE ZZZS

Like everything else about the diaper-and-training-pants crowd, the need for sleep varies dramatically from child to child. Survey any group of toddler caretakers and they will report tremendous variations. Some twelve-month-olds subsist on only nine hours of sleep in any twenty-four-hour period, rarely napping for more than an hour. Meanwhile, some three-year-olds are still sawing enough logs each night to raze a forest and supplement their nighttime slumber with a long afternoon snooze, too, for a total daily sleep time of thirteen hours or more.

SHUT-EYE AVERAGES				
Age	Total Sleep	Nighttime Sleep	Napping Sleep	Number of Naps
12 months	13³/₄ hours	11¼ hours	2½ hours	2
18 months	13½ hours	11¼ hours	2¼ hours	1
24 months	13 hours	11 hours	2 hours	1
36 months	12 hours	10½ hours	1½ hours	1

Baby Basics

The journal *Sleep* reported that nine- to twelve-month-olds averaged two naps per day. At fifteen to twenty-five months, the average dropped to one afternoon nap. Most children continue afternoon naps until age four.

How are parents to decide how much sleep their toddler needs? If a child is relaxed and content, it's doubtful that he's sleep deprived, no matter that parents have deep circles under their eyes from entertaining him eighteen hours a day. But since fussier toddlers tend to have more difficulties sleeping, it can be hard to sort out whether the fussiness is caused by a lack of sleep or whether their high-strung personalities keep them from getting concentrated, restful shut-eye.

Your toddler may be sleep deprived if he is:

- Routinely falling asleep in the car
- Hard to awaken in the morning and from naps
- Cranky and irritable during the day
- Hyperactive before bedtime
- Likely to fall asleep before bedtime

KNOWING WHEN YOUR CHILD NEEDS REST

As any adult insomniac knows, being sleepy and being tired are very different. Being overly tired makes falling asleep difficult because in response to the achiness that often accompanies being overtired, the muscles tense. It's impossible to relax mentally to the point of drifting off when the body is physically primed for action. It is much easier to get sleepy children to close their eyes than it is tired ones!

Parents should make an effort to notice the subtle changes in their toddler's appearance so they can more readily discern whether he's rested, sleepy, or tired. When toddlers are very sleepy:

- Their faces look softer, even puffy
- The muscles around the lips and chin may droop
- Their movements slow
- They become less animated
- They may yawn

If they are tired, on the other hand, they are apt to show signs of tension and increased physical strain:

- Their faces show signs of strain
- The muscles around the eyes tense
- The eyes may appear sunken
- Activity level may increase
- Play becomes less focused
- Crankiness is common

To facilitate getting a toddler to sleep, try getting her into bed when she's sleepy. This means she's physically more relaxed. It's harder when she's physically and emotionally tense from being tired.

Reading the Signals

A common reason that children of all ages don't want to sleep is because life is so grand. They want to live every moment to the fullest. They don't want to be shut up alone in a room while other family members are out in the living room having fun. Even if everyone else is in bed, some youngsters would rather be out in the living room having fun all by themselves than lying awake in a darkened room.

Toddlers don't connect crankiness to a need for sleep. They have to be taught to recognize these bodily sensations and emotional reactions. Then they will eventually recognize the signals. If they actively fight going to bed, they may become upset by the mere comment "You look sleepy now" or "I think you're unhappy because you're tired" because they suspect those fateful words "Time for bed" will soon follow. Nevertheless, parents should continue to share their observations.

Schedules Help!

Whether parents put balky toddlers down for the night and let the tantrums run their course or let them stay up until they collapse from exhaustion in the wee hours, conduct "rise and shine" at the same time each morning and prevent longer-than-usual naps that compensate for missed sleep. Studies on insomnia demonstrate that establishing a schedule is crucial. Being extra tired ups the odds that children will be ready to sleep at the next nap or bedtime.

The invariable routine of a rigid bedtime and nap schedule can go a long way toward regulating toddlers' sleep patterns. The human body operates in circadian rhythms—a predictable cycle that causes people to fall asleep at night and awaken in the morning at about the same time each day. These rhythms change over our life span. If left to their own devices, teenagers would stay up half the night and sleep half the day; on the other hand, senior citizens naturally fall asleep early and awaken shortly after dawn.

Not all toddlers run on the same clock, however, and it is difficult when theirs doesn't match the rest of the family's. Some night owls have a hard time sleeping at night no matter how early they get up; early birds may awaken long before the rest of the family despite having gone to bed late the night before. Instead of having their biological clocks reset by a consistent schedule that conforms to the rest of the family, they lie awake in bed and are chronically sleep deprived.

Resetting the Alarm

There are no guarantees, but many parents can sometimes reset their toddlers' internal clocks by following a rigid schedule that will bring them more in line with the rest of the family. To do this:

- Awaken young toddlers at the same time each morning.
- Put them down for naps at the same time each day.
- Awaken them from naps at the same time.
- Awaken them from afternoon naps by 4 P.M. to ensure sleepiness at bedtime.
- Keep bedtimes consistent.
- Coordinate with other caregivers to be sure the daily routines are the same.

SHARING SLEEP SPACE WITH YOUR TODDLER

So many American parents struggle with getting children to take naps and go to bed at night that, when surveyed, sleep problems routinely appear near the top of the list of child-rearing problems. The bedtime battles being waged across America are by no means universal. In cultures where families bed down together—and that includes most of the world—sleep problems are virtually unheard of.

When foreign parents hear about the accepted American practice of isolating little children in darkened rooms and placing them in beds that have bars like cages, they are shocked. To them, this sounds unspeakably cruel. "Put children to bed by themselves?" they exclaim. "But aren't they frightened and lonely?"

Certainly the continuing after-lights-out attention-seeking from toddlers, and the ongoing worries about monsters and burglars among older children, suggest that fear and loneliness are exactly what they experience. In many cultures, parents get toddlers ready for bed, then allow them to rejoin the family until they express an interest in sleeping. If they don't ask to go to bed, parents wait until they fall asleep on the couch or wherever, then carry them into a shared sleep area.

When American parents wait for youngsters to conk out on their own before carrying them to bed, some find the problems persist. That's because they are taken to their own bedroom. So as not to end up alone, toddlers may fight their feelings of sleepiness and become overly tired. That can end up with them being chronically sleep deprived.

The Family Bed

American taboos are quickly falling by the wayside as more parents find that the age-old solution of letting toddlers sleep with them virtually eliminates bedtime scenes and helps everyone get better rest. But although this practice appears more kid-friendly on the surface, there's no guarantee that it will enhance a toddler's life. The loss of the parent's alone time can make it harder for them to remain patient with their youngster during the day, which is clearly not in a toddler's best interest. Additionally, the loss of private time with their partner can jeopardize marital relationships, which, given the stress of rearing a toddler, may already be strained.

Big-Bed Safety

Toddlers are probably in greater jeopardy from sleeping alone in cribs than from bunking with parents, given the risk that they'll climb over the bars and fall to the floor, or become trapped between the mattress and the bars—or that another emergency will arise that a parent asleep in another room won't hear. Still, accidents in big beds do occur, and there are some precautions parents should take before deciding to sleep with their little one:

- If you push your toddler's bed up against yours, check to be sure he can't become wedged between the mattresses of the two beds or between his mattress and the wall.
- Don't use a slatted headboard, foot railing, or side railing that could trap a child's head.
- Don't sleep together in a waterbed.
- Check out co-sleepers, which are advertised to be a safe alternative. These three-sided cribs are designed to attach to the parent's bed.
- Keep your child's bed away from dangling cords from curtains or blinds; they are strangling hazards.
- Do not sleep together if you are under the influence of drugs or alcohol. That might keep you from being aware of having rolled on top of your child.

Co-sleeping

In a co-sleeping arrangement, the crib or toddler bed is pushed up against the parent's bed or a specially designed co-sleeper is attached. The bars can be lowered as needed for breastfeeding and hands-on comfort, and raised to keep her within her space. When the youngster graduates to a twin bed, her sheets can be tucked in around her so she doesn't gravitate toward her parents.

Bad Bedfellows

Many parents find that having the family snuggled up together in the same bed produces some of their warmest moments. Others find it far from pleasant. Some toddlers thrash, toss, elbow, wiggle, wet, and are generally difficult sleeping companions. Early risers may chatter, hum, poke, and play.

If parents don't want to share their bed, moving the crib or toddler bed into the parent's bedroom can eliminate the loneliness and enhance children's sense of safety and security. This usually translates into less resistance at bedtime. Some children can tolerate being on the opposite side of the room with a curtain or room divider to provide some privacy for the parents.

Experimenting to see whether sleeping together at night is a workable arrangement can prove costly. Once children have discovered the security, warmth, and comfort of sleeping with a human teddy bear, they are likely to be more resistant than ever to going back to a darkened bedroom with the stuffed variety. Of course every child is different, and after spending a few months in a parent's bed, some may feel sufficiently secure that sleeping alone becomes much easier. Some toddlers relish the privilege of being "big enough" to have their very own bed and are delighted to make the switch to sleeping in their very own room.

If parents decide to oust a small bedfellow, the best time to initiate the project is when separation and attachment issues are less of a factor—typically around age three. Otherwise, aim for a period when the child isn't going through a lot of other difficult adjustments, separation anxiety isn't a major issue, the child wants to grow up rather than regress to baby days, and independence conflicts aren't paramount.

WINDING DOWN

Insisting that toddlers nap or go to bed if they aren't sleepy can provoke power struggles. Instead, have them observe quiet time. A noisy environment can certainly interfere with a child's ability to fall asleep. After entering dreamland, some can tolerate a lot of hullabaloo; others remain susceptible to being awakened by sounds, especially during lighter phases of sleep. If you can't produce a quiet environment on cue, classical music can help to mask telltale sounds that suggest interesting happenings are going on elsewhere in the house.

To create a quiet and relaxing transition, help your toddler unwind by providing soothing entertainment, such as listening to music or looking at books. Bath time routines help, too. Discourage continued requests to get up by putting a kitchen timer in his bedroom. Tell him that, unless it's an emergency, he must wait until the alarm sounds before getting up or calling to you.

Once he does relax, sleep may not be far behind. Even if sleep doesn't follow immediately, children need to learn to relax and spend time entertaining themselves. Common strategies parents use to help their toddler fall asleep include rocking them to sleep, singing lullabies, telling stories, giving back rubs, holding their hand, and taking the child into their bed.

....

Baby Basics

To help toddlers wind down at bedtime, check out books like *Goodnight Moon* by Margaret Wise Brown, *Dr. Seuss's Sleep Book*, *Time for Bed* by Mem Fox, and *The Going to Bed Book* by Sandra Boynton.

....

TEACHING HEALTHY SLEEP SKILLS

The downside of rocking and singing and back-rubbing and music-playing to quiet fretful children and help them fall asleep is that they come to depend on someone or something outside of themselves—a real problem if they wake up in the middle of the night. Children need to learn eventually to handle the task of falling asleep—and of falling back asleep—unassisted.

Baby Basics

Nursing and giving children a bottle to help them fall asleep is *not* a good idea, dentists say, because the milk pools in their mouth, rotting their teeth. The same problem applies to juice and other sweet beverages. Remember: only water!

Many parents dedicate themselves to learning how to put their child to sleep, when the goal should be for *toddlers* to learn to put *themselves* to sleep and to put themselves back to sleep after awakening. Sleep experts point out that children need to acquire a specific set of sleep skills. Surprisingly, they don't come naturally to many. Children must learn how to fall asleep, fall back asleep, and sleep through the night.

The first step is for them to learn to spend time alone. Being comfortable spending time alone in a crib or toddler bed is a prerequisite for falling asleep and for falling back asleep. By handing a toddler a stuffed animal after he awakens in the morning or from a nap, leaving the room, and waiting five to fifteen minutes to rescue him, parents can give their child time to practice being by himself in his crib. Some experts say this can also serve a toddler well at night.

Your Role as Parent

When parents exit the bedroom, and leave a little one screaming, they don't have to feel like meanies who are abandoning helpless babes to a dangerous world. They could think of themselves as teachers who are confident that their child is safe, and that with time and practice he can discover the state of relaxation needed to fall asleep.

The problem with continued quick responses to soothe crying tots is that it perpetuates their dependency and helps them avoid the task at hand: learning to fall asleep on their own. As the sleep-teacher, the parents need to:

- Set up the conditions that are conducive for sleep.
- Check from time to time to be sure a wailing toddler is safe.
- Provide frightened youngsters with a comforting pat and reassurance that "you're okay."
- Remain confident that the child can learn.

Holding Firm

In two-parent homes, it may be best to have the adult who is less intensely connected to the child be the one to manage bedtime complaints and middle-of-the-night pleas for attention. Since bedtime brings up separation issues for adults as well as for children, the more connected parent may experience some anxiety that the child picks up on. This can intensify the distress and separation anxiety of both. The parent in charge of putting the child to bed should follow this approach:

1. Say "good night," tell the toddler she'll be fine, give her a comforting pat, and leave.
2. If crying persists, return after two to three minutes to see that she's okay.
3. Give her another pat, tell her she's fine, and leave.
4. Return after five minutes for another quick check to make sure the screaming doesn't mean she's ill or injured.
5. Provide another comforting pat, calm reassurance that she's okay, and leave.
6. Continue checking and providing reassurance at five- to ten-minute intervals.
7. Avoid checking if the intensity of the crying is abating (so as not to disturb her if she is beginning to relax or fall asleep).

The advantage to this approach is that children learn to fall asleep and to fall back asleep by themselves. By continuing to show up at the crib at regular intervals, the parent makes sure that the child is all right and provides reassurance that she has not been abandoned. Try to provide reassurance without reconnecting—hold talking to a minimum; don't pick your child up. Many parents are amazed at how quickly the youngster they thought would never settle down proceeds to do just that.

Meanwhile, others are amazed that two weeks later the child still manages to scream for an hour. With toddlers, there's no way to predict what will happen. Sometimes the parent's attitude plays a role. If the parent is distressed about the child's intense crying, the youngster will sense it. The timed parental visits to the nursery meant to reassure may have the opposite effect.

Handling Hysteria

What happens when parents refrain from running into their wailing toddler's bedroom to help him fall asleep, and he is so upset he vomits? Or he cries so hard, he can't catch his breath and begins gasping for air? This is the point at which many parents decide the "give him time to learn to settle himself down" approach is doing more harm than good. Check with your pediatrician to see whether it's okay to hold firm under these circumstances. If so, be as sympathetic as you would toward any little person who is having such a hard time mastering something difficult. Then change the sheets, clean him up, tuck him in, give him a pat, and tell him he'll be okay. Tell him it's time to sleep, wish him sweet dreams, and leave. Return a few minutes later to check on him to be sure he's not ill.

Handling Wakeups

If a child awakens crying and parents determine that she isn't ill, they can verbally reassure her that she is fine or offer a stuffed animal or other favored toy for comfort. What happens next is up to each family. Philosophies of what's best for toddlers differ. Sleep problems are among the toughest, and what is acceptable to parents in one household is definitely not workable in another. You can:

- Leave and stay away no matter how hard the child cries, so that she can eventually learn to fall asleep by herself. (Be sure the hard crying doesn't signal illness or injury.)

- Remain physically present to provide some reassurance and moral support, moving a chair a few inches farther from the crib each night until you are out the door, thereby helping the child to feel more secure while she learns to fall asleep on her own.
- Hold, rock, sing, carry, and otherwise soothe the child to help her fall asleep.
- Invite the child into your bed.

Whether you sleep together with your child or sleep apart, whether you respond to each call from the bedroom, only go in when your child is hysterical, or resolutely stay away, don't judge others negatively for doing it their way—and don't let them judge you for doing it yours.

. . . .

Baby Basics

Toddlers can be spiritual beings, too. Like adults, they can derive comfort from prayer and from having religious objects in their rooms. Knowing that God is watching over them can help put their minds at ease.

. . . .

HANDLING SPECIFIC TYPES OF TODDLER SLEEP ISSUES

As with most child behaviors, the range of causes of sleep issues in toddlers is vast. Here are some common reasons certain toddler sleepers have a difficult time falling asleep.

They're Independent

When the terrible two's negativity sets in and toddlers feel driven to disagree with every other thing the parent does or says, they may resist going to bed just because they've been told that's what they must do. Letting toddlers be in charge of some bedtime decisions can help satisfy their need to be in control. Let them pick which story is read, which pajamas are worn, which stuffed animals go into the crib, whether the night-light is on or off, and which music you play.

They're Attention Seekers

When older toddlers refuse to stay in bed, some parents have successfully bored them to sleep. They refuse to provide any attention, announce that they themselves are going to bed, proceed with their normal bedtime preparations, and climb into bed, feigning sleep. Ideally, children become bored enough from the lack of attention and ask to be taken to bed, or they wind down and fall asleep on their own. Obviously this trick is only workable if it is safe for the toddler to be up and about the house by herself.

They're Afraid of Monsters

If fears of the dark are keeping your toddler awake, try dousing monsters and assorted goblins in beams from a night-light. Often a fear of a nighttime visit from a wild animal or cartoon character can be overcome by outfitting the child with a special repellant guaranteed to render a beastie harmless. Placing a protective object in the room, such as an oversized teddy bear to stand watch, can be reassuring.

They've Had a Nightmare

Because children in this age group have such a poor ability to distinguish reality from fantasy, it can be impossible to convince them that the monsters and big bad bears they saw in a nightmare weren't real. Nevertheless, provide lots of reassurance that "it was just a dream." When they're old enough, they'll understand the difference.

There are no proven ways to eliminate nightmares, but the following techniques can help:

- Reduce your child's overall stress level.
- Avoid scary bedtime stories.

- Keep bedtime rituals soothing and relaxing.
- Avoid roughhousing before bedtime.
- Avoid mentioning scary things.

Encourage your child to share the bad dreams, since this helps many toddlers feel better. If his vocabulary is limited, try to help him tell it. If he says, "Bear," ask, "Was it a scary bear?" Avoid questions like, "Was the bear trying to eat somebody?" so as not to implant more fear!

They're Experiencing Sleep Terrors

These sudden, unexplained bouts of screaming and wild thrashing within the first few hours of going to sleep can be terrifying to parents who find themselves unable to comfort their youngster. Although children appear to be awake, they are actually asleep during these episodes and have no memory of them on awakening. Sleep terrors are believed to occur at the transition from one phase of sleep to another. The only reported dangers are sleepwalking, which can lead to injury, and some very upset parents! If sleep terrors are occurring regularly, some experts recommend resetting the sleep cycle:

1. Rouse the toddler about fifteen minutes before the episodes typically occur.
2. Keep him fully awake for five minutes.
3. Continue nightly until the episodes stop—usually in about a week.

FROM CRIB TO TODDLER BED

Whether or not your baby is sleeping well in his crib, you'll eventually have to face the transition from crib to bed. After all, cribs are not for climbers—a category that includes many toddlers! Be careful about putting toys into a toddler's crib; if she steps on top of them, it may give her just the boost she needs to make it up the side and over the bars. It is dangerous for toddlers to climb over the bars of the crib because a fall from such a great height poses the risk of injury. Some little monkeys surprise their parents by managing to climb out not long after their first birthday. Put some padding on the floor beneath the crib to soften it in the event of a fall. As soon as your little one begins scaling the bars, it's time to move up to a toddler bed.

Toddler beds are a great next step because they have rails to keep youngsters from falling out—and from feeling afraid they might fall out. They are also lower to the ground and pose less danger to climbers, although if a child is routinely crawling out, it may be better to keep the bars down to reduce the risk of a fall.

Parenting Pointer

Many children are in love with their toddler beds initially because they're so easy to climb out of! Parents must decide whether it's better to lower the bars, which makes climbing less dangerous, or to keep the bars up to prevent a fall while sleeping. Another option is to have the child sleep on the mattress on the floor.

Since many toddler beds use the same size mattress as a crib, it's best to stick with the old one if at all possible. The familiar feel and smell of the old mattress can help smooth the transition from the crib. The quality of toddler bed frames varies dramatically from brand to brand. If you plan to lie down with your child to read stories or sleep, be sure to get a model sturdy enough to support both of you.

Making the Transition

How will your toddler handle the transition from crib to toddler bed? There's simply no way to predict it. It's smooth as silk for some, decidedly difficult for others. If a child is very resistant to change, slow to adapt to new situations, or a sentimentalist, leaving the safety and security of the crib can be trying. Given a toddler's love of predictability and routine, it's a bad idea to let him step into his room to find his beloved crib gone. He may not find his parent's idea of a great surprise to be so wonderful. Perhaps he didn't like his crib at all. Nevertheless, it was the steady friend that kept him safe night after night for as long as he can remember. If possible, provide a gradual transition.

The secret to getting youngsters to give up their crib more willingly, many parents say, is to have them participate in the process from the very beginning. If parents assume the role of enthusiastic cheerleaders trying to whip up excitement about the change, it will be infectious. Try these ideas:

- Have toddlers help pick out their very own "big boy" or "big girl" bed, or at least the sheets.
- Have them assist as you haul the bed into the room and set it up.
- Ask if they want their crib toys moved. If so, hand over the toys one by one and let them do the arranging.
- Let a doll try it out for size, or ask if you can lie on it.
- Play a pretend game of "nite-nite" so the youngster can try it out long before naptime or bedtime, when they're likely to be less frazzled and cranky.

No matter how well toddlers seem to be handling the switch up to this point, it's anybody's guess how they will react when it's time to bed down for the night. Many toddlers find the change upsetting. Here are a few more ideas to help ease this transition:

- Let your youngster choose which bed to sleep in if possible. Some youngsters take to it instantly, but months may go by before they suddenly decide they're ready.
- Raise the bars on the toddler bed so they feel more secure and aren't afraid of falling out.
- Consider leaving the bedroom door open or a night light on to lessen fearfulness.
- Put a gate across the doorway to discourage roaming.
- Avoid making the change when other major upheavals are occurring, such as a change in sitters or the birth of a sibling.

- Provide some extra bedtime TLC to help your toddler calm down so he can drift off.
- If you must remove the crib, it may help to let an upset child sleep on the mattress on the floor next to the toddler bed.

Some toddlers gladly make the move and never again express an interest in their crib. However, for many the excitement and enthusiasm about being "a big boy" suddenly disappears at naptime. Or, a youngster may be happy to nap in his new bed during the day, only to appear shocked and appalled when it's suggested that he sleep there at night. Many children like to take naps on it for a few days before tackling it at night.

Toddlers who are initially very resistant may continue to want their crib for a few days or weeks, then spontaneously opt for the toddler bed. Some continue to ignore it for months before deciding they're ready. Many parents find it's best not to apply any pressure, since toddlers can be so quick to dig in their heels and do the opposite of whatever their parents want. They suggest leaving the crib up and remaining indifferent as to where the child sleeps.

Sometimes a toddler can't have a choice. A new baby is coming, so parents need her to relinquish her crib and move on. Parents in this situation may worry that being ousted because of a sibling will be yet another terrible blow that adds to the toddler's feeling of being displaced.

If the transition turns out to be very hard, sometimes the only consolation is that in a matter of hours, days, or weeks, the new bed will become sufficiently familiar and the toddler will adjust. Sometimes it turns out to be surprisingly easy. The youngster is delighted to participate in the preparations for the new baby, is thrilled because the move makes the coming sibling seem more real, and enjoys her lofty status of big sister. There's just no second-guessing a toddler!

Staying Put

The toddler who won't stay put in a toddler bed poses a real dilemma for parents: What to do with a little one who scurries out of bed the minute parents have finished tucking him in? What to do with the little insomniac who rises in the middle of the night when everyone is asleep and forays into the house? The first step to getting a child to stay in bed is to discuss it.

Explain that it is dangerous for him to be up by himself, that he must stay in bed unless it's an emergency, and that he is to call Mommy or Daddy from his bedroom if he needs something. After that explanation, which a child may or may not understand, make it a policy to studiously avoid further conversation. Limit verbal exchanges to repeating in a firm tone of voice, "You're supposed to stay in bed unless it's an emergency. Go back to bed and call if you need something." (This assumes the parent has a baby monitor or is close enough to his room to hear him call.)

....

Parenting Pointer

As with anything you are trying to teach your toddler, bedtime procedures are established with baby steps. Be patient and consistent as you train your child to stay in bed for the night.

....

Walk him back to his room, help him into bed, issue another reminder to call if he needs something, and leave. Toddlers in this situation are apt to cry or call before you make it through the bedroom door. If that happens, turn around and go right back to his bedside to check on him, just as you promised.

In getting across any new idea to a toddler, you need to go one step at a time and show him how things are supposed to go. Stepping out of the room and turning right back around to go back in demonstrates what is to happen: He calls; you respond. That can provide reassurance that having to be a big boy sleeping in a big bed doesn't mean he is expected to be independent. If a toddler doesn't start climbing back out of bed the moment the parent turned to leave, that should be considered a victory.

Remain calm and matter-of-fact as you approach your child's bed, and say, "I heard you calling/crying. Is everything all right? What do you want?" Provide a drink of water if a child says he's thirsty, do the monster check if he's scared; then give him a pat and tell him he's doing fine, that it will take a while to get used to the new bed. Repeat the procedure several times, avoiding all conversation except:

I heard you call. What do you want?

No. You're fine now. It's time to get some sleep.

Good night.

Begin extending the time between visits to the child's room. Difficulty with the transition to a strange bed is understandable, too. Many adults have a hard time sleeping when they're away from home for the very same reason.

....

Baby Basics

It may seem inhumane to install a door protector and close the door to contain a toddler who keeps popping out of a toddler bed after everyone else is asleep. But given the danger youngsters can get into roaming the house, it may be the only safe recourse. Be sure to completely safety-proof the bedroom first!

....

EXHAUSTING WORK

It's not surprising that so many toddlers resist bedtime. Having to make their sleep/wake cycles conform to those of other family members isn't easy when your body is running on a different biological clock. The bad news is that lots of youngsters continue to resist bedtimes throughout their childhoods, and getting teenagers to cooperate with lights out can be even more difficult since their biological clocks begin to change, turning them into night owls.

The good news is that it's far easier to deal with the crankiness of a sleep-avoidant older child than with a sleep-deprived toddler. Parents can anticipate that even if they're not getting much rest now, once children have mastered basic sleep skills, things will get better!

PART 4

DIAPERS AND POTTY TIME

Chapter 10

DIAPERING 101

As a new parent, you are expected to instinctively be an expert on taking care of a baby—from washing her hair to cutting her toenails. If you had your baby in a hospital, you might come away thinking the most important thing to know is how to give your baby a bath, but the numbers tell a different story. The bath to diaper-changing ratio suggests that you'll need to know a lot more about the care of a baby's body than how to bathe her.

WET DIAPERS

When baby first starts eating, it's important to count how many wet diapers she has (six to eight in a twenty-four-hour period is good) as a judge of whether she is getting enough milk. Once your milk has come in, some babies urinate every one to three hours, while others only four to six times a day. If she's sick or if it's very hot outside, she may urinate less and it would still be normal.

Urination should never be painful. If you think your baby is in distress while urinating, call your doctor, as this could be a sign of a urinary tract infection.

If you see actual blood in your baby's urine or bowel movements, talk to your health care provider. It could be simply a result of diaper rash, but it could also be a sign of something more serious.

THE SCOOP ON POOP

In your baby's first few days, his poop will look like tar—black, sticky, and hard to remove. This is meconium, a thick, dark green or black paste that fills a baby's intestines in utero and must be eliminated before he can digest normally. If you're lucky, he'll have eliminated most of the meconium in the hospital. If not, you'll be wiping it off at home. (It's sticky stuff, and may not come off with plain water. Try a little baby oil on a cotton ball.) Following the meconium, your baby's bowel movements will turn yellow-green.

If you're breastfeeding, your baby's poop will resemble seeded, slightly runny Dijon mustard once your milk comes in. It will be more tan if you're formula-feeding, and thicker than peanut butter.

The most amazing thing about this bodily function is how much noise can be generated from such a small person. There you are, holding your precious, dozing baby as relatives coo over how sweet he is, when you hear the sound of a volcano erupting. It's definitely a conversation-stopper, and a clue to head to the changing table after the noises stop.

Your baby will typically dirty several diapers a day, but he may have bowel movements as often as ten times a day or as infrequently as once a week. Both are normal. The ten-times-a-day baby does not have diarrhea, and the once-a-week-baby is not constipated (unless the poop, when it comes, arrives in pellets). If your baby is eating well, growing nicely, and seems comfortable, don't be concerned about how often he poops.

CLOTH VS. DISPOSABLE DIAPERS

Be forewarned: You will need lots of diapers. First, though, you have to choose which type—are you going to be on Team Cloth, or Team Disposable?

There are women who can argue about their diaper choices for hours. One concern is the impact on the environment (disposables become solid waste that must be disposed of in landfills; cloth diapers use energy and water for laundering and, if you're using a diaper service, transporting). The other concern is the health of the baby (cloth diapers are more natural and you're likely to change them more often; disposables keep baby drier, but leak synthetic pellets when they get overloaded). Luckily, there is a middle road—natural, hypoallergenic disposables such as Earth's Best TenderCare Chlorine Free Diapers.

Team Cloth

The main complaint about cloth diapers is that too often "poop happens." In other words, the poop leaks out of the diaper and stains the baby's clothing, especially in the first couple of weeks when explosive bowel movements are common. More changes and more laundry ensue. Plus, unless you use disposables when you're out of the house, you're left carrying around dirty diapers. Still, environmentally speaking, cloth diapers are the best choice and, with good planning and organization, may work for your family.

Reasons to Use Cloth Diapers

There are many good reasons to use cloth diapers:

- Cloth diapers have a hundred other uses (including a peek-a-boo toy, burping rag, and, sooner than you might think, dust rag and silver-polisher).
- You'll be more attentive to your baby's needs since you'll have to change her diaper more quickly when she wets.
- Kids may potty train earlier because they can feel the wetness when they urinate in cloth diapers. Disposable diapers wick the moisture away from the skin.
- They are less expensive than disposables.
- Fewer chemicals are touching your baby's skin.
- They're environmentally correct.
- Even taking into account the cost of doing laundry or using a diaper service, cloth diapers are generally cheaper to use than disposables.

Applied Skills

Unlike disposable diapers, you may need to prepare cloth diapers for use. Below are the different styles of cloth diapers.

- **Prefold Diapers:** Prefold diapers have a thick center and thinner edge sections, and are rectangular in shape. They can double as burp cloths and be used as inserts for pocket diapers. Prefold diapers require some sort of closure and a waterproof cover.
- **Pocket Diapers:** Pocket diapers consist of an outer layer of waterproof material and comfy inner layer of microfleece or suedecloth. This keeps your infant dry and prevents diaper rash.
- **Fitted Diapers:** Fitted diapers feature elastic and built-in fasteners, and provide excellent protection against leaks and explosive events. Like prefolds, they require some sort of waterproof cover.
- **All-In-Ones:** All-in-one diapers are often easy to use, but can be difficult to clean.

The Best Way to Wash Cloth Diapers

First, after removing from baby, rinse messy diapers in the toilet. Keep wet diapers in a diaper pail that's about half full of water; add one-half cup of vinegar to the water. Keep a secure lid on the pail. Put diapers in the washing machine and first run the machine on the spin cycle to remove excess water. Then reset the machine to the full wash cycle in hot water, using mild detergent and bleach. Add one-half cup vinegar to the final rinse, and either machine dry at highest heat or line dry in the sun.

Team Disposable

One possible reason disposables are more popular is that putting them on is more intuitive. Open one up with the tapes or Velcro tags underneath your baby, put her bottom in the middle of the diaper, bring the front of the diaper up between her legs, and fasten the tabs at her waist. Some disposables contain substances similar to barrier creams (e.g., Desitin or Balmex). If your baby develops a diaper rash, it may be a reaction to the built-in protective cream. Change to a different brand (or try cloth diapers).

Reasons to Use Disposable Diapers

- Disposables are required by most day-care centers and preferred by babysitters.
- They're less bulky so your baby's clothes will fit better.
- You have less financial commitment up front, and you don't need pins or wraps.
- Used diapers go right out to the trash.
- You'll have fewer changes and less laundry to do.
- Fewer changes also mean better chances that your baby will sleep all night.

Tricks of the Trade

There are a few tricks to diapering with disposables.

- While your baby still has her umbilical cord, fold the top of the diaper down to turn it into a low-rise bikini before fastening.
- Make sure the leg edges are turned out, not folded back under the elastic. This creates a better seal.
- If your disposables fasten with adhesive tapes, make sure not to get anything on the adhesive—lotions, water, or powder will ruin their stickiness. If your disposables fasten with Velcro tabs, don't pull the tabs too hard or they might rip off.
- When you're diapering a boy, make sure his penis is pointed down in the center of the diaper. If you accidentally diaper his penis up, or tucked out a leg edge, you will end up with a wet lap.

- Even though today's disposables are unlikely to leak until they weigh more than your baby, change them once they get a little squishy. Otherwise, the little pellets of super absorbent gel burst out of the diaper and are pretty much impossible to get off of your baby's skin unless you give her a full bath.

....

Parenting Pointer

According to the California Integrated Waste Management Board, disposable diapers represent about 50 percent of the personal garbage produced by parents of a single child.

....

Eco-Friendly Disposables

Although more expensive, biodegradable disposable diapers like Nature Boy and Girl are made of cornstarch instead of plastics. Critics, however, maintain that these diapers aren't better for the environment or the health of babies. The real issue is that regardless of whether the diaper is biodegradable, no diaper can break down in an airtight landfill. Furthermore, those who argue the environmental benefits of using cloth diapers can be confronted with the idea that cloth diapers excessively use a precious resource, as well—water, especially important in drought-stricken areas. Consider: You need water for the growing cotton plants, you need water to wash the diapers, and you need water for the extra loads of laundry necessary when cloth diapers leak.

Base your decision about which kind of diaper to use on what works best for your family.

Generics

The amount of advertising dollars spent on promoting brand-name disposable diapers is staggering. Do brand names make a difference? One advertising exec commented that parents buy brand-name diapers for their firstborn and then happily buy the generics or store brands for subsequent children. Do the math: Is it still a bargain if you have to double the cheaper diapers to get the same leak-proofing? You might use generic during the day when you can change the baby more often, and a more absorbent brand at night when your baby's sleeping. Try different brands to find the one that works for your baby.

GEARING UP FOR DIAPERING

Whether you go cloth or disposable, you will spend a lot of time with diapers over the next couple of years. Over time, you'll discover what brands and methods work best for you and your baby. If you have a two-story home, set up changing stations on both floors to save precious time and energy. While you're perfecting your technique, there are a few things all changing stations need.

- Make sure your changing surface (changing table or empty counter) is tall enough so you don't hurt your back when bending over it.
- If you plan on using disposables, keep one bag in the current size and one bag of the next size up waiting in the wings.
- If you're using cloth, you'll need three to four dozen in each size.
- You'll need three to six diaper wraps to go over the cloth diapers.
- Use washcloths for the first month before switching to diaper wipes.
- Get a diaper pail designed for whichever type of diapers you're using.
- Get a variety of changing pads—one for the changing table, one for traveling, and a larger, waterproof pad for naked time.
- Keep two pad covers in rotation (one on the pad, one in the wash).
- Have cream or ointment for diaper rash. Odds are you'll need it eventually.
- Invest in a waterproof flannel crib pad or disposable bed pads, put underneath the sheet. You'll need them now, and they're a good idea to keep for the crib-to-bed transition.
- Above all, keep your sense of humor.

DIAPERING, STEP-BY-STEP

Make sure you have everything you need within reach before you put your baby on the changing table, countertop, bed, or floor to change him. Use the dirty diaper to do as much preliminary wiping as you can before you bring out the clean cloths or wipes.

Try not to look disgusted; you want your baby to think getting his diaper changed is fun. Sing, spin a mobile, or hold a toy in your mouth—anything to keep your baby entertained and on his back. For the first month, consider cleaning the baby's bottom with plain water (using an infant washcloth, cut-up towel, soft paper towel, or cotton balls). Save commercial diaper wipes for later, as they may irritate your baby's skin.

For a girl, make sure you wipe front to back, using a clean section of washcloth or piece of cotton each time, to prevent spreading poop to the vagina. Although you don't typically need to clean the inside of the lips of the vulva, it sometimes seems as if poop is in every fold, back and front.

For a boy, toss an extra diaper over his penis while you're cleaning him. This reduces the chance of getting a fountain in the face. This isn't a bad precaution when changing a girl, either.

When you're done diapering, put your baby down in a safe place (never leave your baby alone on the changing table, even if he is belted in). You want to dump whatever is loose from the dirty diaper into the toilet. (This goes for disposable diapers, too. Their biggest environmental hazard may not be the amount of paper in the diapers, but rather the problems caused by leaching bacteria.) When you're done, wash your hands thoroughly.

Diapering gets more challenging as your baby gets more control over his body and can kick away your hands, flip over, and, eventually, try to stand up. If he's persistent in wriggling, move the scene of operation to a washable rug on the floor. You may have to swing a leg over his torso to gently hold him on the floor during some of the wrigglier stages. And once your baby learns to stand up, you may have to learn to change his diaper while he's vertical.

DIAPERING TIPS

Here are some strategies to improve the quality of time spent diapering:

- First and foremost, get all your gear together BEFORE you open a dirty diaper. You'll be glad you did.
- If your changing table has a strap, slip your hand between your baby's belly and the clip before you try to fasten it to avoid pinching your baby's delicate skin.
- Speed counts—the faster you can get your baby diapered and dressed the happier you're both likely to be.
- Accuracy counts—if the diaper isn't lined up correctly on your baby before you fasten it, it will probably leak.
- Treat diaper rash at the first signs—don't let it get out of hand.
- Put a towel or extra cloth diaper under your boy or girl baby and another one over your boy baby while you're changing. Babies do pee when their diapers are off.
- If you have an active child, give up your changing table and get good at diapering your child on the run.
- Stash several special toys in a box near your diaper table, and let your child see these toys only at changing time.
- Always have some diapers on hand that are one size bigger than the diapers that your baby is currently wearing. Babies can grow out of diapers seemingly overnight and too-small diapers contribute to diaper blow-outs.
- Use a cloth diaper or a waterproof flannel mattress pad as a changing pad when you're away from home. The cute little changing pads that come with diaper bags are so waterproof that any accidents run right off the pad onto the couch/chair/lap you're changing her on.

- Good quality paper towels moistened with water can substitute for diaper wipes.
- Cut up a cloth diaper into four squares and use the squares as an extra liner (for either cloth or disposable diapers) at night.

DIAPER RASH

Diaper rash can be as mild as a little redness or as severe as bleeding sores. Some babies seem to get it all the time; others hardly ever. Peak diaper rash times are when babies start to eat solid foods, when they sleep through the night in a dirty diaper, and when they are taking antibiotics. The best way to treat it is to prevent it.

Change diapers frequently (immediately if they're messy). As often as you can, expose your baby's bottom to air and light (even a light bulb helps). This is pretty easy when your baby's an infant. In a warm room, put him belly down on a disposable absorbent pad (the kind you sat on in the hospital) or use a waterproof crib pad with a cloth diaper on top of it. Do not leave him alone.

Once your baby is mobile, it is less likely he'll stay put. If it's summer, let him run around bare-bottomed outside. If it's winter, you might consider heating up your bathroom and giving him a little extra naked time after his bath.

It's not necessary to slather on ointment with every diaper change to prevent diaper rash. If you notice a little redness—the first symptoms of diaper rash— begin treating it immediately. Don't just hope it will go away on its own as it's likely to get worse and become a lot more uncomfortable for your baby and a lot harder for you to treat. Also understand that, left untreated, a simple case of diaper rash can become a yeast infection, which is a lot harder to get rid of than ordinary diaper rash. (A yeast infection typically comes on quickly and intensely, characterized by a bright red rash around the diaper area with small red pimples here and there in the surrounding areas.)

The AAP recommends that you don't use any baby powders. The concern is that, if inhaled, powder can cause breathing problems and lung damage. If you do use a powder, use the cornstarch-based product sparingly, shake it into your hand (away from the baby), and don't allow it to build up in the neck or groin folds.

Rash Remedies

Ointments come into play when your baby has diaper rash and can't be naked. These are typically oil-based (Vaseline, A&D ointment, or plain olive oil) or zinc-oxide-based (Desitin, Balmex, or Johnson & Johnson). Ointments create a barrier, protecting your baby's skin, and have to be spread on thickly to work. If standard ointments are ineffective, you might ask your drugstore to order a thick cream called Triple Paste or Aquafor. Both are hard to find and expensive, but some moms swear by them. Others reach for Bag Balm, an ointment intended for use on cows with chapped udders. Bag Balm, used to treat a variety of skin problems, soothes soreness and inhibits bacteria growth, but it is only FDA-approved for use on animals. Check with your health care provider before using.

Don't apply over-the-counter hydrocortisone cream unless you've discussed it with your doctor. Extended use of hydrocortisone cream can thin a baby's skin.

If you suspect a yeast infection, ask your pediatrician to prescribe an antifungal ointment or use an over-the-counter antifungal cream like Lotrimin. However, if your doctor prescribes a combination steroid-antifungal cream like Lotrisone, only use it as long as recommended. Do not use it as a regular diaper cream, because the steroid can lead to serious side effects in children, including thinning of the skin.

Nonmedical Ideas

In Hawaii, where the humid climate makes diaper rash a real problem, moms use pure cocoa butter to prevent diaper rash. Cocoa butter is available at most drugstores and comes in solid bars or sticks that must be warmed. (Put it in a jar, then sit the jar on a sunny windowsill or in a bowl of warm water. Test it on your own skin to make sure it's not too hot before applying to your baby.) If you live near a grocer that caters to a Latino community, you have access to another remedy—plantain leaves. Crush fresh leaves, and use them to line your baby's diaper.

If you're battling diaper rash and using home-washed cloth diapers, add vinegar to the rinse water. Urine is irritating because it is alkaline, and the acid in vinegar can make it less so. (Diaper services often treat their diapers in this way as a standard practice, or will upon request.) You can also add vinegar to your baby's bath water. Use about one cup of white vinegar in about six inches of water in a normal tub, or less than one-third cup in a sink or baby tub.

If you're using disposable diapers, consider peeling off the outside plastic cover and fastening a cloth diaper around it. That combination will prevent leaks while allowing air to get through.

If your baby has graduated to wipes, you should go back to using plain water to clean your baby's bottom while she's rashy. Diaper wipes may make the rash worse.

INTIMATE CARE

Keeping your baby's private parts clean goes hand-in-hand with diapering and will reduce the risk of infection. Don't panic if you see a spot of blood the first time you change your baby's diaper. In the early days red spots are not a concern. They can come from urates, which are normal crystals in a baby's urine that turn to a salmon color on the diaper. Talk to your health care provider if you see any blood after the first couple of days.

Just for Girls

In girls, spots within the first week home may also be a small amount of bloody vaginal discharge caused by the mother's hormones. Talk to your doctor if you see blood in your baby's diaper after the first couple of days.

Penis Care

You will be asked in the hospital if you want your son circumcised. If there are no religious or cultural reasons to circumcise your son, you need to decide if this is the right decision for your family. The benefits of circumcision include:

- Reduced risk of urinary tract infections during the first year.
- Possibly reduced risk of cancer of the penis.
- Possibly reduced risk of sexually transmitted diseases.
- Decreased association with AIDS.
- Easier genital hygiene.
- If father is circumcised, he may want his son to be also.

Critics argue that circumcision:

- Can be painful.
- May reduce sexual pleasure and performance (proponents disagree).
- Is a violation of human rights when performed on an infant since he can't make an informed decision about this permanent medical procedure.

If your son is circumcised, don't clean his penis at all for the first four days. After that, wipe it gently with a wet cotton ball, then pat it dry with a clean cloth diaper. You'll probably be given a tube of sterile petroleum jelly from the hospital. For the first four days or so after the circumcision, squeeze some onto a gauze pad and cap the pad over the tip of the penis every time you change him. This keeps it from sticking to the diaper. After a few days, you may see a yellowish discharge that forms a crust. This is normal, as are a few spots of blood. If the penis oozes blood, call the doctor.

If your son is not circumcised, don't retract his foreskin for cleaning; if you force it, you could cause bleeding and scarring. Normal bathing will keep him clean.

Chapter 11

POTTY TRAINING

Today's toddlers tend to complete potty training much later than prior generations. Twenty-five years ago, 90 percent of toddlers were trained by age 2½. Now, one third of children are still in diapers after their third birthday. Parents who wish to pursue a more lenient approach should prepare themselves for later completion of toilet-training (or "toilet-learning"), as well as questions and an occasional raised eyebrow from older friends and relatives.

THE PARENTS' MINDSET

It's not surprising that many parents approach potty training with such trepidation. Psychologists once thought that the methods they used had a major hand in children's personality development. Sigmund Freud went so far as to state that parents' toilet-training methods dictated a child's eventual career choice! The good doctor believed that overly lax methods would result in the kind of sloppiness that would prompt adults to enter careers like painting. Harsh training methods would lead to controlled youngsters who would enter fields emphasizing the traits of frugality, obstinacy, and orderliness, which Freud considered typical of bookkeepers and accountants.

There is absolutely no evidence that a parent's approach to potty training has anything to do with forming personality, much less career choices! Yet people still refer to exacting, overcontrolling adults as having "anal personalities," and many believe these traits stem from their potty training experiences. Indulge their fantasy if you wish, but know that the research suggests that they're wrong.

Parenting Pointer

In potty training toddlers, parents can do absolutely everything "right," but youngsters won't be successful until they are physically ready, are intellectually capable, have mastered the complex mechanics involved, and decide to refrain from wetting and soiling. All parents and caregivers can do is teach children what they need to know to be able to use the potty, help them acquire the specific skills, try to increase their motivation, and remain confident that if nothing else, the social pressures of kindergarten (if not preschool and day care) will provide an incentive powerful enough to zap the thorniest resistance.

SIGNS OF READINESS

In order to be potty trained, children should exhibit physical, cognitive, and psychological signs that they're capable of getting the job done.

Physical Readiness

Children must be capable of controlling bladder and bowel, which means their central nervous system must have matured to the point that they can control the sphincter muscles that stop and start the flow of urine and expulsion and retention of stool. To achieve nighttime control, the child must be awakened by the sensation of a full bladder, so staying dry at night typically comes later.

It's not possible to be certain whether a youngster's muscles are still automatically giving way when the bladder fills to a certain point. A toddler may have enough physical control for successful potty training if he:

- Remains dry for three to four hours at a time
- Awakens from a nap with a dry diaper
- Passes a substantial quantity of urine at one time
- Has bowel movements at predictable times
- Has well-formed stools
- Routinely goes to a specific place to urinate or have a bowel movement (e.g., a corner of the living room)
- Is able to stop the flow after urination has begun

The bladder is the most reactive organ when it comes to stress, and people of all ages can and do respond to emotional upset by literally "peeing in their pants." By applying pressure to perform, parents can cause youngsters to feel anxious. This undermines bladder control. Accidents in kindergarten are common, and often happen in first grade classrooms, too. Be kind! Be patient!

Parenting Pointer

There is no way to be certain that after experiencing the urge to urinate, the child has the physical control of the sphincter to stop the flow. Punitive methods can cause youngsters who cannot comply with demands to feel incompetent, ashamed, and humiliated. Parental kindness and patience are in order.

Cognitive Readiness

Using the potty is a complicated affair. In addition to being able to recognize and communicate the need to go to the bathroom, and follow instructions on where and how to use the toilet, children must be able to:

- Understand how urinating and passing stool happens (that it comes from them)

- Understand the purpose of the toilet (that they are to "go to the bathroom" there)
- Discern when their bladder is full (recognize the physical sensation of the urge to urinate)
- Recognize the urge to have a bowel movement (recognize the physical sensation of the urge to pass stool)
- Consciously contract the muscles of the abdomen to push out urine and stool while simultaneously relaxing the sphincter muscles

Psychological Readiness

Youngsters must also be emotionally up to the challenge. Psychological readiness includes:

- Being proud of their accomplishments
- Enjoying independence
- Wanting to wear underwear
- Disliking wet or soiled diapers
- Being able to sit quietly for five minutes
- *Not* being in the midst of a phase of toddler negativism
- *Not* being distracted by other major stresses

Learning to use the potty requires a lot of effort on the toddler's part. Don't begin when he or she is coping with other major adjustments, such as the birth of a new sister, an older brother starting school, a change in a parent's work schedule, or an illness.

Parent Readiness—Yes, Parents!

Parent readiness matters, too! Choose a time when you aren't under a lot of stress so you can be patient. You should feel very comfortable with your baby taking yet another giant leap toward independence, and have the time to be on call for at least two days. Children need far more than two days to learn, but working parents can at least help toddlers have some concentrated practice to get them started. Then the methods being used at home need to be discussed with day care center staff and baby sitters so potty training can continue during the week.

SEEING IS BELIEVING

Before toilet-training can begin, toddlers must be aware that their urine and stool come from them, and that elimination is an act on their part. If they are always in diapers, they may think all those wet and soiled clothes happen by magic. They may have better luck making the connection by:

- Having the opportunity to watch others use the bathroom. Some parents aren't comfortable with this, but it can really speed things along! Sometimes an older sibling is willing to demonstrate. Many children have opportunities to witness peers using the potty at day care.
- Being repeatedly told that they are having a bowel movement when they are grunting or straining. If you can tell when your child is going in his diaper, be sure to point it out!
- Observing themselves in the act. Letting them go around the house without clothes is messy, but toddlers simply must be able to observe that urine comes from their own body. Letting them be naked in the backyard in summer is a solution for some families.
- Watching the contents of their diaper being put into the toilet. This doesn't guarantee they'll make the connection, but may help some youngsters make sense of what is supposed to happen.

Baby Basics

Reading can facilitate potty training in several ways. Read toddlers a story to prepare them. Then, after buying a potty, read to them daily while they sit on it. Check out *Everyone Poops* by Taro Gomi or the *Once upon a Potty* series by Alona Frankel.

ON YOUR MARK . . .

Buying a potty seat can be an opportunity to begin generating enthusiasm for training, but no matter how excited toddlers seem, parents shouldn't expect miracles. Once it's out of the box, they may be more interested in wearing the seat on their heads than in sitting on it. It's better to start toilet training with a self-contained potty unit that sits on the floor. Sitting on a toilet so far from the ground can be scary for toddlers. Later, parents can provide a stepping stool and a specially designed toilet seat insert. The insert offers additional security by ensuring they don't fall in.

Baby Basics

Once toddlers start learning to use the bathroom, they may want to use every toilet in every store, gas station, park, zoo, church, and museum they enter! Since getting to a public facility takes longer, toddlers quickly learn they must announce their need to use the toilet further in advance, well before the urge becomes intense. That, combined with their keen interest in exploring the bathrooms of the world, makes it hard for them to decipher whether their faint urge to "go" stems from physical need or emotional desire. In time, they'll learn to more accurately predict their needs and understand their sensations and feelings. Until then, happy exploring!

When buying inserts, parents should beware of brands that have a raised splashguard. Eventually most toddlers bump into it, and that can be painful enough that they refuse to use the toilet again. Some potties can be moved onto the toilet when the child is ready, and the continuity can make the transition easier.

Parents will need to explain what the potty is for: "This is where people put their poop and pee so they don't have to wear diapers. I'm going to teach you how." Having a teddy bear sit on it and discussing the bear's pride in being a big boy with a potty all his own can give a toddler a chance to observe and become comfortable with the situation before he tries it. Here are some other tips:

- Unless a child wants to remove her clothing, it's a good idea to suggest she remain dressed so the feel of the cold, hard plastic doesn't alarm her. The goal should be to get the child to sit on it every day for a week with clothes on. (But of course, if she wants to remove her pants and/or diapers, so much the better!)
- Some children are more amenable to sitting on their potty while their parent uses the toilet or while being read a story, singing songs, or reciting nursery rhymes. Forcing them to spend time sitting on the potty can lead to power struggles, so parents should decide in advance whether they're going to adopt the firm "you need to do this now" approach or let the child proceed at his own pace, although later they may decide to switch tactics.
- Whether or not their youngster sits on it, parents should be sure their toddler understands that he can use it whenever he wants, and should ask if he wants help. Take your toddler with you to the bathroom after each diaper change, and reinforce the message: "Your pee goes here" (point out the potty). "Your poop goes here" (scrape it into his potty so he can see it).

Put down the potty lid, but don't transfer stool to the toilet for flushing until the toddler has left the room. Children may enjoy flushing, and the chance to pull the handle on the tank may serve as a big incentive to use the potty. But unless parents are certain that their youngster isn't afraid of the sound and motion, it's better not to let them do it. Flushing can take on a whole new meaning when youngsters realize that it causes something of theirs to disappear—a fact they may not have grasped when parents cleaned or discarded their disposables.

GET SET . . .

After toddlers have become comfortable sitting on the potty fully clothed, the next step is for them to become accustomed to the feel on bare skin. This is a good time to introduce training pants that can be pulled on and off.

Disposable training pants may prevent children from feeling the wetness. Since they need to be able to distinguish the difference between wet and dry, cloth may be a better choice while they're awake. However, disposable training pants may be more convenient at night while children are still bed-wetting.

Parents can explain, "Kids wear Pull-Ups when they're learning to use the potty. I'll help you pull them down, or you can do it yourself." Being sensitive and responsive to toddlers' desires to handle all or portions of the chore themselves is important for keeping them motivated! During the week that the child practices sitting on the potty seat without clothes, continue to reinforce the idea that bowel movements are supposed to go into the potty. The toddler should accompany them into the bathroom to watch the contents of their messy diapers being emptied into the potty bowl.

GO!

Lots of concentrated practice in a few days is better than practice spread out over a period of weeks. Provide salty foods to increase thirst, and encourage youngsters to drink lots of liquids. If the toddler agrees, have her spend the day without clothing so you can catch her in the act and take her to the potty when nature calls.

After each wet or soiled diaper, you may wish to note the time and day. This information can be used to determine the times of day or the time intervals during which the child needs closest attention.

Baby Basics

Praise for being a "big boy" or "big girl" can backfire when toddlers are vacillating between "me do it" and "Mommy do it." Saying "Mommy doesn't want her baby to have to wear wet diapers anymore" may provide more incentive than saying "Big kids use the potty instead of going in their diapers." Applying some cornstarch or cream after youngsters have used the potty and exchanging tickles and kisses can reassure them that mastering this skill won't turn their world upside-down.

TEACHING HYGIENE

Using the potty will be messy for little boys who insist on standing to urinate. Learning to aim takes practice, and splashing is inevitable. If they won't sit, having them climb onto a stool to urinate into the toilet is an option. Make sure the stool is stable and doesn't slide. Teach children basic hygiene.

- Show them how much toilet paper to use.
- Teach girls to wipe from front to back so they don't introduce bacteria into the vagina.
- Consult your pediatrician for ways to care for an uncircumcised penis as your son goes through the potty training process.
- Provide a stepping stool so they can reach the sink.
- Help them turn on the cold water, apply soap, rub their hands together, rinse, and dry them with a towel.
- Explain the danger of turning on the hot water.

Many stomach and intestinal upsets that parents believe to be a mild case of flu are actually bacteria from poor bathroom hygiene. Toddlers spend a lot of time with their hands in their mouths; they must be taught to wash carefully every time they go to the bathroom.

REWARDS AND PRAISE

Lots of parents recognize that their personal interest in potty training is much greater than their youngster's, so they happily invest in a quantity of Hot Wheels, stickers, cookies, or other items to make the potty experience worthwhile. At first, rewards can be given for simply sitting on the potty for five minutes. Later, the parent can up the ante. To be effective, keep these tips in mind:

- The child must understand exactly what to do to earn the reward, whether it is just sitting on the potty for a specified period or urinating in or having a bowel movement in the toilet.
- Don't require the child to go for a whole day without an accident in order to earn a prize.
- Give rewards immediately; they should *not* consist of a promise of good things to come later unless the child is unusually good at planning ahead.
- Don't give the reward if the child doesn't complete the required task. You can, however, reassure the child that he'll have another chance to earn one later.
- Change the type of reward if the toddler loses interest.

When you give rewards for desired behavior, accompany them with verbal praise, since the ultimate goal is for the child to progress beyond the need for tangible goodies. However, if a toddler is in an oppositional stage, it may work better to refrain from verbal praise and simply say, "Here is your prize for having used the potty" or "You should be proud of yourself." Effusive comments like "I am so proud of you!" can trigger the rebellious impulses that make so many two-year-olds want to do the opposite of whatever they sense their parents want. Instead, try, "Aren't you proud of yourself?" This is a bit less confrontational.

TRACKING PROGRESS

With a large piece of paper and a box of stars or stickers, parents can make a chart to help their toddler track her progress. After each successful use of the potty, the child gets to add a sticker to a chart under the correct day. (Instead of a chart, you might consider letting the child place stickers directly on the potty!)

....

Baby Basics

When parents turn potty time into a game, most kids can't wait for the chance to play. The standard procedure is to draw a bull's eye with a magic marker on a circle of tissue paper. Drop it into the potty, and see if your toddler can take aim, fire, and score a hit. Alternatively, drop a Cheerio or a square of marked toilet paper into the potty and see if the child can hit it. (This is easier for boys, but fun for all.) Boys can also try to roll a Ping-Pong ball around the bowl. (Disinfect both the ball and the hand that retrieves it afterward.)

....

Sometimes toddlers consider stickers a great incentive; sometimes an additional motivator in the form of a prize after the child has earned five stickers boosts enthusiasm. So you don't start the troublesome battle of "if I do what you want, what will you buy me?" consider bestowing the gift you can feel good about giving and the present toddlers love most of all: spending time with *you*. For instance, try an extra bedtime story, ten minutes longer in the bathtub, a leisurely walk around the block to study the dandelions and worms, a trip to the park, or extra time to finger-paint. Just remember that rewards work best when they're immediate!

UP WITH UNDIES, DOWN WITH DIAPERS!

Have your child help select underwear that can be worn as her reward for sustained continence. Let her break out her new attire when she's made it through a full day without an accident.

Baby Basics

Musical potties, available at many stores, have a moisture-activated sensor, so that when children tinkle, they receive instant positive reinforcement: a song! No tinkle, no tune. It provides toddlers with that all-important sense of personal control—only they can make it work.

To increase interest in using the potty for toddlers who are intently working on independence and autonomy issues (that is, going through a very oppositional stage), parents can try making a studied show of having lost interest in it themselves. Employing a bit of reverse psychology works best if a youngster has demonstrated some enthusiasm for learning, but the pattern has been for enthusiasm to quickly fade. Some of these strategies are a bit harsh; parents need to beware, since by using them they risk creating still more control struggles:

- Suggest your tot relinquish Pull-Ups and return to diapers.
- Allow the youngster to experience the discomfort of wet and soiled diapers by being less responsive to changing them. (Delaying a few minutes is enough—the point isn't to torture little ones or to cause diaper rash!)
- Pick her up for a diaper check or change when she's engrossed in a fun activity.
- Eliminate the fun and games when changing him.
- Be less solicitous and more businesslike.

BEDWETTING

At age three, an estimated 50 percent of three-year-olds still wet the bed. Within six months, the figure drops to 25 percent; at age four, it's down to 20 percent. Bed-wetting is considered normal until age six, but the figures remain high for young adolescents, too: 8 percent of boys and 4 percent of girls. The reasons for bed-wetting are not well understood. Genetics may play a role, since studies show children who achieve nighttime continence late often have a parent who had a similar problem. Sleep patterns of hyperactive and depressed children are such that they may not awaken when they need to use the bathroom.

To help eliminate bed-wetting, try the following:

- Limit fluid intake before bedtime.
- Have youngsters use the bathroom right before going to bed.
- Try to determine the time at which the bed-wetting usually occurs, set an alarm, and walk your toddler to the bathroom during the night.

Children who wet the bed need to be handled with compassion. Parents need to trust that children don't like to wake up in a cold damp bed, and should avoid using shame, humiliation, and punishment. Instead, parents should use a plastic sheet and involve older toddlers in the cleanup. They should be able to help with removing the sheets and putting them into the laundry basket.

Bed-wetting problems should be discussed with the child's pediatrician to rule out the possibility of a medical problem and to see about exercises to help increase bladder control. Older children can sometimes overcome the problem by using a moisture-activated device that awakens them.

BOWEL PROBLEMS

Many toddlers continue to have a bowel movement everywhere and anywhere, except the potty. Some are trained for a time and then regress. Is this yet another sign of the uncanny affection toddlers have for their poop? Is it a reaction to the discomfort or embarrassment of sitting naked on a potty for an extended time? Could it be a last-ditch effort to hang on to babyhood? Or perhaps it's an assertion of toddler autonomy?

Most parents never do decipher this puzzle. One thing is certain: If it's a struggle for control, parents are probably doomed to lose. Those who become angry and punitive may find themselves dealing with chronic soiling, known as encopresis (explained later). Here is a hodgepodge of things parents have tried to enhance children's motivation, with varying degrees of success:

- Have toddlers sit on the toilet for five minutes every day at the time they are likely to have a bowel movement. As soon as the time is up, reward their success for having remained seated.
- Immediately offer more desirable treats and toys when toddlers get their stool in the right place.
- If you've already tried the enthusiastic "hip-hip-hurrah" approach to drumming up pride of accomplishment, switch to being matter-of-fact when toddlers get it right, as if using the potty were nothing unusual.
- If your approach all along has been matter-of-fact, try staging victory celebrations.
- Put them back in diapers. However, know that some youngsters then regress to wetting in them, too.
- Ask your child why he doesn't like to use the potty. You probably won't get an answer. Tell him if there's anything that bothers him about it, to let you know. Maybe at some point he will. Maybe it will be a problem you can fix.
- Have your toddler tell you when he needs to go, hand him a diaper, and let him retreat to wherever to do his own thing.
- See if spending time in an environment where other children use the potty, like a preschool, makes a difference.
- Wait for kindergarten peer pressure to solve the problem.

So why do some children insist on having bowel movements anywhere *but* the toilet? In the absence of an underlying medical problem, resistance that develops into full-blown encopresis—constant soiling—often develops from a predictable chain of events:

1. The child is slightly constipated, so her stool is a bit harder than normal. Because passing hard stool is painful, she tries not to have a bowel movement, worsening the constipation and pain.
2. If she uses the toilet, the hard stool causes the cold water to splash, hitting the child's bottom.
3. The combination of pain from passing stool and the surprise and discomfort of being splashed makes the child nervous—even a bit afraid—about pooping in the toilet again.
4. A vicious cycle is created wherein the child's reluctance to use the toilet causes her to become increasingly constipated. Bowel movements become increasingly hard and painful, which further increases reluctance.

The situation can escalate to the point that a mass too large and hard to pass through the rectum forms in the bowel. Liquid that can't be absorbed leaks around the mass. The child cannot inhibit the flow, and continuous involuntarily soiling occurs.

To break the cycle, increase her intake of fruits, vegetables, and fruit juice, and keep her well hydrated with water. If that doesn't help, check with the child's pediatrician about administering a stool softener. A good stool softener will make it impossible for children to contain bowel movements once it takes effect.

Once the child has been having regular soft bowel movements for ten days, rectal soreness should be completely healed. At that point, it is time to work on having bowel movements on the potty. Because children in this situation have come to associate the potty with physical pain and discomfort and the whole situation may have become traumatic, breaking the negative associations and creating new, more positive ones may take some time and a lot of patience. The goal is to help toddlers recover from trauma so they can have a fresh start.

For starters, have the child sit on the potty or toilet for five minutes every day at the time she usually goes, wearing Pull-Ups while seated. Wearing Pull-Ups should add to her feelings of safety and ensure no splashing occurs if she is on the toilet and does have a bowel movement. If her resistance is too strong to be overcome by reassurance and pep talks alone, offer stickers, toys, or special privileges. Set a timer and engage in a quiet activity she enjoys, such as reading a book, playing with an Etch-A-Sketch, or reciting nursery rhymes. Reassure her that the point isn't for her to have a bowel movement; it's to learn to relax while sitting on the toilet.

Once she's sat for five minutes without a struggle for at least three days in a row, it's time to up the ante. Make rewards contingent on having a bowel movement there. Leave on her Pull-Ups to add to her feeling of comfort and to prevent splashing, if she's on the toilet. If she doesn't go during her daily five-minute regimen of sitting on the potty, provide verbal praise and tell her she can still earn the reward if she goes while sitting on the potty later. Ask her to tell you when she needs to go.

After a week of having regular bowel movements on the potty, her memories of the trauma are fading (let's hope!). At that point, have her remove her training pants and try having a bowel movement in the potty or toilet. Continue to set a timer to ensure that she sits for five minutes, but only provide a reward after she actually uses the potty, which may be later in the day.

PART 5

SAFETY FIRST!

Chapter 12
SAFETY BASICS

Babyproofing the house before your baby first comes home is fairly easy because newborn babies and even younger infants aren't very mobile and can't get into too much trouble. There are still very important things to address, even when your baby isn't moving around at all.

CHILDPROOFING THE HOUSE

Even before your baby gets moving, it is time for you to get on all fours, crawl around the house, and make sure that everything is safe. Remember that your main goal in getting your house childproofed is creating a safe environment for your baby to explore and play in.

....

Parenting Pointer

It is never too soon to childproof your house, but do it at least by the time your baby is six months old. If you wait much longer your infant may already be crawling, cruising, or walking, and then you probably won't discover hazards until they have already hurt your child.

....

General Tips

There are many basic safety measures to take care of in each room. Things to watch for range from the little plastic caps on door stops, which kids can choke on, to heavy items on low carts or tables that can easily tip over, especially TVs. Check out the next chapter for even more specific childproofing information.

Your Shopping List

Whether you need these items depends on the layout of your home and your childproofing decisions. For example, do you want to latch your kitchen cabinets, or do you want to rearrange the contents so that all hazardous and breakable items are stowed high out of reach with only child-safe items (pots and pans, Tupperware) in the lower cabinets?

- Outlet covers or caps
- Gates
- Drawer and cabinet latches
- Toilet locks
- Foam strips or corners for table edges
- Window guards
- Window latches
- Oven locks
- Doorknob covers
- Stove knob covers
- Bathtub faucet covers

Basic Childproofing for Crawlers:

- Cover electrical outlets.
- Remove or block access to furniture that is easily tipped over (like floor lamps).
- Either remove furniture with sharp edges or install soft guards.
- Place finger guards on doors so they don't slam on your infant's fingers.

- Move breakables or other dangerous knickknacks out of reach.
- Regularly hunt for dropped coins or other potential choking hazards.
- Hide, coil, cover, or block access to electrical cords.
- Knot blind cords out of reach, or cut through the loop and shorten the strings.
- Gate stairs.
- You shouldn't put your baby in a walker, but if you do, never use a walker around stairs.
- Make sure your pool, if you have one, is solidly fenced and the gate is kept closed and locked. Hot tubs should be kept closed and locked when not in use, and toilets should be locked. Don't even leave a pail of water unattended.
- Cede the lower shelves of your bookcases to your child; move your books out of reach, and restock shelves with baby books.

Additional Childproofing for Cruisers and Walkers:

- Install window guards.
- Place nonskid backing on rugs that your child might slip or slide on.
- Lock kitchen cabinets and drawers that contain anything dangerous (knives, etc.).
- Turn pot handles toward the back of the stove when cooking.
- Make sure bookcases will not topple over.
- Secure the TV so it won't fall if tugged on or pushed.

POISON CONTROL

If you do a good job of childproofing your house, your infant shouldn't be at too much risk of getting into any real poisons. If she does get into a poison—one of your own medicines, household cleaners, or something even more serious, such as a pesticide—do you know what to do?

In Case of Emergency

The AAP no longer recommends that parents keep syrup of ipecac in their homes to induce vomiting. Instead, you should just call Poison Control. This used to mean remembering your local poison control number, but getting help got a lot easier a few years ago when the system was switched to a single nationwide toll-free number. To call your nearest poison control center from anywhere in the United States, you now simply dial 1-800-222-1222, and a poison safety expert will help you figure out what to do for your child.

To prevent poisonings, remember to use products with child-resistant caps, even vitamins and herbal supplements. Store your household cleaners, chemicals, and insecticides out of reach in a locked cabinet. Also keep all hazardous products in their original containers, instead of transferring them to a milk or soda bottle to use them.

Lead Poisoning

As your infant becomes more mobile, paint chips become a potential source of lead poisoning. If you live in a new house, your kids aren't at risk, but if you live in a house that was built before 1950, or that was built before 1978 and is now being remodeled, these paint chips can be a hazard to them. If you have an older home with deteriorating paint, be sure to have your home and your child tested for lead. You also can keep your kids safe from paint chips and dust contaminated with lead by washing their toys and pacifiers often and covering or sealing places that might be covered with lead paint. In addition, you may want to consider having the lead paint professionally removed from your home.

Parenting Pointer

The U.S. Department of Housing and Urban Development estimates that 25 percent of houses still have "significant" amounts of lead-based paints. Most parents do a poor job of estimating how old their home is, potentially putting their children at risk.

If you have a job or hobby that involves working with lead, it is important to change your clothes before entering the house, and to wash your clothing separately from your family's clothes.

Baby Basics

Baby walkers are one product for infants that have always had a bad reputation. If you are considering buying or using a mobile baby walker, keep in mind that the AAP has actually called for a ban on their sale because they are associated with so many injuries, and they won't help your baby learn to walk any faster. An alternative to a mobile baby walker can be a stationary walker or activity center. These include lots of bells and whistles to keep your older infant entertained.

CHOKING PREVENTION

Parents often worry about their baby choking on food once he starts finger and table foods, but the average house has a lot of other choke hazards that put infants even more at risk. These hazards can range from large pieces of food to coins your baby may find on the floor to your older children's toys.

Parenting Pointer

First aid for a choking infant usually involves placing the child face down on your lap and giving five back blows with the heel of your hand to the area just between the infant's shoulder blades. If that doesn't work, the next step is placing the infant face up and giving five compressions to the infant's breastbone. A CPR class can teach you more first aid to help a choking infant.

Younger children naturally put everything in their mouths. This is the way that they learn to explore the world around them, so it is impossible to "teach" them not to put things in their mouths. Instead, it is the parents' responsibility to keep the house free of choking hazards—which can be a daily chore.

The following tips can help keep your baby safe from choking:

- Once your infant is eight to nine months old and you start offering finger foods, cut them up into small, bite-size pieces.
- Avoid giving "choke foods," such as grapes, peanuts, hard candy, popcorn, and chewing gum, to your infant or toddler.
- Let your infant play only with age-appropriate toys (no parts smaller than one and one-quarter inch in diameter and two and one half inches long).
- If you have older kids, consider putting their toys, which often have small parts, in a separate room that your infant can't enter.
- Warn older children not to give their younger siblings foods or toys that they might choke on.
- Let your younger infant play with Mylar balloons instead of rubber or latex balloons, which can be a choking hazard if they pop.
- Look for and pick up small objects, like coins, pins, batteries, marbles, and buttons, each time you put your baby down on the floor.

It is also important to learn CPR so that you know what to do if your baby starts choking.

RECALLS AND PRODUCT ALERTS

Although it seems that most child products, household products, and toys are being built to high safety standards, each year many children are hurt or killed by unsafe products that have already been recalled. Do you know whether any of the products in your home have been recalled?

Parenting Pointer

A new website, *www.recalls.gov*, makes it easy to find all types of recalled products, including consumer products, motor vehicles (including cars and car seats), boats, food, medicine, cosmetics, and environmental products.

....

The Consumer Product Safety Commission (CPSC) recalls hundreds of products each year, including toys, cribs, playpens, and other baby equipment. Unfortunately, it is often up to parents to identify which products have been recalled, and then either repair these unsafe products or remove them from their homes. Even if you send in your product registration card, there is no guarantee that you will be notified if the product has been recalled, so regularly watch the news, magazines, and websites for recall alerts and information.

Even more of a concern is the rise in popularity of buying used products, some of which may have been recalled, from online auction sites. As long as you check to be sure a product hasn't been recalled, most used baby accessories can be safe. However, don't buy a used car seat on the Internet, since there is no way to make sure that it wasn't damaged in a car crash.

SUNSCREEN

Keeping your kids safe from the harmful effects of the sun is very important. Remember that most people get 80 percent of their lifetime exposure to the sun before age eighteen. Increased exposure means increased risk of skin cancer, so it is never too soon to start limiting that exposure.

In addition to using sunscreen, sun safety can include keeping your child covered up with light, loose-fitting clothing, a hat, and sunglasses. It's also best to avoid being outdoors during the hottest part of the day, between about 10 A.M. and 4 P.M.

When to Start Using Sunscreen

Younger children often are forgotten when the family puts on sunscreen, because the parents think it isn't necessary or just not appropriate for infants. In fact, the AAP recommends that you start using a sunscreen on your infant once he is six months old, and that you apply it at least thirty minutes before you take him outside. You should then reapply it about every two hours, or sooner if your child was in the water.

The SPF, or sun protection factor, of sunscreen refers to how much protection it gives from the sun. The higher the SPF, the more protection the sunscreen offers. In general, you should use a sunscreen with an SPF of at least 15 on your infant.

What about Younger Infants?

Just because you don't start using sunscreen until age six months doesn't mean that protecting your younger infant isn't important. Sun exposure can be even more harmful for younger infants than for older ones, and the usual recommendation is to just keep them out of the sun. If you must have your younger infant out in the sun and can't keep him covered up, you can still apply sunscreen to his skin. Just use small amounts and only apply it to small areas that are exposed to the sun.

INSECT REPELLENTS

Insect bites used to be considered a simple nuisance. The biggest problem they caused was an itchy, or sometimes painful, red spot. The rise in West Nile disease and other insect-borne illnesses makes it even more important to keep your children safe from insects.

Parenting Pointer

Alternatives to DEET include natural insect repellents, including those that contain citronella or soybean oil. They may not work as well as insect repellents with DEET, but they are a good alternative if you aren't convinced that DEET is safe to use on younger children.

The most commonly used insect repellents are those that are made with DEET, which can be safely used on infants as young as two months of age. Although you shouldn't put the insect repellent on your infant's hands or around her mouth or eyes, you can put it on other exposed areas of skin or clothing. Always be sure to wash it off once you get back inside.

POOL AND WATER SAFETY

Drowning is a leading cause of death for younger children, so it is important to keep your backyard pool safe. Even if your young children know how to swim, they should not be considered drown-proof and should always be supervised around the water. In addition to not leaving your children alone around a pool, you can keep your kids safe by:

- Putting a fence around your pool with a self-closing and self-latching gate
- Locking or childproofing all exits from your house that lead to the pool
- Leaving a telephone by the pool so that you can quickly call for help if you need it
- Keeping toys away from the sides of the pool so that you don't attract younger children, who might fall in
- Storing rescue equipment near the pool so you are ready in an emergency

Infant Swimming Lessons

Although the AAP doesn't recommend formal swimming lessons until age five, that doesn't mean that you can't take your infant in the water. Aquatic programs are also popular at this age, and although these are not really swimming lessons, they can help you get your baby used to being in the water. Just remember, whether as part of a class or in your pool at home, if your baby is in the water, keep your hands on her at all times.

Indoor Water Safety

Pools aren't the only drowning risk for younger children. A crawling baby can pull up on a bucket, fall in, and quickly drown. Other hazards include the bathtub, toilet, and any other container of water. Remember to never leave your infant alone near any water, not even for just a few seconds, which is more than enough time for your baby to drown. Don't assume that a bath ring or seat will be enough to keep your baby safe—these are meant to make bath time easier, not provide supervision.

KIDS AND PETS

Having a family pet is a popular tradition in many families. For your infant's safety, remember that no matter how kid-safe you think your dog or cat is, you should never leave your baby unsupervised around an animal. Any pet, even one that is usually tame and playful, can bite or attack if it feels threatened by an aggressive infant who is pulling on its ears or invading its space.

Some families also enjoy having more exotic pets, like iguanas, turtles, snakes, and frogs. Because of the risk of salmonella to children who touch or handle these pets, which can cause fever, vomiting, and diarrhea, younger children shouldn't have any contact with these types of reptiles and amphibians. You should even be careful to wash your hands and any surfaces that touch these pets with soap and water so that you don't contaminate your younger children. Small baby turtles with a shell less than four inches in length are especially dangerous, because younger kids can put them in their mouths. In fact, sale of such turtles has been banned by the FDA.

FIRST AID

As the parent of a small child, you'll be administering a lot of first aid—particularly once your child is getting around on his own. You can minimize hazards by childproofing, but your baby will still get his fair share of "owies" the first year.

The First Aid Kit

Once your baby becomes mobile, you'll be patching up scrapes and bumps, pulling out splinters, and administering other forms of first aid. You'll need:

- First-aid manual
- Telephone number for Poison Control
- Sterile gauze
- Steri-Strips or butterfly bandages
- Soap
- Adhesive strip bandages (Band-Aids)
- Adhesive tape
- Antiseptic wipes
- Elastic bandage
- Papain (this natural meat tenderizer soothes bee stings)
- Antibiotic ointment such as Bacitracin
- Hydrocortisone cream
- Tweezers
- Old credit card (to scrape bee stings)
- Calamine lotion
- Cold packs (instant, or keep one in the freezer; use a bag of frozen vegetables in a pinch)
- Cotton balls
- Scissors

Parenting Pointer

When your baby does get hurt, how you react will influence her reaction. If you are matter-of-fact about the injury ("Oh, you scraped your knee. Come on, let's get a bandage"), administering first aid will be a lot easier for both of you.

Common Injuries and Treatment

The following are some common childhood injuries and simple treatments. Don't hesitate to call your doctor if you think the injury is more serious or should be examined.

- **Burns:** Soak the burned area in cool water for at least twenty minutes or until the pain fades. You can hold the burn under cold running water or put ice and cold water in a bowl. Don't use ice alone; it can increase the damage to the skin. Do not put butter or other greases on a burn—they'll trap the heat and make it worse. Simply cover any blisters that develop with a bandage, but don't pop them. Redness and slight swelling are signs of a first-degree burn (the least serious); blistering and significant swelling indicate a second-degree burn; areas that seem white or charred indicate a third-degree burn. If you suspect a second- or third-degree burn, see a doctor immediately.

- **Poison ingestion:** Take away the poisonous substance, if your child is still holding any, and remove any left in her mouth with your fingers. Keep anything that you remove for later analysis. Check for severe throat irritation, drooling, breathing problems, sleepiness, or convulsions. If you see any of these symptoms, call an ambulance. If not, call your local poison control center.

- **Tick bite:** The faster you get the tick off, the less likely your baby is to get a tick-borne disease. Clean the area with alcohol if it's available, water if it's not. If you have nothing to clean with, skip this step. Pull the tick straight up from the skin using your fingers (tweezers are more likely to break the tick, leaving part embedded). Save the tick in case you need to bring it to a doctor. Mark the area, but not the bite, with a pen, and watch that skin for a few days for a bull's-eye-shaped rash. This rash may indicate Lyme disease, for which your baby will be treated with antibiotics. Depending where you live, you should also watch for signs of Rocky Mountain Spotted Fever (rash on hands and soles of feet, fever).
- **Sand in the eye:** Try to keep your baby from rubbing her eye, but otherwise do nothing as tears will usually wash out the sand. If not, you can help them by washing the eye with water. If nothing you do seems to work, call your doctor.
- **Bee stings:** If the stinger is visible, try to remove it by scraping across the skin with a credit card. Do not squeeze it. Wash the area with soap and water and apply an ice pack to reduce swelling. You can also counteract some of the effects of the venom by sprinkling it with meat tenderizer (unless it is near the eye) or spreading a paste of baking soda and water on it. If your baby has a severe reaction—swelling that extends far beyond the site of the sting, a rapid heartbeat, clammy skin, hives, or trouble breathing, call 911. Talk to your doctor once the initial crisis of a severe reaction has passed. Although such allergies are rare, if your child does have an allergy to bee stings you will need to carry a bee sting kit that includes an epinephrine shot that will dilate the airways and allow your baby to breathe.
- **Sunburn:** If you're like most parents, your first reaction to your baby's sunburn will be guilt. "Oh, how can I have forgotten to put lotion on? Why did we stay at the park all afternoon? Why didn't I go home when I realized I forgot her hat?" After you're done beating yourself up about

this, give your baby a bath in cool water or soak some washcloths in water and lay them over the burned area. After she's dry, spread aloe (100 percent) on the burned area.

You can also soak your baby in a lukewarm bath with either a quarter cup of baking soda or a cup of comfrey tea (comfrey reduces swelling). Give her some ibuprofen. If the sunburn blisters, if your baby gets a fever or chills, or if she seems very sick, call the doctor.

- **Cuts:** Stop the bleeding by applying pressure directly to the cut. If the cut "smiles" (the edges gap apart farther in the middle than on the ends), is deep, or may have dirt or glass stuck inside, see a doctor. Otherwise, wash it thoroughly with soap and water, apply an antibiotic ointment, and put on a bandage. If the cut isn't particularly deep or long, it will probably stay closed on its own. Or you can bring the edges together and fasten with a butterfly bandage or Steri-Strip before covering it with a regular bandage.

- **Splinters:** Wash the area with soap and water. If the splinter protrudes, stick a piece of tape over it and pull the tape off—the splinter may come off with the tape. Still stuck? Move on to the tweezers. If the splinter is embedded, soak the area for ten minutes, wipe with an antiseptic, then numb the skin with ice or a local anesthetic intended for teething—like baby Orajel or Anbesol. Sterilize a sewing needle by holding it in a flame for a few seconds (make sure to wipe off any carbon on the needle) or dipping it in alcohol. Then gently, using the tip of the needle, try to tease the splinter out. If it's still stuck, try again after your baby's bath. Don't poke around for more than five minutes; it's unlikely you'll remove the splinter and you may damage your baby's skin. You can also try gently rubbing the skin over the splinter with a pumice stone—if you take away a thin layer of skin, the splinter may be easier to grab. Call your doctor if it is deeply embedded, if it is glass or metal and you can't get it all out, or if the area becomes infected.

- **Bug bites:** These are not a major deal for most babies and usually look worse than they feel. If your baby seems itchy, put ice, cortisone cream, or a paste of baking soda and water on the bite. If the itching doesn't seem to stop or the area keeps swelling, call your doctor, who may prescribe an antihistamine.
- **Scrapes:** Run cold water over the scrape and wash it with soap. Pat it dry with a clean cloth, dab with antiseptic cream, and bandage. Go to the doctor if the scrape is deep, bleeding heavily, embedded with gravel or dirt, or if later you see increasing redness or pus.

Chapter 13
BABYPROOFING FOR EXPERTS

What can toddlers get into? The obvious answer is, everything within reach. But how far, exactly, can they reach? Much farther than you might think possible! Consider everything that can be climbed on, fallen off of, pulled open (or over), and used to extend their reach. The list of hazards is endless. Use common sense and watch carefully to see the kinds of danger your child might get into. Your child is rapidly growing, and what was safe one day might be unsafe the next.

ROOM-BY-ROOM SAFETY

Once you've done the basic safety measures from Chapter 12, it's time to delve deeper into each room to be sure you've checked everything.

The Kitchen

One of the biggest dangers in the kitchen is the stove. There are now many devices to make the stove safe, including locks for the knobs and adjustable covers or guards to keep your baby away from things cooking on the stovetop. You should also secure your other kitchen appliances. Even the dishwasher and refrigerator can be hazards, so place a locking strap on both to keep your kids out.

Kitchen cabinets are often harder to secure than you would think, and they contain many things that could be hazardous to a young child. There are many safety products to help childproof your cabinets. You can choose either a system that latches on to the outside of cabinet handles, which is simpler to install but easy to forget to put back on, or one that installs inside the cabinet as a latch. Or use a combination of the two, especially on the cabinets that contain cleaners, poisons, or breakables.

The Bathroom

As in the kitchen, you should secure the drawers and cabinets in your bathroom. Also consider installing toilet lid locks to prevent drowning, and keep hot appliances such as curling irons out of your infant's reach. A nonslip mat and a faucet cushion can help make the bathtub safe, too.

Bathtub Seats

About 1 million bathtub seats are sold in the United States each year. But if you think these handy devices mean you can sneak out of the bathroom for even a minute, you're wrong! An analysis of CPSC data revealed that bathtub seats were involved in the deaths of thirty-two children age five to fifteen months between 1983 and 1995. In twenty-nine of these deaths, the drowning occurred when the child was left in the seat unattended. Several toddlers managed to crawl out, then slipped and fell. So if you use them, keep these points in mind:

- Collect everything you need—towels, shampoo, soap—before filling the tub.
- Don't trust an older sibling to supervise. According to the study, eleven deaths occurred when a big brother or sister was left in charge.
- Ignore the doorbell, the telephone, your pager, and the soup boiling over on the stove.
- Ignore your other child's call, too. The study showed that 24 percent of the deaths occurred while a parent ran to check on the other child.
- If you leave the bathroom for even a second, take your dripping baby with you!

Some deaths occurred in the presence of a caregiver who couldn't get the straps off fast enough when the child ended up face down in the water. It may be better to forget bathtub seats altogether!

The Fireplace

While a warm fire is nice on a cold night, fireplaces are hard to keep childproofed. Among the dangers are the sharp edges around the hearth and the risk of getting burned when there is a fire going.

The easiest way to childproof a fireplace is to simply place a heat-resistant safety gate around the whole thing. That way you don't have to worry about your kids getting into the fireplace and playing with ashes, falling on the sharp corners of the hearth, or getting close to the flames. If your fireplace is fueled by natural gas, be sure to secure your gas key, place a cover on your gas valve, and install a carbon monoxide detector.

The Garage

Many people don't consider the garage as being part of the house and so don't take steps to keep it childproofed. With all the dangers that a garage may hold, including gardening products, insecticides, lawn equipment, and power tools, it is especially important to keep it safe in case your child manages to get inside by himself. In addition to securing these dangerous items, you should keep your car locked and your keys out of reach so your kids can't accidentally lock themselves inside.

Parenting Pointer

Certain plants can be poisonous. Check with your local nursery and your pediatrician if you're unsure if any plants in and around your home could be dangerous.

OTHER IMPORTANT SAFETY MEASURES

When you think you've thought of everything, watch your child to see what hazards she discovers . . .

Firearms

Parents must keep guns and ammunition locked, and they must store them separately.

Teaching preschoolers (and teens!) about the dangers of guns can help but can also make them more interested in them. They must be locked up! (And if you have youngsters, consider not keeping any firearms in your home at all.)

Toy Chests

When the toddler reaches inside a toy chest and the lid falls on his hand or head, the result can be serious injury or even death. When a child climbs inside and lowers the lid, the result can be asphyxiation. The safety standards for a toy chest include the following:

- A hinged lid that will stay open rather than falling shut
- NO latch, so a child who has crawled inside and lowered the lid can push it open
- Air holes for ventilation

When shopping for a toy chest, check for all three safety features; especially check the lid's hinge or select a box with a lightweight top. If you're using a metal trunk or another box to store toys, remove the lid.

Chemical Potpourri

Modern households are filled with substances that parents may never have thought of as being particularly dangerous . . . but that's because they never considered eating them! Everything from ammonia to bleach to dyes to gasoline to ink to polishes to white correction fluid can be extremely dangerous. One particularly dangerous substance is alcohol. Glue is yet another item to watch out for.

Cosmetics

It's one thing to put dye on your hair—quite another to put it in a stomach! Products whose safety you never thought to question should be kept well out of reach of little hands, including creams, hair coloring agents, lipsticks, perfumes, and shampoos.

Poisonous Insects

Exposed roots, rough stones, and sharp sticks are a potential danger in their own right, but they are also perfect tools for digging, poking, and exploring the great outdoors. While a toddler is outside, she can also be exposed to a variety of nasty bugs: fire ants, bees, wasps, hornets, and dangerous spiders.

Childproofing for the Holidays

Holiday decorations are bright, colorful, and often sparkly and dangly—all perfect to engage your child's curiosity. So go ahead and decorate for the holidays, but make sure that you also make it safe for your baby. You'll need to be on high alert during the holiday season.

- Put a baby gate around the Christmas tree to keep your baby from getting too close and trying to pull off any ornaments or use a branch to pull herself up to stand.

- If you don't close off the tree, don't put any ornaments or lights on lower branches and put breakable, precious ornaments on higher branches.
- Don't put nuts or hard candies within reach on a coffee or side table. Choking is a major hazard for small children.
- Place candles and menorahs out of reach to avoid burns or tipping over.
- Don't put any holiday greenery, especially those with berries like poinsettias and holly, within reach of little fingers. Much of it is poisonous if swallowed.
- Make sure your fireplace is properly screened, and never leave a baby alone in a room where there has recently been a fire. Ashes can burn if touched.
- Check your tinsel—older versions were made with lead and shouldn't be used.
- Make sure that any alcoholic drinks are kept at adult height. Even a small amount of alcohol can be toxic if sipped by a baby.

LIFESAVING SKILLS

Basic lifesaving skills are familiar to many people, but used by few. This is the time to refresh those skills—with the hope they'll never be used.

CPR

Every parent should take a basic course in CPR, cardiopulmonary resuscitation. The Red Cross and American Heart Association offer courses in communities across the country. In them, students learn to administer artificial respiration to people who have stopped breathing, chest compressions if someone's heart has stopped beating, abdominal thrusts for choking, and basic first aid. The cost of these courses is nominal; they are readily available in most communities, so there's really no excuse not to take one. Not all include the specific techniques for reviving infants and toddlers, which are different than those used for adults. Check to be sure that what you need to learn will be taught.

Young children account for more than half of the 7,000 drownings that occur each year, so it really is worth parents' while to acquire CPR skills. An online video demonstration can be viewed at *www.heartinfo.org/cpr/cpr.html#retpulse.*

Artificial Respiration

Five minutes without oxygen is enough to cause permanent brain damage; a few more minutes and death is probable. The exception is if the body is very cold; it then needs less oxygen, sometimes enabling youngsters to survive for longer periods. If a child has stopped breathing due to swelling of the air passages caused by a medical problem such as asthma, an allergic reaction, or a respiratory infection, artificial respiration should be started immediately. However, if the child has stopped breathing due to an object stuck in his windpipe, artificial respiration might force it farther into the child's windpipe or even the lungs. Before attempting artificial respiration, a rescuer should follow the instructions for choking (see the section "Treating a Choking Victim").

For artificial respiration, follow these steps:

1. Place the youngster face up on the ground, lift the chin up and tilt the head back to keep the tongue from blocking the air passages. Examine the mouth and remove any visible obstructions with a curled finger.

2. Cover the child's nose and mouth tightly with your mouth and give two gentle breaths lasting 1 to 1½ seconds each. Be careful not to blow too

much or too hard; this will cause the child's lungs to hemorrhage. When properly done, you should be able to see the child's chest rise. His head must remain tilted up throughout to keep the wind passages open.

3. If the child does not resume breathing on his own, administer additional breaths at the rate of about twenty per minute until a medical team arrives.

4. If vomiting occurs, as is often the case, turn the child's head to the side to prevent choking. Then quickly clear the mouth cavity before resuming assisted breathing.

Chest Compressions

The heart delivers oxygen-enriched blood to the brain. If the child has collapsed and is non-responsive—that is, he doesn't moan, cough, or move even when his shoulder is tapped and his name is called—check for a pulse at the carotid artery. The easiest way to find the carotid artery (either of two large arteries on each side of the neck that carry blood to the head) is to place your fingertips (not the thumb, which can confuse the issue because thumbs have a pulse) in the groove of the child's neck, next to the windpipe, near the jaw.

If you can't find a pulse, someone trained in CPR needs to manually pump the blood via chest compressions while you call 911. Compressions can damage the heart if it is already beating, so it's important to be sure there is no pulse before beginning. Here is the procedure for carrying out chest compressions:

1. Place a flat hand on the child's chest on the lower half of the breastbone, which is located between the nipples, and push down with the heel of your hand.

2. The child's chest should depress one-third to one-half the depth of the child's chest, far less than is needed for an adult.

3. Repeat this action at the rate of 100 compressions per minute.

When you combine mouth-to-mouth breathing and chest compressions, deliver five chest compressions for each breath until help arrives, and check occasionally to see if the heart has begun beating on its own.

Treating a Choking Victim

If a child is eating or playing with a small toy and begins to choke, his air passage may be partially or completely blocked. Signs of a partially blocked air passage include choking or coughing that starts very suddenly, gagging, or breathing that is noisy and high pitched.

If a child can manage to breathe a little bit, call 911 or get her to an emergency room immediately. Trying to dislodge the object could end up making matters worse by cutting off the child's air completely. If a child's ability to breathe is almost completely cut off or if breathing has stopped altogether, the situation is desperate and the child must have immediate assistance to keep her alive until an emergency medical team arrives.

Symptoms of desperate trouble include:

- The ribs and chest are sucked in when the toddler tries to breathe.
- The toddler can't get enough air to cough.
- The toddler can only wheeze softly or make soft high-pitched sounds.
- The toddler can't make any sound at all.
- The lips and skin are bluish.

If the toddler is unconscious, look in the child's throat and try to remove the blockage. If that doesn't work, administer two rescue breaths. If the child doesn't start breathing on her own, start chest compressions. Sometimes the compressions will eject the object from the windpipe.

If a toddler can't breathe but is still conscious, the goal is to force her to cough; something she can't do on her own because she is unable to take in enough air. Begin by explaining that you will help her. Quickly position her in front of you, reach around her with both arms, make a fist, and place it so that your thumb rests just above the navel and below the breastbone. Grasp your fist with your other hand. Give five quick thrusts, pressing upward and in. The object may be expelled. If not, give five more abdominal thrusts. Keep trying until the object is ejected.

If the child loses consciousness, lay the child down, lift her chin, open her mouth to look for the object, remove it if you can, and help her breathe with artificial respiration. If her heart stops, start chest compressions until medical help arrives.

MEDICATION SAFETY

While it might be tempting to refer to medicine as "candy" when you're trying to get some down a reluctant toddler's throat, don't! Just think what will happen if he gets into a bottle or a box when you're not around. Many parents don't realize that overdoses of vitamins can be dangerous, too. Follow these basic safety strategies:

- Call medicine by its real name.
- Use products with child-resistant packaging.
- Don't confuse "child-resistant" with "childproof." The name changed when it was discovered how quickly toddlers could get the covers off. Very few items are toddler-proof!
- Keep medications in their original containers to avoid confusion down the road.
- Avoid storing liquid medicines in cups or soft-drink containers that might tempt a thirsty toddler.
- Install childproof locks on cabinets, drawers, and closets where medications are stored. (Don't depend solely on locks! Little fingers can sometimes work them open.)
- Keep track of how much medicine has been used. If you discover his hand in the bottle and pink syrup ringing his mouth, or her hand in the pills and white powder on her tongue, you'll have an idea how much has been ingested.

- Treat vitamins containing iron like the medicine it is; an overdose can be fatal.
- Check the dosages and use a proper spoon or vial for measuring before each administration. A teaspoon from your set of measuring spoons is NOT the same as a teaspoon from your silverware drawer.
- Don't mix medications without your pediatrician's approval.
- If the phone rings while you're administering medication, take it with you. Don't leave unattended drugs around a toddler!

Don't take your own medication around a toddler—you don't want her to mimic you. Children need to learn that when it comes to prescriptions and over-the-counter medications, they are to take *only* what a caretaker administers. That includes vitamins.

Herbal Safety

There's no guarantee that an herb is safe, and some homeopathic remedies can pack a big punch. Before administering alternative remedies to a toddler, check the following:

- That it has been tested on youngsters
- That its effectiveness has been established
- The kinds of side effects and adverse reactions that may occur
- That it won't interact with other prescription and over-the-counter medications your toddler is taking

CAR SAFETY FOR TODDLERS

Toddler car seats can face forward in your car and are used for babies who are at least two years old. Most toddler car seats are designed to carry children until they are 60 to 80 pounds, though state laws vary on how old and how large your child has to be before he can leave a car seat. There are also older child options for those too small or young to leave a car seat but too mature to sit in a baby seat. Usually boosters will do the job—there are several types. Younger children will likely still want a car-seat-like booster that has a five-point harness. As the child gets bigger, the car seats generally get smaller and more compact. Ask your pediatrician and visit your local baby supply store to read labels and find a seat that matches your child's height and weight and fits in your car properly.

Parenting Pointer

When you buy a new car, be sure it comes equipped with the new LATCH (Lower Anchors and Tethers for Children) system for safely securing car seats. This is the most up-to-date and simple car seat system available in vehicles. Car seats can work in older cars, but the LATCH system makes things a lot easier.

A toddler car seat attaches to the car via the seat belt in your car. It can be moved from car to car, but it is less convenient than the infant car seats. It does not double as a carrier. Speak to other parents about their toddler car seat choices before purchasing your own.

PART 6

MEDICAL CARE AND BASIC BABY HYGIENE

Chapter 14

CHOOSING A PEDIATRICIAN

For many parents, their pediatrician is one of the people they have the most contact with outside the house during their baby's first year. That makes choosing a good one important. Having a pediatrician that you will be comfortable with will also help you feel confident that your child is growing and developing normally and that you are making the right choices about his care.

THE SELECTION PROCESS

Deciding which pediatrician you will trust with the care of your new baby is a big decision, and one that is made differently by different parents. Although there might not be one best way to choose a good pediatrician that you will be happy with, there are some things that you should not do.

- Don't just pick a doctor from the phone book or from a list provided by your insurance company.
- Don't pick whoever is "on-call" when your baby is born.
- Don't go to a pediatrician that someone else likes unless you ask what she likes about the doctor.
- Don't go to a doctor just because the office is in a convenient location.

It is important to choose a pediatrician before your baby is born so that if anything goes wrong, you will know who is taking care of your baby and advising you on medical decisions that you must make. Choosing the right doctor may mean avoiding unnecessary tests or treatments from a provider who is overly aggressive or, on the other hand, avoiding a doctor who misses something important because of an inappropriate "wait-and-see" attitude.

Getting Recommendations

Your choice is fairly easy if you already have a pediatrician who has been caring for your other children or if your own pediatrician is still practicing. If not, the best way to find a pediatrician is to get recommendations from friends or family members who have a pediatrician that they like. But it is important to find out *why* they like their doctor. Is it simply because the office is efficient and they can get in and out quickly? Or is it because they always get an antibiotic when they want one?

When accepting someone's recommendation, make sure that you are comfortable with the reason why they like the pediatrician, and that this reason has something to do with being an educated and competent doctor (not a personal preference for the way the waiting room is decorated, for instance). The same applies when a person recommends against a doctor, because the reason for being unhappy with that particular pediatrician may be something that wouldn't bother you. Your own OB/GYN doctor might also be a good source of a recommendation, but again, ask why she is recommending the pediatrician.

Parenting Pointer

The American Board of Pediatrics reports that there are 77,328 board-certified pediatricians in the United States, and an additional 2,500 new pediatricians graduate from residency training programs each year. Only 9 percent of them practice in rural areas, though, so whether it will be easy for you to see a pediatrician is likely to depend on where you live.

Practicing Styles

Although parents often focus on office hours, hospital affiliations, and length of wait times, one of the most important things to consider when selecting a pediatrician is his style of practicing medicine. Does he wear a white coat and tie and seem very formal, or does he dress casually and have a playful, informal style? Does he spend a long time explaining things, or does he provide you with reference material that you can take home and read?

Recognizing the pediatrician's style is important, because just as you become friends with different types of people, there will likely be a particular pediatrician's style with which you will be most comfortable.

Your Expectations

It is also important to consider your own expectations when you choose a pediatrician. Do you want to always be able to talk to the doctor when you call for advice, and not have to speak with a nurse? Do you expect these calls to be able to last fifteen or thirty minutes?

If you have moved or your previous pediatrician is no longer practicing, you can't always expect to have the same relationship with your new doctor. Just because your previous pediatrician gave you her home phone number to use at any time does not mean that your new pediatrician will do the same thing. The one thing you should expect is that building a relationship takes time on both ends, although with time you may get those same privileges from another doctor.

Parenting Pointer

The most common reasons for a child to go to the doctor, besides well visits, include having an ear infection, an upper respiratory tract infection, and gastroenteritis, with diarrhea and vomiting.

SOLO VERSUS GROUP PRACTICE

As you look for a pediatrician, you will notice that some doctors practice all by themselves in a solo practice, while others work with a group of doctors. While it shouldn't be the most important factor when you choose a pediatrician, you should understand some of the differences between solo and group practice pediatricians, as well as the major pros and cons of each.

Solo Practice Pediatricians

One of the main benefits of going to a pediatrician in practice by herself is that when you have a visit, you will always see your pediatrician. You don't have to worry about explaining your child's whole medical history to another doctor or seeing someone you don't necessarily like or trust. Even when you call after hours, you will get to talk to your own doctor.

Another benefit is that a small office will have a small staff. That means that the receptionist, nurses, and office manager are likely to recognize you when you come in and better understand your family's specific needs. You will probably also be able to get common tasks, such as getting a copy of your child's immunization records, done quickly.

Of course, such a small office can be a problem if you don't like or get along with even one of the office's staff members. Another downside is that without any other doctors covering for your pediatrician, you may not always get an appointment when you want one. A small office also may not have the latest medical technology available, so you might have to go elsewhere for simple lab tests and other procedures.

Group Practice Pediatricians

A pediatrician in a group practice shares an office with one or more other pediatricians. With more doctors being available, you probably will be able to get an appointment whenever you want one. You may not be able to see your own doctor or talk to your own doctor after hours, though.

Another downside is that with a larger office, there will be more office staff and you may not get to know everyone in the office. However, a larger office will have more resources, and will likely be able to provide more services than a solo practitioner will.

MAKING YOUR CHOICE

Before making your final choice for a pediatrician, you should consider some practical matters:

- Is the pediatrician on your insurance plan?
- Is she in a convenient location so that you don't have to drive for an hour with a sick child?
- Are the office hours convenient for you?
- How long do you have to wait for an appointment?
- Will you always see your own pediatrician?
- How long will you be kept waiting in the office?
- Is someone available when the office is closed if you need help?
- Is the office affiliated with a children's hospital?

Although you could wait until your prenatal visit to consider these questions, you could also do a little homework on your own and call the offices to save some time. One "wrong" answer may not be enough to disqualify a potential doctor, but if you get several unsatisfactory answers, especially for the questions that are most important to you, then scratch that doctor's name off of your list of candidates.

Next, find out if the pediatricians that you are considering agree with your positions on important matters, like breastfeeding, antibiotic overuse, circumcision, and so on. If not, are they at least flexible and willing to help you do things the way you want to, even if they disagree with your methods?

Once you find a pediatrician that you like, be sure to take some steps to keep the relationship healthy, such as by showing up for your appointments on time, not showing up without an appointment, and not waiting until after hours to call with non-urgent problems.

The New Parent Consult

It is usually best if both mom and dad go to any prenatal visits to meet the doctors that you are considering. After you make a list of candidates from recommendations and the questions found in this chapter, try to schedule a prenatal visit to meet each doctor. While some doctors charge for these "interviews," most provide them as a free service.

You will want to ask several questions about issues that are important to you, but the main point of these visits is simply to find out if you feel comfortable with the pediatrician and to see how her office works. For example, if you see a waiting room that is overflowing with frustrated parents who seem to be waiting for long periods of time, you might end up waiting for your visits, too, unless there was an emergency that put the office behind schedule. If you show up early for your prenatal visit and see a regular stream of kids come in and quickly go back to see the doctor, then you have likely found an office that is run very efficiently and which you might want to go to yourself.

You Can Change Your Mind

Even with a lot of recommendations and a good prenatal visit, it will still take a few "real-world" visits to find out if you have found the right pediatrician for you. The office may have a policy you didn't know about, or maybe the doctor was simply on her best behavior for the "interview." If you later encounter problems with your pediatrician or her office and you can't resolve them, start the process over and look for another pediatrician.

Chapter 15

WELL VISITS

Your infant will make lots of visits to your pediatrician's office during his first year of life. While most of these visits ideally will be for well-child checkups and immunizations, you may also have to go in for a few sick visits when your child is not feeling well. Knowing what to expect can help you make the most of these visits.

PREPARING FOR YOUR VISITS

You don't often hear parents complain about spending too much time with their pediatrician, so it is important not to waste what time you have in the office. Taking care of your sick child and supervising his siblings running around the room are just a few of the things that can distract you during your visits. Preparing a list of questions can help you to not forget anything important. (You'll learn more about what to put on this list later in this chapter.)

The first step in preparing for your visits to the doctor is deciding who actually is going to take your baby to the office. Will it be mom, dad, a grandparent, or another caregiver?

Although you often don't have much choice because of work schedules and other constraints, ideally both mom and dad would come to each visit. That way each parent can ask his or her own questions and get a better understanding of how the baby is growing and developing.

WELL-CHILD VISITS

There will be a number of visits to your pediatrician for checkups during your baby's first year. These checkups, or well-child visits, include an evaluation of your baby's growth, development, and feeding habits; a complete physical examination; a discussion of what you should be doing to take care of your baby's needs; and usually some vaccines. Because appointments for well-child visits are planned far in advance, both parents should make every effort to attend. This is especially important in your baby's first months, when it's likely that both mom and dad have a lot of questions.

Recommended Checkup Schedule

Most pediatricians stick to a standard timing schedule for well-child visits as recommended by the AAP. This schedule calls for visits at these ages:

- Two weeks
- Two months
- Four months
- Six months
- Nine months
- Twelve months

The first visit to the pediatrician is usually well before two weeks though. The AAP recommends that all babies see their pediatrician within three to five days of leaving the newborn nursery to make sure they are feeding well, not losing too much weight, and aren't becoming jaundiced.

What to Expect

At each well-child visit, in addition to a standard history and physical, your pediatrician should have your baby's height, weight, and head circumference recorded and plotted on a growth chart to make sure that he is growing well. It is also important that the exam include a testing of your baby's red reflex, which is part of an eye exam, and a hip check to evaluate for developmental dislocation.

Parenting Pointer

If your pediatrician is leaving out major parts of a traditional well-child visit, such as not measuring his height, weight, or head circumference, or not checking your child's hips or eyes during the physical exam, you might want to change to another doctor.

Other tests will include getting a hematocrit or hemoglobin level to screen for anemia. This test is done sometime during the first year, often at the nine-month checkup. It's likely that your baby also will be either screened or tested for tuberculosis and lead poisoning sometime during his first year of life.

When attending a well-child visit, be prepared to answer the following questions about your baby:

- How often is he breastfeeding or taking a bottle of formula?
- What new foods have you introduced since the last visit?
- What new milestones has your baby picked up, such as rolling over, sitting up, or standing?
- How well is he sleeping at night and during naps?

- In what position is he sleeping?
- Where is he sitting in the car, and in what kind of car seat?
- Has he had any reactions to his immunizations?
- Are you giving him a vitamin or any other medications?
- What concerns do you have about his development?

Parenting Pointer

If your child has a chronic condition, such as asthma or eczema, don't wait until your well visits to talk about them. If you do, it will take away much-needed time for your pediatrician to talk about your child's nutrition, growth, development, and safety. A separate visit to talk about your child's illnesses is usually a better idea.

Be prepared so that your baby's doctor can more easily determine how well your child is doing. Questions you might ask your doctor include which foods to start next, what milestones to watch for, and what things you should avoid doing.

RECOMMENDED VACCINATIONS

Just like antibiotics, vaccines also can be seen as both an extraordinary medical advance and a threat to your child's health. Even though vaccine experts generally agree that no vaccine is 100 percent safe or effective, it is clear that they are helpful for the majority of children. If you are uncertain whether you want to immunize your child, be sure to talk to your pediatrician about your concerns so that you can make an informed decision. Most of the common problems from vaccines are limited to local reactions at the location where your child got the shot, such as redness, swelling, and soreness. Many vaccines can also cause rashes and fever, but severe reactions, like a serious allergic reaction, seizures, or high fever, are very rare.

Routine Vaccinations

There are several vaccines that are commonly given to children at their routine checkups. These include all of the following, which are listed in the Recommended Childhood and Adolescent Immunization Schedule that is published by the AAP each year.

Hepatitis B

This vaccine, which protects against the hepatitis B virus, a common cause of liver disease, is given as a three-dose series to infants. The first dose is often given at birth or before hospital discharge. The second dose is usually given when infants are one to four months old, and the last dose when they are between six and eighteen months old.

DTaP

The diphtheria, tetanus, and acellular pertussis vaccine has fewer side effects than the older DTP vaccine. The first three doses are given at two, four, and six months.

IPV

Although kids used to get the oral polio vaccine (OPV), because of the risk of it causing vaccine-associated paralytic polio, this vaccine is now given as an inactivated shot. Your infant will get doses of this vaccine at two and four months, and a third sometime between six and eighteen months.

Hib

This vaccine protects against the *Haemophilus influenzae* type b bacteria, which can cause meningitis, epiglotitis, pneumonia, and skin, bone, and blood infections. It is given at two, four, and six months, with a booster dose at twelve to fifteen months.

Prevnar

Although often thought of as the "ear infection vaccine," this vaccine also protects against meningitis, pneumonia, and blood infections caused by the *Streptococcus pneumonia* bacteria. Like Hib, it is given at two, four, and six months, with a booster dose at twelve to fifteen months. An older Prevnar 7 version of this vaccine is now being replaced with the newer Prevnar 13 vaccine that provides better coverage against more subtypes of the Strep pneumo bacteria.

Rotavirus Vaccines

Depending on the vaccine brand that is given to your infant, Rotarix versus RotaTeq, she will get either two or three doses of this oral vaccine to protect her from infections caused by certain strains of rotavirus, a common cause of vomiting and diarrhea in children.

Twelve-Month Shots

In addition to the booster doses of the Hib and Prevnar vaccines, infants get the MMR (measles, mumps, rubella) and the chickenpox vaccine when they are twelve to fifteen months old.

Flu Shots

Parents are often surprised at the idea of giving a flu shot to their baby, but it is approved for infants six months and older. Why would you want to give your baby a flu shot? One of the main reasons is that younger children are thought to be at big risk for flu complications, just as elderly people are. So even if your baby is healthy, a flu shot might be a good idea to help her avoid getting sick. In fact, it is now recommended for all children who are at least six months old. Keep in mind that infants do have to get two doses of the flu shot at least one month apart the first year that they get their flu shot.

Combination Shots

Nobody likes the fact that infants have to get so many shots, especially if they have to get four or five separate shots during a single visit. Your baby might get fifteen separate shots before her first birthday, including three doses of several vaccines. However, that number can be greatly reduced with the use of combination vaccines.

One of these, Pediarix, combines the DTaP, IPV, and hepatitis B vaccines into a single shot, which can cut the number of shots from fifteen to only nine (or ten if your baby also got the birth dose of the hepatitis B vaccine). Pentacel is another that combines DTaP, IPV, and Hib. If you are concerned about your baby's reaction to all those needles, speak with your pediatrician about the possibility of receiving combination shots.

ALTERNATIVE IMMUNIZATION SCHEDULES

Few people would describe the childhood immunization schedule as being very flexible. Sure it advises that some vaccines can be given within a certain age range, for example, six to eighteen months for the third dose of Hepatitis B, but it still advises that all of the vaccines in the schedule be given to all children.

Even though most parents get their child's vaccines on time, concerns about vaccine side effects have led some parents to seek alternative immunization schedules. Some of these parents are still worried about thimerosal, even though there are thimerosal-free versions of all of the vaccines in the current vaccine schedule, even the flu vaccine. Others are worried that children are getting too many vaccines at too early an age. And of course, the underlying worry is that there is some connection between vaccines and autism.

On the other end of the debate are parents and health experts who fear that stopping vaccines will simply cause an increase in vaccine-preventable illnesses, such as whooping cough and measles. They understand that even delaying vaccines can be a problem, as many children are at highest risk for many vaccine-preventable infections as infants, including whooping cough, Hib meningitis, and pneumococcal meningitis, etc.

Can an alternative immunization schedule decrease your child's side effects and still protect him from vaccine-preventable infections? When considering this question, it is important to keep in mind that there are actually no research-proven alternative immunization schedules. The current schedules that some parents use, in which they pick and choose which vaccines they want their kids to have, likely work because most other kids are still fully vaccinated.

EARLY INTERVENTION

Babies develop at different rates. Some may walk at ten months while others may not reach that milestone until they're fourteen months old. Some babies crawl at seven months, while others are ten months or older. Some babies skip that step and go directly to walking. Some talk early, and some talk late. Parents, especially first-time parents, worry. Remember, there is a wide range to normal.

If your child was born very early; has been diagnosed with a developmental delay; or has a visual or hearing impairment, motor problems, a language disorder, a chromosomal disorder, or any other serious condition, early intervention is critical. These first few years, from birth to three, is when the rate of learning and development is most rapid. Getting the right help for your baby can make a long-term difference.

You want to get a specific assessment of the issue(s) and a clear plan of therapy. Early intervention has been proven, both in long-term studies and on an anecdotal basis, to be effective. In fact, the earlier the intervention, the more effective it is.

Trust your instincts and talk to your doctor if your baby is not reaching developmental milestones or you suspect your baby has a hearing or vision problem. Be persistent and ask for a second opinion if you are not satisfied with your doctor's assessment.

Chapter 16
SICK VISITS

With luck, most of the visits to your pediatrician during your baby's first year will just be for well-child visits, but there may be times when your baby is sick and needs to see the doctor. Keep in mind that just because your child doesn't have a runny nose, cough, or fever doesn't mean that she isn't sick.

Behavioral problems might also be a good reason to schedule an appointment with your pediatrician, instead of just trying to get advice over the phone. Such problems might include the child not sleeping well, being very fussy most of the time, not feeding well, or refusing solid foods.

....

Parenting Pointer

When your child is sick, don't wait until the last minute to make an appointment. The earlier you call once your pediatrician's office opens in the morning, the sooner you will get an appointment. If you wait until late in the day you might be asked to wait until the next day for an appointment, even for a problem that has been going on for several days.

....

You should usually expect a same-day appointment when your child is sick, unless your child's condition is a long-term or non-urgent problem, such as acne or bowlegs. It is unreasonable to expect a parent or child to wait even one or two days when the infant has an ear infection, fever, or difficulty breathing. You probably should look for another doctor if you are regularly made to wait several days for appointments when your baby is sick.

What to Expect

During sick visits your child should be weighed and have his temperature taken. Next, after talking about your child's problems and symptoms, your pediatrician should perform a complete physical exam. Doctors who quickly prescribe an antibiotic each time you walk in the door or regularly leave out parts of the exam, such as not looking in your baby's ears or mouth, may not be providing adequate care. If your child has a fever and was up all night crying, your doctor should look at her ears before concluding that she has an ear infection.

Questions the Doctor May Ask

Parents often assume that a doctor can tell what is wrong with a sick child just by the physical exam. In reality, the history (or story of the child's illness) is often even more important. For example, suppose a child has a cough and runny nose. If she is eating and drinking well, isn't too fussy, and isn't having trouble breathing, and the symptoms just started yesterday, then she likely just has a cold and doesn't need any antibiotics. If, however, she has had two weeks of symptoms that are now worsening, and has developed a fever, she might have a sinus infection and may need antibiotics. Both cases would likely have the same physical exam; it is the description of the illness that would get her the right treatment.

Some questions that you should be prepared to answer during each visit can include:

- How long has your child been sick?
- What are all of her symptoms?

- When are the symptoms worse?
- How have the symptoms been changing?
- What makes the symptoms better?
- How has being sick affected her eating and sleeping?
- Has she been around anyone else who's been sick?
- What medications have you been giving her?
- Why do you think she hasn't been getting better?
- What are you most worried about with this illness?

Questions to Ask Your Doctor

Parents seem to have a million questions that they want to ask their pediatrician, but they often forget them during the visit. Preparing a list of questions and bringing them to your visits can help to make sure that you get all of your questions answered. Some good questions to start with at a sick visit include:

- What is my child's diagnosis?
- What causes this?
- What treatments are you prescribing, if any?
- What are the side effects of those treatments?
- Are there any alternatives to those treatments?
- When should she start getting better?
- What are some signs to watch for that might mean she is getting worse?
- When can she return to day care?
- Do I have to limit her diet or activity?
- Should I bring her back for a recheck?

Getting answers to these questions (and making note of the answers) is especially helpful if only one parent can make it to the visit and needs to explain everything to the other.

INFANT ALERT: SICK VISITS DURING THE FIRST MONTH

You're more likely to need to call the doctor while your baby is a newborn. Symptoms that are not worrisome in an older baby can indicate real trouble during a baby's first month.

- Call your doctor immediately if your jaundiced baby becomes dehydrated or feverish.
- Call your doctor during her regular office hours if your baby looks deep yellow or orange, has fewer than three bowel movements a day, or still looks yellow after she is fourteen days old.
- Call the doctor if your zero-to three-month-old baby's temperature is above 100.4°F rectally. A fever in the first two months may be a sign of a serious infection, and an infection at this age can quickly overwhelm the developing immune system. Your baby may be hospitalized and treated with antibiotics.
- Diarrhea in newborns can quickly lead to dehydration. Babies normally have several bowel movements a day, and these are typically runny. If the stool looks more like water than like mustard, however, it could be diarrhea. If you suspect diarrhea, and your baby is pooping more often than she is eating, call the doctor.

- Projectile vomiting (vomit that shoots out of the mouth instead of dribbling down the chin) may mean your baby has an obstruction in the valve between the stomach and small intestine. Call your doctor immediately.
- While a newborn doesn't have a lot of muscle control, she typically kicks and squirms and waves her arms around. If she feels floppy all over or seems to lose muscle tone, she may have an infection, and you'll need to call the doctor.
- A quivery chin is cute, but if your baby seems to quiver all over, your doctor needs to find out why.

Older Baby Symptoms

If your baby is more than a month old, you don't need to be quite so quick to dial the doctor. But you should call if your baby:

- Is three to six months old and has an axillary (under the arm) fever higher than 101°F.
- Is over six months old and has an axillary fever higher than 103°F.
- Has a fever for more than two days.
- Has a fever and a stiff neck, symptoms of meningitis. (Check for this by holding a toy level with her face and then moving it toward the ground. If she can't follow its path by bringing her chin down to her chest, she may have a stiff neck.)
- Is too sleepy. (You may be relieved if your baby suddenly starts to sleep all day and night, but a big jump in sleepiness is not normal and may indicate an infection.)
- Cries excessively.
- Vomits persistently (after every feeding within twelve hours), or if the vomit contains blood.
- Seems dehydrated. (If your baby seems to be peeing a lot less than usual—i.e., if you're changing fewer diapers—there is a problem.)

- Has trouble breathing (the skin between her ribs may suck in with each breath), or breathes extremely rapidly (more than forty breaths a minute).
- Has persistent bluish lips or fingernails (babies can briefly turn blue from the cold, or from crying).
- Has a cough that lasts longer than two weeks (although you should check with your doctor when your baby first develops a cough), or has a whooping or barking cough.
- Has eye inflammation or discharge.
- Has a rash that covers much of her body.

CHILDHOOD FEVER BASICS

"Does she have a fever?" That is one of the first questions you'll be asked whenever you call your doctor with a question about a sick baby—and it will soon be one of the first questions you'll ask yourself.

....

Parenting Pointer

Do not try to lower a fever by rubbing your baby with rubbing alcohol. Isopropyl alcohol is quickly absorbed through the skin, and large amounts applied topically can be inhaled, which can lead to alcohol poisoning and other problems.

....

Fevers do have a purpose, although their exact role is unclear. They may increase the number of white blood cells (which kill viruses and destroy bacteria) or raise the amount of interferon, an antiviral substance, in the blood and thus hinder bacteria and viruses from multiplying. Fevers aren't dangerous in themselves (although they serve as a warning of other problems), except when they rise very quickly or reach extremely high levels—above 106°F.

You will notice that your baby's fever will climb in the afternoon from a morning low. This is normal, and doesn't mean your baby is getting sicker.

Thermometers

Thermometers come in different styles: glass, digital, and tympanic. Avoid using a mercury-filled glass thermometer because of concerns about mercury. The American Medical Association issued a statement that non-mercury fever thermometers are as effective as and safer than mercury-filled ones. Disposable strips aren't accurate enough for a baby under a year, and definitely not for newborns. You can take a baby's temperature rectally, under her arm (axillary), or by reading the heat off of her eardrum (tympanic). You can't, however, take her temperature orally; holding the thermometer under her tongue would be uncomfortable and she might gag or choke. Also, she might bite off the end.

Taking Your Baby's Temperature

For babies under three months, most doctors want you to take a rectal temperature. It's the most accurate and, at this age, every degree is significant because treatment of a fever will be based on temperature.

If you are using a non-mercury glass thermometer to take your baby's temperature rectally, make sure you have one intended for rectal use. If you are using a digital thermometer, designate one for that purpose by marking it with an indelible "R." First clean the thermometer by wiping it with rubbing alcohol or washing it with soapy water. Then make sure it is reset by shaking the thermometer until the temperature gauge reads below 98.6°F. To reset a digital thermometer, turn it off and then on again.

Put a dab of petroleum jelly on the tip of the thermometer. Lay your baby stomach down on the changing table and hold her with one hand placed firmly on her back; add another dab of petroleum jelly at the opening of her anus. Insert the thermometer tip a half inch into her rectum (never forcing it), and hold it there between your second and third fingers, with your hand cupped over her buttocks. Wait two minutes for a glass thermometer, or until a digital thermometer beeps. A rectal temperature of 100.4°F and up in a baby under three months is considered a fever.

For older babies, open up or remove her clothing to take a temperature under her arm. Put her in a comfortable position, lying in your arm or against your chest. Put the glass or digital thermometer in her dry armpit and tuck her elbow against her body. Cuddle her, making sure she doesn't move her arm. (You can pace the floor with her; just keep her arm firmly over the thermometer.) Wait four minutes, or until the digital thermometer beeps its all-done signal. An axillary temperature of over 102.2°F is considered a fever.

How to Treat a Fever

If your baby has a fever, make sure she isn't dressed too warmly and that her room isn't hot. You can strip her down to her T-shirt, but keep a light blanket handy for when her temperature begins to drop.

With your doctor's permission and confirmation of the dosage, give her a fever-reducing medicine, like acetaminophen (Tylenol) or ibuprofen (Motrin). You should see the fever start to come down thirty minutes later, sometimes sooner. If it doesn't, or spikes back up again quickly, these medicines can be alternated. While doses of Tylenol are meant to be given four hours apart and Motrin six hours apart, pediatricians sometimes recommend giving a dose of Motrin only two hours after giving Tylenol. Just don't give a second dose of the same medicine any sooner than prescribed. Talk to your doctor about what he thinks is most effective in treating fevers.

You can also try to bring your baby's fever down by giving her a bath in a few inches of lukewarm water, using a washcloth to spread water over her, and letting her air-dry. Give your feverish baby lots to drink—she's sweating out fluids, and dehydration can make her feel worse.

Febrile Convulsions

You should, however, be aggressive in fighting fevers in children who are susceptible to febrile convulsions. Two to four percent of children, most between six months and six years old, are susceptible to these kinds of seizures, characterized by symmetrical rhythmic convulsions, eyes rolling back in the head, and a loss of consciousness. Convulsions can last as long as ten minutes, but usually disappear in less than two minutes. Although it's less common, some susceptible children experience them every time they get a fever. The seizures usually have no permanent effects and are not a form of epilepsy. A seizure is likely related to fever if:

- The seizure occurs within twenty-four hours of starting a fever
- The seizure lasts less than five minutes
- The seizure affects the whole body and is not confined to one side

While your child is having a seizure, you want to focus on her care—you can call the doctor once the seizure is over. If your child has a seizure:

- Turn her on her side
- Remove any hard objects she might slam into
- Look at your watch

You need to time the seizure—your doctor will want to know its duration. If the seizure lasts longer than five minutes, call your physician or local paramedics. After five minutes the child should get emergency care and be evaluated; but seizures of that duration are rare. If your child is prone to these seizures, you will probably want to administer fever-reducing medicine sooner, rather than later. Call your doctor after the seizure is over and review the incident.

MEDICINES 101

You'll be treating a lot of minor illnesses, so have the following on hand. For nonprescription medicines, check the label for the correct dosage. If no information is given for your baby's age or weight, call your pediatrician's office for the correct dosage.

- Thermometers—at least one oral and one rectal
- Infant acetaminophen drops or suspension

- Infant ibuprofen drops
- Topical anesthetic (useless for teething, but may help with splinter removal)
- Vaseline
- Pedialyte (oral electrolyte solution designed to replace fluids and minerals lost when child has diarrhea or vomiting)
- Benadryl (an antihistamine for allergic reactions)
- Calibrated syringes or droppers for giving medicine
- Nasal aspirator
- Saline nose drops
- Diaper rash cream
- Hydrocortisone cream
- Aveeno (an oatmeal bath, soothing for many skin problems)

Giving Medicines

"Give him one dropperful of Tylenol," or, "Give him one teaspoon of antibiotic," your doctor says. You dutifully fill the dropper or syringe up to the correct line, put it in your baby's mouth, and squirt it in. It immediately comes dribbling back out, at which point you madly try to shovel it back in with your finger. Giving a baby medicine is not intuitive. If you're lucky, your baby will like the taste and lap it up—but don't count on it.

The cheek pocket strategy is a good one. Use a finger to pull out a corner of your baby's mouth to make a pocket in his cheek, and drop the medicine into the pocket a little at a time. Keep the pocket open until all the medicine has been swallowed.

Distractions can help make the medicine go down. If you can call on another adult or sibling to wave a toy or make faces at your baby, do so. Otherwise, dangle a toy from your mouth as you use both of your hands to give the medicine.

If giving your baby medicine orally is always a struggle, ask your drugstore for acetaminophen suppositories. The dosage, in milligrams, is the same as that for oral medication, but is less preferable than the oral form because the amount that is absorbed can vary.

Eye Treatments

You may also someday find yourself having to give your baby eye medication, in the form of drops or ointment. You'll need to have someone hold your baby's hands so she doesn't rub away the drops immediately, or you can wrap her in a blanket. Balancing your hand on her cheek, but being careful not to touch the dropper to the eye, aim the drops for the inside corner of her eye. (Her eye does not need to be open; when she blinks, the drops will get in.)

If you're administering ointment, you do not need to force her eye open. Instead, squeeze out a line of ointment along the roots of her upper eyelashes (kind of like eyeliner). Keep her hands away from her eyes until the ointment melts into them. You can also pull down her lower eyelid to make a pouch and put the drops or ointment inside that. If your baby really fights the eye medication, try applying it when she is asleep.

Other Ideas

Here are some other strategies for administering medicines:

- When taking your baby's temperature rectally, keep a cloth diaper or a diaper wipe nearby while you're waiting for the reading, just in case he poops.

- Try refrigerating your baby's liquid medicines—they may taste better cold. But check with the pharmacist to make sure refrigeration won't alter the medicine's effectiveness.
- If he really hates the taste of a medicine, have your baby suck on a Popsicle first to partially numb his mouth.

Your baby will get sick and you will get through it. Rely on your good sense, and know that your baby will probably be better in the morning.

COMMON MEDICAL PROBLEMS

Your baby's first year will bring a lot of fun and exciting firsts, including her first smile and first steps. The first day that she's sick, whether she has a runny nose, vomiting, or a sore throat, won't be one of the firsts that you are looking forward to, though. Being prepared will make it easier for both of you.

Diarrhea

When caused by a virus, as diarrhea typically is, the basic treatments are aimed at preventing your child from becoming dehydrated. If the only symptom is diarrhea and your child is eating and drinking well, you often can just continue her regular diet and give a few ounces of an oral rehydration solution each time she has diarrhea. You might try the typical BRAT diet, which stands for bananas, rice, applesauce, and toast. Yogurt, with acidophilus, is also thought to help treat diarrhea, and might be helpful for your older infant.

Vomiting

Vomiting accompanied by diarrhea and a low-grade fever, particularly when other people are sick with the same symptoms, is often caused by a simple stomach virus. Vomiting can be a symptom of more serious conditions, though, some of which are medical emergencies. Call the pediatrician if you're unsure.

Dehydration

Although the average infant with diarrhea can drink enough to stay hydrated, if he has large amounts of very watery diarrhea it is possible for him to quickly get dehydrated, especially if he is also vomiting. Being able to recognize dehydration is important and can help to make sure your baby gets the medical attention he needs. Early treatment can also help you avoid unnecessary trips to the doctor or emergency room.

One of the first signs of dehydration to watch for is whether your child is still urinating. If he is having a soaking-wet diaper every six to eight hours, then he likely isn't dehydrated. If he is still having wet diapers, but they are not as wet as they usually are, then he is mildly dehydrated and might get worse without treatment.

The next sign that an infant is dehydrated is a dry and sticky mouth. It is a good sign if your infant's lips and tongue still seem moist or if you can see saliva in his mouth. Late signs of dehydration, which can indicate a medical emergency, can include not making tears, sunken eyes, a sunken fontanel or soft spot, and a lot of weight loss. If you think your infant is dehydrated or if you can't tell, be sure to seek immediate medical attention.

Constipation

As long as the bowel movement is soft and watery and not big and firm nor small, hard, little balls, than your child likely isn't constipated. Although exclusively breastfed babies rarely get constipated, infrequent bowel movements can be normal beginning at around two to three months of age and until you start baby foods. Again, as long as the bowel movements are soft, this slowdown is likely normal, even if your child has only one dirty diaper a week. Infrequent bowel movements can be more concerning in the baby's first few weeks of life, though, when it can be a sign that she isn't getting enough breastmilk to drink.

Your infant also may get constipated when you introduce solid foods, like cereal. Once she gets used to her new diet, the constipation often goes away without treatment.

For an infant with persistent constipation, it can help to give her extra water, juice, and baby foods with fiber. If your baby drinks formula and has a great difficulty with constipation, you might have to change to a soy or elemental formula to soften her stools. Rarely, a stool softener might be needed. Things to avoid are regularly giving your child suppositories, or using enemas. You might ask your doctor about Hirschsprung's disease if your child has never had a normal bowel movement on her own.

Colds and Coughs

The common cold is the most frequent cause of a runny nose in younger kids. As with most other viral infections, there is no treatment for the common cold, and you often just have to treat your child's symptoms until he gets over them on his own.

These symptoms typically begin with a clear runny nose, low-grade fever, and a cough. Over the next few days the symptoms may worsen, with a higher fever and worsening cough. The runny nose might become yellow or green before going away over the next one to two weeks. It is important to understand that this is the normal pattern for a cold and does not mean that your child has a sinus infection or needs antibiotics. The belief that any runny nose that turns yellow or green is a sinus infection has led to the great overuse of antibiotics and the creation of resistant bacteria that are difficult to treat. Of course, if your child is very fussy, is not eating or drinking, or has trouble breathing, then a trip to your doctor is a good idea.

To help your infant feel better during his cold, you might use saline nasal drops and frequent suctioning with a nasal aspirator to clear your infant's nose, a cool-mist humidifier or vaporizer, and an age-appropriate dose of a pain and fever reducer. Keep in mind that the FDA now warns against using cold and cough medicines in children under age two years, though, so they should be avoided. Also, when considering using a pain and fever reducer, remember that children and infants should not take aspirin because of the risk of Reye syndrome, a life-threatening liver disorder.

While a yellow or green runny nose is typically caused by a common cold, if the infection lingers for more than ten to fourteen days and is worsening, or if the child has a high fever for more than three or four days and appears ill, then he may really have a sinus infection that requires antibiotics.

Bronchiolitis

Often starting out with typical cold symptoms of a runny nose and mild cough, infants with bronchiolitis will develop wheezing, a worsening cough, and trouble breathing as the infection gets in their lungs.

Usually caused by the respiratory syncytial virus (RSV), bronchiolitis can quickly turn into a serious infection that sometimes requires hospitalization so the patient can receive intravenous fluids, oxygen, and further care. Younger infants, especially those born prematurely, are especially prone to serious infections and complications from bronchiolitis.

Bronchitis

The same viruses that cause the common cold can also cause bronchitis, an infection of the bronchial tubes that lead to the lungs. Symptoms are also similar, with a cough, but the cough might be more productive than it is with a cold, and your child may not have much of a runny nose. Although the cough from bronchitis might last several weeks or longer, it doesn't usually need treatment with antibiotics. Over-the-counter cold and cough medicines are also not recommended, especially in light of the FDA warnings about using them in children under two years of age.

Croup

Croup is one of the scarier respiratory infections that your infant can get. Unlike most other viral infections, which start with mild symptoms that gradually worsen, an infant with croup usually wakes up in the middle of the night with a loud cough that sounds like a barking seal, and he may have trouble breathing.

Initial treatments might include going into the bathroom, closing the doors, and turning on all of the hot water. This "steam room" treatment will usually help your child to breathe. Just be sure to keep him away from the hot water. Other treatments might include using a cool-mist humidifier or simply walking outside if it is a cool or cold night.

More serious cases of croup are usually treated with steroids or a nebulized medicine called racemic epinephrine. Call your doctor or go to the emergency room if your child with croup is very irritable or is having a hard time breathing.

Whooping Cough

You should also be aware of the symptoms of whooping cough, or pertussis, which has made a recent resurgence because the vaccine wears off after several years. When younger children get pertussis, after a few days or weeks of cold symptoms, they often get coughing spasms or fits, which can be followed by the typical "whoop" as the child gasps for air. Many children also vomit after these coughing fits, which is known as post-tussive vomiting.

Routine immunization with the DTaP vaccine protects most infants from the bacteria that causes whooping cough, although it takes at least three doses to be protected, which leaves many infants unprotected until at least their six-month well-child checkup, when they get their third dose of DTaP. Unfortunately, the protection wears off in teens and adults, who can get sick and expose younger infants to pertussis. A newer vaccine—Tdap—can now protect teens and adults too.

To protect your younger children from whooping cough, you should keep them away from any older child or adult with a chronic cough or bronchitis, which is often the only symptom at that age. Because this condition is often overlooked, be sure to tell your doctor if you are worried that your child might have whooping cough. In addition to treatment with the antibiotic erythromycin, younger infants who have whooping cough are often hospitalized because of the risk of apnea, a condition that may cause a child to stop breathing.

Allergies

Infants with allergies are often misdiagnosed as having colds and sinus infections. Because the average child has six to eight upper respiratory tract infections each year, it is possible that kids who almost always have a runny nose do indeed continually get sick. However, a more likely reason for a chronic runny nose is allergies, especially if your child typically has a clear runny nose and no fever.

In addition to being difficult to diagnose, allergies can be difficult to treat at this age, because few medicines are approved for use in children so young.

Parenting Pointer

Although it was long thought that having pets was bad for kids at risk for allergies or asthma, several recent studies have shown that children who grew up around allergens might have a decreased chance of developing allergies and asthma later in life. Some experts believe that the recent increased incidence of allergies and asthma is because we live in too "sterile" an environment, and pets may help to make it less so.

Asthma

Asthma can also be difficult to diagnose at this age, when kids may just have a chronic cough and not the typical wheezing that older children with asthma often have. Some features that might indicate asthma as the cause of a chronic cough include worsening of the cough at night or with any kind of activity, especially once your child starts walking and running around.

The importance of daily preventive medications to manage asthma is now well known. Medicine such as inhaled or nebulized steroids can prevent further asthma attacks and allow your child's lungs to heal, so early diagnosis is important. Avoiding triggers will help a lot as well.

Rashes

After colds and ear infections, a rash is one of the more common reasons for a visit to the pediatrician. Rashes can range from small red bumps and itchy, crusted plaques to welts from head to toe.

Eczema

Eczema is one of the more frustrating rashes, both because it is so itchy and because it usually keeps coming back. It often affects children with other allergic-type diseases such as allergies and asthma. Usually beginning at about age six to eight weeks, infants with eczema develop itchy, red patches on their cheeks, elbows, knees, and eventually the rest of the body in severe cases.

Treatments for flare-ups of eczema usually include a topical steroid cream, either over-the-counter for mild cases or prescription strength for persistent cases, and regular use of moisturizers as a preventive measure. Flares also can sometimes be prevented if you can find and avoid common triggers, such as harsh soaps, wool clothing, overheating, and frequent baths without using a moisturizer.

Hives

Hives are large, red, raised areas that come and go quickly and are very itchy. Unlike most other rashes that affect children, each hive usually only lasts a few hours before it disappears and another pops up somewhere else. Hives are a common allergic reaction in children, often triggered by foods such as peanut butter, egg whites, milk, and soy. They also can be triggered by medicines or even by infections. If possible, try to find and then avoid known triggers. You usually can treat hives with an oral antihistamine, like Children's Benadryl, but ask your pediatrician first, especially to review the dosage for a younger child.

Hand, Foot, and Mouth Disease

This is a common viral infection that is often overlooked because most parents aren't able to get a good look in their infant's mouth when she is sick. A child with hand, foot, and mouth disease (HFMD) usually has a fever, irritability, and ulcers in the back of the mouth. This infection is easier to recognize if the child also has the typical blisters on the palms of the hands and soles of the feet.

Unfortunately, there is no treatment for this common illness. The symptoms can last for seven to ten days, during which time your child will be contagious to others. Symptomatic treatments with pain and fever reducers and making sure your child drinks enough so that she doesn't get dehydrated can be helpful until she recovers. Appropriate pain and fever reducers might include ibuprofen if your infant is over six months old, or acetaminophen. Remember to not give your child aspirin because of the risk of Reye syndrome.

Tonsillitis and Strep Throat

Parents often confuse the term "tonsillitis" with strep throat. It can help to remember that "tonsillitis" is a generic term for an infection or inflammation of the tonsils, but it doesn't refer to whether the problem is caused by a virus or bacteria. So even if your child has enlarged tonsils that are red and covered with pus, it doesn't necessarily mean that she has strep. Tonsillitis also can be caused by a viral infection, which, unlike strep throat, doesn't require treatment with antibiotics. Younger children are much less likely to get strep than are older children, but you might have your child tested if she has direct contact with someone who does have strep.

INFECTIONS AND OTHER PROBLEMS

Other common childhood problems that you may get some experience with include ear infections, chickenpox, and other infections.

Ear Infections

Parents often suspect that their child has an ear infection when he starts pulling on his ears, but unless there are other symptoms, like a fever or irritability, the ears are usually normal.

Parenting Pointer

Some of the risk factors that increase your child's chances of getting frequent ear infections include: having a parent who smokes, not breastfeeding, drinking a bottle while lying down, using a pacifier, having uncontrolled allergies or gastroesophageal reflux, and attending a large day care.

More typically, your child will develop an ear infection a few days or weeks after having a cold. A child will experience ear pain, irritability, fever, and a decreased appetite when he gets an ear infection. Although symptoms often go away without treatment, doctors still commonly prescribe antibiotics, especially for children under the age of six to twenty-four months.

An ear infection shouldn't be confused with simply having fluid in the middle ear, which commonly occurs after an ear infection. This fluid doesn't usually require treatment and will often go away in two to three months. If it isn't going away, a child may need treatment with ear tubes, especially if it is causing a hearing loss. Frequent or persistent infections can also be a sign that your child needs ear tubes.

Chickenpox

Chickenpox is much less common since children began getting routine immunizations that protect against it. However, because children don't get this immunization until their first birthday, your child can be at risk if he is exposed to someone with chickenpox during his first year.

Symptoms usually begin ten to twenty-one days after exposure to a person who has chickenpox, and include fever and a rash. The rash begins as small, itchy, red bumps that quickly become blisters. These blisters will crust over before fully healing in about seven to ten days. They can be treated with an anti-itch medication, like calamine lotion, or an Aveeno oatmeal bath.

Thrush

In addition to causing diaper rashes, yeast can also cause an infection in your child's mouth. Once infected, an infant develops white patches inside the mouth, typically on the tongue, the inside of the cheeks, and on the lips, gums, and the roof of the mouth. This common infection is typically treated with the oral anti-fungal medication Nystatin, although persistent infections are often treated with fluconazole, a stronger medication. Be sure to clean your baby's pacifiers and the nipples for bottles, which can sometimes be the source of the yeast that causes thrush. Breastfeeding mothers should also be sure that they don't have a yeast infection of their nipples, which would also require treatment.

Roseola

A common infection of younger children, roseola begins with a high fever and mild upper respiratory infection symptoms, like a runny nose. After a few days, the fever breaks, and the child develops a pink or red rash all over his body.

It is the characteristic pattern of the rash developing once the fever breaks that makes this infection easy to recognize. Unfortunately, that means that you usually can't make the diagnosis until the end of the illness, and so your child might have to go through testing to look for other more serious causes of fever, like blood and urine infections, while he has the high fever.

Fifth Disease

Although not very common in younger children, Fifth disease has such a characteristic presentation that it is important to be familiar with it. Like most other viral infections that cause rashes, Fifth disease typically results in mild cold symptoms, but in this case children's cheeks become red. This redness gives rise to the other name for this illness, "slapped-cheeks" disease. After a few days, the redness is replaced by a pink, lacelike rash on the child's arms and legs. And although the rash may come and go for several weeks, it requires no treatment and will go away without problems.

Adults who are exposed to someone with Fifth disease and who aren't immune can get a more serious infection that is accompanied by arthritis. Pregnant women are also at great risk if they get Fifth disease. If a pregnant woman is exposed to a child who is infected with this disease, she should call her obstetrician.

Baby Basics

Although parents worry when their kids get sick a lot, it is important to remember that the average child gets six to eight upper respiratory tract infections, such as colds and sore throats, and two to three episodes of diarrhea each year, especially if he is in day care.

Chapter 17
KEEPING YOUR BABY CLEAN

There's no big rush to give your baby her first bath—the nurses bathed her at the hospital. Infants don't get all that dirty, so one bath a week is plenty until she's eating solid foods (and smearing them all over herself) and crawling in the dirt. Just be sure to wash her face, hands, neck, and diaper area daily. If your baby likes her bath, feel free to bathe her every day. It won't bother her skin as long as you limit her bath to no more than ten minutes, use water and a mild soap only, and, if she has unusually dry skin, use a lotion afterward.

GEARING UP

The first few baths are relatively simple—you're just concentrating on keeping your baby warm, making her feel secure, and getting her clean. As she grows, of course, toys and boats and ducks will take up more room in the tub than she does. In the meantime, stock up on some simple, yet highly recommended, bath aids:

- Cotton balls (for cleaning eyes and ears)
- Plastic cup or spray bottle
- Soft brush
- Baby washcloths (lots, for washing, warmth, and play)

- Several towels
- Giant bath sponge (for baby to lie on, or use another towel)
- Baby soap or no-tears shampoo (the two are pretty much interchangeable), or mild glycerin bar soap
- Baby bathtub, dishpan, or clean sink
- Foam pad to kneel on when you're bathing your baby in an adult tub (Special pads are available for this purpose, or you can use kneelers designed for gardening.)
- Nonskid mat (for use in the adult tub)
- Protective faucet cover (for adult tub)

The Sponge Bath

If you decide that your baby's first bath should be a sponge bath, your best location choice is a counter next to the sink, if your counter is big enough. This has several advantages. Cleanup will be easy since it's waterproof, it's high enough to keep you from wrecking your back, it provides a ready source of warm water, and it makes it easier to rinse your baby's hair.

You'll need something soft to lay your baby on. A thick, folded bath towel is fine. If you have a baby bathtub that came with a thick contoured sponge, save the tub for later but place the sponge on the counter.

Make sure you have everything that you need within reach. You'll need several towels. In addition to the one on which your baby's lying, you'll need one to keep parts of him warm while you're bathing other parts, and another one to dry him. You'll also need:

- At least two washcloths (you don't want to wipe a spot of milk from his face with the same washcloth you just used to wipe his backside).
- Cotton balls or another clean washcloth for his eyes.
- Baby soap or mild bar soap (like Dove).
- A clean diaper.

- Clean clothes
- Diaper rash ointment, if you're using it
- A plastic cup

Strip the baby down to his diaper and lay him on the towel. Cover him with the other towel; you'll uncover only the piece of baby you're washing at the moment.

Wipe inside the corners of his eyes, from inside out, using a clean cotton ball or different corner of the washcloth for each eye. You can use cotton balls to wipe his ear folds as well, but don't try to wash inside the ear canal, even if you see wax. The wax protects the inner ear. Then move on to washing his limbs and the front of his torso.

Parenting Pointer

When bathing your baby, pay special attention to all the creases around his neck, which may be filled with gunk. With a newborn, this gunk is likely to be skin cells sloughing off; with an older baby, the gunk is likely to be dried food.

To wash his hair, wet it with the washcloth, add a dab of soap, and gently massage the entire scalp, including the soft spots. (You don't really need a special baby shampoo; liquid baby soap is an all-purpose cleaner at this stage.) Hold your baby so his head is being supported by one hand, and tip it slightly back over the sink. Using the plastic cup, pour warm water back over his head, avoiding his eyes. If some soap does get into his eyes, wipe them with plain, warm water; he'll open his eyes once the soap is gone.

Next, take off his diaper and wash his bottom and genitals. (If you're bathing a girl, remember to always wash from front to back.) Finish by sitting him up, leaning him forward on your hand as if you're going to burp him, and wash his back. Check to make sure all the soap is rinsed off, and dry him with a clean towel, again paying particular attention to the creases in his neck.

INTO THE TINY TUB

When you're ready to get your baby off the counter and into the tub, you don't need an official baby bathtub. You can bathe your baby in a clean dishpan, the tiny plastic basin the hospital gives you to hold your supplies, or even the sink itself.

Whatever type of tub you choose, think of your back when you're positioning it. Having the tub in the sink or up on the counter will be easier to manage than crouching over it on the floor. When you are trying to bathe two kids at once, put the baby tub with its stopper unplugged right inside the big tub—there should be room left for your older child.

Gather up all your supplies while your baby is still dressed. Line the baby tub with something soft (a special-purpose bath sponge or a towel), fill it with only two or three inches of lukewarm water, and test the temperature on the inside of your wrist or elbow. The idea here is that most of your baby's body and all of her face should be well above the water line. You'll keep her warm by layering extra washcloths over her stomach and pouring warm water on them regularly. (This is a great job to give a sibling.)

. . . .

Parenting Pointer

Babies lose heat especially quickly when they are naked, so get your bathroom nice and toasty, around 75°F, before bath time starts. You can either turn up your thermostat or let the shower run and steam up the bathroom before tub time begins.

. . . .

BATH-TIME TIPS

Try these strategies for improving bath-time efficiency, safety, and fun:

- Turn your hot water heater to a low setting (about 120°F) to avoid dangerous burns.
- Don't answer the phone, even a cell phone, while bathing your baby. Let the calls go to voicemail. It's too distracting to be talking on the phone while bathing a slippery baby.
- Remove shaving razors from the sink and edge of the tub.
- Put liquid baby soap into a clean pump dispenser for one-handed use.
- Save the spray bottle the hospital gave you for cleaning your perineum and use it to rinse your baby's hair.
- Bring on the washcloths—the more the merrier. Besides the one you're using for washing, spread a few others across your baby to keep him warm. If you have another child, give him a washcloth to soak with water and drip onto the baby's tummy. You may be rewarded with tandem giggles.
- Pat your baby dry. Don't rub, as this can irritate delicate baby skin.
- Heat the towels in the dryer, and let them cool slightly—your baby will love the snuggly warmth.
- The kitchen sink makes a great place for a baby bath if you have a spray hose and faucet that turns out of the way and all the dishes are done.
- Make your baby comfortable in the baby bath or sink and reduce the chance he'll slide around. Put a folded towel or special-purpose bath sponge on the bottom before you put your baby in the water.
- Bathe with your baby. It's a lot easier on your back than leaning over the tub, and you're bound to get wet anyway. (If you have a hard time finding enough time for your own bath in a normal day, this idea is for you.) Have another adult nearby to pass the baby to you when you get in the tub and so you can hand off the slippery baby when it's time to get out of the tub.

- Get a spray hose that attaches to the tub faucet; you can use it to rinse your baby with clean water, and it makes hair washing much easier.

GRADUATING TO THE BIG TUB

Your baby is ready to graduate to a regular bathtub once he can sit steadily without support (usually some time after six months).

You'll find that baby stores sell bath seats or rings for this stage. These will give your baby extra support, but probably aren't worth a trip to buy them. Your baby won't use a bath ring for long; as soon as he starts crawling, he'll want to explore the tub. A bath ring or seat may give you a false sense of confidence. Even when your baby is in a bath ring or seat, you need to stay within grabbing distance—these devices don't keep a baby from tipping over and slipping under the water.

Since a towel or sponge on the bottom of a regular tub will slide all over, get a non-skid mat if your baby seems not to like sitting on the bathtub's hard surface. This will be softer to sit on, as well as safer.

BABY HYGIENE 101

Following are some basic care methods for babies and small children.

Scalp Issues

Some babies are born as bald as a cue stick while others sport a full head of hair at birth. But even those who appear to be bald at birth have fine, downy, very light-colored hair. Your baby may lose her hair in the first six months. It can also come in a different color than what you saw in the delivery room.

"Telogen effluvium" is the technical term for your baby losing his first hairs. All hair has two stages: growth and resting. When it's in the resting stage, the hair remains in the follicle. When new hair comes in, the old hair falls out. Stress, fever, and hormonal change can make hair stop growing and go into the resting stage . . . and then fall out. Your baby's hormone levels plummet after birth, which is why his newborn hair falls out.

You may be surprised to find that the new hair is a different color and texture.

Cradle Cap

When you're washing your baby's head, you may see thick, yellow scales. This is cradle cap, and, although it looks pretty yucky, it's benign. You can let it go away on its own, or try this instead: Rub baby or olive oil onto the scalp, let it soak for a few hours, then scrub the cradle cap away with a baby hair brush, baby toothbrush, or nail brush, followed by a dandruff shampoo to get the oil out.

Bald Spots

Your baby may develop a bald spot or two. Study how he sits and sleeps. If he sleeps with his head on the same side or rubs the same spot of his head against his mattress, he may develop a bald spot in that place.

To remedy the problem, alternate where you put him down for his nap and at night. For his nap, put him down with his head going toward one end of the crib; at night, put him down with his head at the opposite end of the crib. He will turn his head to look out of the crib, which will relieve the pressure on the bald side.

Trimming Nails

Of all the baby-care tasks, nothing seems to panic parents more than the idea of cutting their baby's nails.

Clippers or Scissors?

Parents are evenly divided between clippers and scissors. Clippers seem safer than scissors, but can actually cause more damage. The best guide is probably what you're more comfortable using on your own nails—experience counts. And you may discover that your own manicure scissors are actually less likely to draw blood than blunt-tipped infant nail scissors. The blunt tip does keep you from stabbing your baby, but that isn't so much of a risk. The bigger problem is that the blades of baby scissors tend to be a little thicker and difficult to slip easily under your baby's nails, making it more likely that you'll pinch skin.

Trim Time

Wait until your baby is in a deep sleep when you're learning to trim nails. This means her arms and legs flop when lifted, and her hand is resting open, not in a fist. Hold the scissors or clippers in one hand; with the other, pull the tip of her finger down away from the nail. You should now have better access to the nail, so go ahead and cut. Cut straight across. If you're worried about sharp corners, you can gently file them later. If you do cut your baby, press on the cut and the bleeding will quickly stop. You can also dab on antibiotic first-aid cream.

You will get better with practice—and you will get plenty of practice. Your infant's fingernails may need to be trimmed several times a week. (The good news is you don't need to worry about cutting your baby's toenails. Don't worry if they look weird; they'll grow out slowly.)

BEGINNING TOOTH CARE

Do you really need to start thinking about tooth brushing when your baby won't have any teeth for ages? Well, yes, actually, you should start thinking about tooth brushing now. You need to get your baby used to having his gums cleaned before his teeth come in. The first few times you try it, he's likely to bite you, and you're much better off getting those bites over with before they can draw blood. Still, it's not likely to be fun.

The best toothbrush for an infant is a gauze square (sold in the first-aid section of a drugstore) wetted with plain water. It's amazing how much gunk this can remove.

An alternative is a fingertip brush—a brush with rubber bristles that sits like a cap over your finger. You can also go straight to a toothbrush; infant toothbrushes are very soft. (The downside is that they are quickly chewed into oblivion.) Hold your baby against you when you brush, facing into a mirror so you can see what you're doing—and your baby always enjoys mirror time. Your baby is less likely to clench his mouth shut or wriggle away when you come at him from the front.

Don't introduce toothpaste at this point. Babies will swallow it, and swallowing excess fluoride can damage the enamel of the teeth yet to come in. That said, babies over six months of age do need a certain amount of fluoride in their diet to prevent future cavities. If the water in your community is not fluoridated, you can purchase bottled water that is or ask your pediatrician to prescribe fluoride drops for your baby.

AFTER TEETH ARRIVE

Most children have some teeth when they enter the toddler years. When they leave them at age three, most children have a full set of choppers. Beginning around age six months, the two lower middle teeth appear. Next the two upper middle teeth (the incisors) come in. Then the teeth on either side of the two front teeth appear (more incisors) followed by more bottom teeth. By age two, most children have sixteen sparkling teeth. However, both the timing and pattern can vary dramatically. Eventually they should end up with ten on top and ten on the bottom, including:

- Eight incisors (the front four teeth, top and bottom)
- Four canines (one on each side of each set of incisors)
- Eight molars (the rest)

These baby teeth, also called milk teeth or primary teeth, will gradually be replaced by a set of permanent ones beginning after age five. The health of the baby teeth affects the permanent teeth, so they need to be well cared for!

Toddlers will need parents to brush their teeth for them until they are coordinated enough to make the proper motions. (At the first dental checkup, typically at age three, the dentist will give them a lesson.) To teach proper brushing techniques, parents can simply place their hand over their toddler's and guide them through the process. Expect toddlers to chew and otherwise mangle the toothbrush bristles. Here are some tips to make tooth brushing easier for you and your child:

- Use a soft-bristled kiddie-size brush. If you buy several, you can let the toddler choose which to use at each brushing.
- Brush a doll or Teddy's teeth first to give your toddler a chance to witness what is going on and become comfortable with the idea.
- Use your child's natural urge to mimic by brushing your teeth while she brushes hers.
- Provide a pea-size spot of toothpaste (choose a brand formulated for children) and try to keep her from swallowing.
- Give her a "once over lightly" to make sure the job is done properly.
- Schedule a trip to the dentist, then cloak yourself in the voice of authority: Remind your child that the dentist said she must brush her teeth every day to keep them healthy.

Teething Blues

One significant reason for older babies to cry is teething, which typically starts at six or seven months (although a few babies don't get their first tooth until twelve or even eighteen months old). The gums swell just before a tooth appears, and this can hurt your baby for days. You can help soothe her with things to chew on—teething toys, a leather band, a cold washcloth, a frozen bagel (take it away when it starts to soften). You can offer her a bottle of ice water to suck (although sometimes sucking makes the pain worse), or try rubbing her gums. There are mixed reports on topical anesthetics, like Baby Anbesol or Orajel. It can be hard to apply, they tend to work only for a limited time, and they taste terrible. Ask your health care provider before using.

Teething babies fuss, cry, and wake up more often. While most experts do not believe that teething causes loose stools, runny noses, or fevers, many parents are convinced that there is a correlation between these symptoms and teething. To be safe, check with your doctor if your child has a temperature of 101°F or higher (100.4°F or higher for a baby younger than three months). Do not give any medication for teething, including acetaminophen and ibuprofen, without checking with your health care provider.

PART 7

DISCIPLINE AND ENCOURAGING INDEPENDENCE

Chapter 18

HOW TO DISCIPLINE

Many parents believe that "discipline" is the same thing as "punishment," and it is unfortunate that the two concepts have become synonymous in so many people's minds. Really, the word "discipline" means "teaching" or "learning," and from discipulus, *which means "pupil." Disciplining toddlers involves—teaching young pupils. It falls to the most important teachers in their lives, their parents, to serve as their principal instructors.*

LITTLE DISCIPLES

Although youngsters like learning much more than they like being punished, it's no easy task to be a student. "There are so many rules. How will I ever learn them all?" Larry sighed as his mother was explaining how he should behave the next time he had friends over to play. And at age six, this tyke was fluent in English and had dedicated many more years to learning rules than a toddler!

Teaching little disciples is a long, slow process. They have little experience on which to build, and their still-developing language skills prevent them from understanding much of what is said to them. In addition, their memory skills are so poor that they forget much of what they've been taught from moment to moment and from day to day. Finally, they lack the intellectual skills to use what they learn in one situation to guide their behavior in another.

When it comes to disciplining toddlers, patience and repetition are the teacher's most important attributes!

TEACHING ABOUT NO-NOS

When parents say "no-no," it is clear to *them* exactly what they want the toddler to stop doing or to stay away from. But what is obvious to them may not be at all clear to the toddler. How do you teach what "no-no" means? Here are a few ideas:

- Change your tone of voice when you say it.
- Accompany your words with a frown and shake of the head.
- Try to get your child to repeat your words, or at least your gestures.
- If your child mimics your words or gestures, smile and gush, "That's right!"

Toddlers may still not associate the phrase and gesture with an expected behavior, but at least they are being helped to focus on those two important words.

Parenting Pointer

Instead of saying "no-no," some parents prefer "That's not okay." Either way, it takes many repetitions for youngsters to decipher their parent's meaning and longer still to relate the words to their behavior.

Don't Just Say No

The problem with "just saying no" is that toddlers don't learn what they *can* do. A child may not be *trying* to create chaos and ill will as she goes from one forbidden activity to the next. She doesn't know what is off limits and what is permissible. Follow up "no-no" and "don't" with an "it's all right to" or "you can" when appropriate.

Offering alternatives may not prevent toddlers from becoming upset if they're very taken with something. Still, offering alternatives provides an important lesson: When the road we want to go down is blocked, we need to find another one.

Too Many No-Nos

The danger of constantly bombarding toddlers with no-nos is that an especially spirited, energetic youngster may find himself in trouble every time he turns around. When children despair of pleasing their parents, or if their need to explore is continually thwarted, they may tune out reprimands and admonishments altogether and allow Mother Nature to dictate their actions.

The easiest way for parents to reduce the number of "no-nos" and "don't touches" is to childproof the home by putting away and securing as many dangerous and fragile objects as possible, and to provide lots of objects for them to manipulate.

Ultimately, the goal is for toddlers to learn to control themselves instead of relying on adults to control them. But developing self-control won't be accomplished in a matter of days, weeks, or even months or years. Until then, you may be better off putting more energy into controlling the environment. That way, you can spend less time struggling to control your youngsters and more time enjoying them.

The Problem with "No"

As anyone who has studied a foreign language knows, learning to understand and use negative words is no small task. In English, things get particularly confusing. Even adults aren't always sure what answering "yes" to a question means; for example, "You're not going to touch the stove, are you?" When addressing toddlers, keep things simple!

Since negatives like "don't" occur at the beginning of sentences, toddlers often miss them. They don't even realize they're being spoken to until the parent has made it halfway through the sentence. So when you say, "Don't touch the stove," the toddler may only hear ". . . touch the stove" or ". . . the stove." It's no wonder toddlers so often do exactly the opposite of what their parents are telling them!

Make it a habit to tell toddlers what to do rather than what not to do. Instead of "Don't yell," you might say instead, "Use your soft voice!"

Why Not?

It's not always necessary to provide reasons for "no." Sometimes "no" can simply be "because I said so." But as children become increasingly independent, an adult won't be present at every moment to supervise. They need to be able to assess objects—and eventually situations and people—to determine what and who is safe. For example, if youngsters understand that they can't play with the lamp because it has an electric cord and a glass bulb, by middle childhood they will better be able to protect themselves when they come upon other interesting appliances and objects containing glass.

Distraction

To keep very young toddlers away from things they're not to touch and dissuade them from forbidden pastimes, distraction is the simplest, most straightforward, least confrontational way to achieve compliance. With this technique, simply remove the forbidden object or move the toddler away from it, and say, "No, don't play with that." Frown, and shake your head, and then offer an alternate toy or activity.

....

Baby Basics

Distraction works especially well before youngsters have achieved object constancy. Until then, they don't understand that objects still exist even if they can't see them at the moment. To them, out of sight really does mean out of mind.

....

Redirection

When toddlers have matured to the point that they can remember the item their parent took away (which they demonstrate by trying to search for an object that has been removed), a teaching device known as "redirection" works well. Redirection simply involves the following:

- Setting a limit ("No, don't play with the lamp.")
- Giving a reason ("It's dangerous. The bulb could break. And you mustn't play with anything that has a cord.")
- Enticing toddlers into a different activity ("Let's find something else for you to play with. How about your flashlight?")

Like distraction, redirection is a simple, straightforward way to minimize or avoid confrontations. The challenge in redirecting a child is to find an activity as enticing as the one they've chosen. Here are some common no-nos and possible alternatives:

- **Jumping on the furniture:** Slip old cases over pillows, place them on the carpet (or on blankets folded to make a pad), clear the area of end tables and other hard objects that could hurt them, and let them jump! Or purchase a beanbag chair children can jump on.
- **Throwing toys:** Give them a dishtowel tied in string, two socks rolled together, a foam rubber ball, a sponge, and let them toss. If they need the sound of the *thunk*, consider letting them hurl a plastic bottle onto a linoleum floor or into a large metal pot.
- **Tearing up books:** Offer old newspapers, magazines, or a phone book instead.
- **Playing in the toilet bowl:** Fill a plastic dish tub half full of water, set it on towels on the laundry room floor (or, on wash day, empty the dirty clothes hamper onto the floor), and let them play.

Sometimes parents come up with great alternatives, but toddlers feel compelled to say "no" because they are practicing independence. This can set the scene for many conflicts. Prime times for resistant behavior are shortly after learning to walk and during the second year.

Offering Choices

When simple redirection fails, try a different approach. Let's say that Jenny wants to paint. Offering choices gives toddlers an opportunity to practice making decisions and to have more control over their lives. Jenny's mother could say, "Painting is messy, and we have company coming over soon. You can play in your sandbox or read a book. Which would you prefer?" Jenny may need to finish wailing her disappointment over not being allowed to paint before she'll be ready to move on, in which case her mother can say, "When you decide whether you want the sandbox or a story, let me know."

In such instances, if the tears don't stop quickly, the new toy or activity probably isn't very appealing, or the upset is about something else entirely. Like adults, toddlers get cranky. Because they have more to cope with and less experience handling their emotions, small disappointments can set them off. A big reaction to a small deprivation can be a sign that they are tired, hungry, ill or coming down with something, going through a stressful period, or going through a spurt of independence.

DANGEROUS SITUATIONS

The time for parents to step out of the teaching role into that of policing is when their toddler is approaching danger. That way, they can stage an immediate rescue.

For instance, sooner or later most youngsters will want to explore electrical cords. When a young toddler reaches for one and suddenly hears his parent's loud voice, he is likely to pause, smile, and reach for the cord again. The parent may believe the child's pause means he understood the "No, don't touch!" warning. From the child's ensuing smile and renewed attempt to reach for the cord, adults may assume the kind of defiance that makes them want to tear their hair out by the roots.

However, the pause may simply be a response to the parent's voice; it doesn't mean that he understood the warning. Even if he does surmise from the parent's tone that he is being warned about *something*, he may not realize he is being warned away from the cord. How can toddlers comprehend that a cord is dangerous when they don't know about either cords or danger, and haven't even touched one yet?

When a toddler is approaching danger, follow these steps:

1. Say, "No! Don't touch!" or "Stop!" in a firm, authoritative tone.
2. If the child pauses, be sure to smile, nod, and provide positive reinforcement by saying "Thank you" to let him know he responded correctly: She paused.
3. Don't wait to see what will happen next; grab him fast.
4. Explain, "That's *dangerous*, honey. It will hurt you."
5. Say "No-no," shake your head, and frown to convey your message nonverbally.
6. Try to get him to say "No-no" and shake his head.
7. Move him away from the danger.

If the child toddles back to the cord, you will need to either repeat the process as often as needed, distract him by providing something different to do, or offer him choices for alternate toys or activities.

If you physically move him away from the cord, he may conclude that you are playing a wonderful chasing game. He may head back in that direction the moment he is released, hoping for more. Once again, you may see his actions as defiant. It's important to consider that by this point the cord may be the farthest thing from his mind.

TIME-OUT

Providing time-outs is an excellent teaching device to help toddlers learn to adhere to important rules and regain control when they are unable to contain themselves. Simply tell your toddler to sit down until she can settle down and observe the limit you have set or behave in accordance with the rules you have established.

Parenting Pointer

Many parents send toddlers to their rooms for time-out, but this isn't an option for youngsters who need to be watched at every moment, and being sent away can make toddlers feel rejected. The point of time-out is to teach, not to punish, although until children learn the advantages of being contained, they may certainly *feel* punished.

The rule of thumb is to assign one minute of time out per year of age, so a two-year-old should be required to sit for two minutes at most. If toddlers weren't upset to begin with, they may become very angry about being prevented from engaging in the activity they have chosen. Therefore, you may not wish to start the clock until the child has settled down.

When the child has regained control, discuss the event that precipitated the time-out to help him learn from the experience so he knows what to do if the same situation arises in the future. It helps to begin the discussion by praising the toddler for having regained control. Besides starting the discussion on a positive note, praise helps little ones focus on their important accomplishment, and keeps both the parent and child from being overly focused on the misdeeds.

Reviewing what transpired and figuring out what to do differently is beyond younger toddlers and will be too hard for older toddlers until they are familiar with the process. In the beginning, you may have to do most or all of the talking for your toddler.

The point of time-out is to teach several important lessons children can use throughout their lives:

1. Important rules must be followed.
2. If people disregard rules, there are consequences, which may be unpleasant.
3. If people don't control themselves, someone else will control them.
4. When people are upset and out of control, taking a brief time-out can help them calm down.

And indeed, most children learn the value of time-outs in short order. In fact, once they have become accustomed to the procedure, toddlers will begin sitting down or running off to their rooms when they are upset over a parental demand or prohibition. During their self-imposed time-out, they will finish crying and re-emerge a few minutes later when they have settled down.

Parenting Pointer

Time-outs aren't just for kids! When parents are upset with their toddler and sense they are losing control, they should give themselves a time-out to settle down and rethink what is happening.

SPANKING

While spankings may more quickly control a child who is repeatedly engaging in forbidden behavior, the fatal flaw is that the parent is controlling the child's behavior. Children need to learn to control their own behavior. Corporal punishment is controversial, but even some social worker champions of abused youngsters consider spanking to be a reasonable course of action in situations involving imminent danger, such as running into the street, reaching for a hot stove, provoking an animal, or running around a swimming pool. They recommend an on-the-spot administration of three swats on the bottom with the open hand (never an object) accompanied by an explanation such as, "Running into the street is a no-no! It's dangerous!" Like hitting a puppy with a newspaper, the goal is for the sound of the swat and the parent's angry voice (not pain) to evoke the correct response to danger—fear.

Parents should not remove the child's clothes, since a hard hand against a soft bottom can cause bruising, which is considered abuse. Also, grabbing a toddler by the arm and jerking, or even holding on tightly while swatting, can cause spiral fractures if the child twists.

Parents who don't spank can usually elicit the same reaction by swooping the child away from danger while shouting, "Stay out of the street! It's dangerous!" and then refusing to comfort the crying child for a few minutes, saying, "No, I'm not giving you a hug right now. I'm upset. You're not supposed to run into the street!"

Relying on corporal punishment is a known risk factor for child abuse, perhaps because parents of strong-willed children find they must hit harder and harder to have an impact. Even if parents are not abusive, a common result is that children mimic their parents and relieve their frustrations by hitting others. If you think that hellion in the grocery store is spoiled rotten and needs a good spanking, you've probably got it backward, because being frequently spanked is associated with poorer behavior, not better.

Although toddlers may appear to be learning self-control from lots of hard spankings, they may only be learning to be subservient to the parental thumb. As soon as children find themselves in a situation where the parent doesn't spank— for example, in public—toddlers' lack of self-control becomes evident. So there's a good chance that the parent with the out-of-control toddler in the grocery store is the most frustrated shopper on the scene and will spank the toddler as soon as they get to the car or arrive home.

Delayed punishments may relieve the parent's frustration, but a toddler's poor memory won't allow him to understand the reason he was hit. By the time the toddler is punished, breaking the pickle jar, refusing to stay in the cart, throwing a tantrum at the candy counter, and swinging on the metal rail in the check-out line will probably be just a blur for the parent, too. Even if the parent could recite the list of broken rules, the child wouldn't be able to remember all these no-nos the next time he's at the store.

HANDLING TANTRUMS

Not every toddler has tantrums, but most do. They are most common between ages two and three, when there can be as many as one to two daily for several weeks, and others intermittently. Not all tantrums were created equal. Telling them apart can be tricky.

Stress Tantrums

The toddler is stressed (tired; hungry; ill; or cranky due to a number of small disappointments, changes, and/or defeats), when some unpleasant thing happens. Perhaps he hates to have his diaper changed, and Dad insisted on it. Or Mom kept her hands on the grocery cart when he wanted to push it himself. Or his toy broke. That one small incident becomes the straw that broke the camel's back, and suddenly the toddler loses control. The screaming and carrying-on is out of proportion to the problem at hand because the upset isn't about a single event. It's the result of an accumulation of stress that has taken its toll on a tyke who, because of his age, doesn't have a lot of emotional control to begin with.

....

Baby Basics

In a stress tantrum, the child isn't trying to get something; instead, she is trying to get rid of the unpleasant feelings that have accumulated. Having a momentary whim gratified helps a stressed toddler feel better, but not for long. The next small crisis produces another upset of similar or even greater intensity because the real problem—feeling generally overwhelmed—remains.

....

Trying to sidestep a stress tantrum may merely be postponing the inevitable. As things heat up, it becomes increasingly clear that the toddler is trying to provoke a struggle. Even if the parent tries to grant the toddler's every wish, the toddler suddenly rejects an offer. Give her the cookie she demanded, and she's apt to hurl it against the wall. Say something soothing and conciliatory, and she escalates. She's out of control.

To manage stress tantrums:

1. Hold the child firmly but lovingly and provide reassurance that she'll be okay in a bit. This assumes you can hold her. Children may thrash too wildly to be safely held.
2. If she's endangering herself, other people, or property as she rolls about the floor, clear the area if you can. Otherwise, move her to a safe place, like a carpeted floor.
3. Let her cry it out. Tears are a great tension reliever.
4. Empathize with the fact that she's having a hard day.
5. When the tantrum ends, ask if she'd like to sit on your lap and have you rock her, or lie down and have you rub her back.
6. Provide reassurance that things will get easier for her when her new tooth comes through, she's rested, she's adjusted to her new day care center, or the stressful situation has passed.

When it comes to stress tantrums, the best cure lies in prevention. Consider them a signal that your toddler is under more pressure than she can manage and see if there's a way to help lessen it. Remember that toddlers are already under a lot of stress because they are struggling with their personal sense of inadequacy that comes from wanting to do things and being unable to do them, having lots to communicate and being unable to say much, and wanting to be independent while being emotionally needy.

Manipulative Tantrums

Some children learn to throw tantrums to get something. Their manipulative tantrums are their way of saying "I want something and I want it now!" Once their end is achieved—freedom to run around the store, liberation from the car seat, permission to eat the cookie or to have a toy—they settle down. Tantrums in public are common because many children have learned if they stage a big one, they will immediately be taken home, which is exactly what they want.

It can be hard to hold firm in the face of manipulative tantrums. Their fearsome intensity can quickly melt parental resolve. But of course, every time you appease the child by giving in, you drive home the lesson that screaming, hitting, kicking, thrashing, breath-holding, fainting, and even head-banging and vomiting are workable ways to achieve goals.

If the behaviors during manipulative tantrums are particularly dramatic, discuss the problem with your pediatrician to satisfy yourself that the quickest, most effective way to end this kind of tantrum—ignoring it—is a safe option. Behaviors that warrant a professional opinion include banging his head or other self-injurious behavior, or holding her breath to the point of turning purple, passing out, precipitating an asthma attack, or vomiting.

To end manipulative tantrums:

- If she's a raging puddle on the floor, tell her you'll talk to her when she's settled down.
- Carry her to an open space where she can't harm herself or something else, preferably with carpet to soften the blows, if she's flinging herself around.
- Step over her and busy yourself nearby (but out of kicking range) by studiously ignoring her.
- Remain alert to what is happening so you can intervene if she tries to hurt herself or something else.

The challenge is to not take manipulative tantrums personally. See them for what they are: a child's rage at rules and limits. By failing to give in and not paying attention to her, you're showing what happens when people are assailed by crushing disappointments: Life goes on. When a tantrum ends and the child has settled down:

- See it as the victory it is—the child regained control on her own.
- Don't attempt to discuss what transpired before or during the tantrum—let the subject drop.
- Be warm enough to show her you're not angry with her—respond to her desire to be held, hear a story, or have you participate in another quiet activity once she's settled down.
- Don't try to compensate for having held firm by being overly solicitous.

If throwing a tantrum has worked in the past, the predictable short-term result when parents don't give in is an *increase* in both the intensity and frequency of tantrums. The confused youngster works harder to employ the strategy that has worked so well in the past to get his way. It may take a number of scenes before he grasps that tantrums are no longer a useful method for getting what he wants. Then, a new inner strength will emerge as he demonstrates himself capable of carrying on even when the world doesn't gratify his wishes, and you will feel better knowing that your youngster can cope with disappointment.

Communication Tantrums

Sometimes toddlers throw tantrums out of sheer frustration over their inability to communicate their needs. For instance, it's very clear that your toddler wants something. It's clear to your toddler that you have it. Try as you might, you can't figure out what your child is asking for. He tries every way he can think of to get the message across, and then dissolves.

Or it is all too clear what your toddler wants: ice cream. He is sure it is in the freezer, because that's where it's kept. Except that there isn't any ice cream there or anywhere else because you're fresh out. He's sure you're withholding it, and you can't find a way to explain it to him. Maybe he wants to watch a particular video, but the tape is broken. Or he wants his pacifier, but it's lost. It's hard to be treated like the devil that is ruining his life when your intentions are good. The only recourse is to provide reassurance that you would give him what he wanted if you could and let him rage at the injustice of it.

It's not easy being any age, but it can be particularly hard to be a toddler. Parents who remain sympathetic as children struggle through these trying moments may also feel helpless. Remember that by demonstrating your love for your youngster when he is at his very worst, you are in fact helping a lot.

Chapter 19

THE ROAD TO INDEPENDENCE

The toddler years are a time of great emotional intensity. At no other age are the smiles quite so pure, the sadness so heartfelt, the rage so total, or the delight so genuine. Each small disappointment, fear, and frustration can produce tears of sadness or anger; then in the twinkling of an eye those frowns can turn to smiles once again!

THE ROLLER COASTER YEARS

After experiencing the ready smiles and relatively easygoing attitudes of baby days, many parents are shocked when behavior markedly deteriorates as tots begin to walk. It is common for them suddenly to resist their parents' requests and directives at every turn. It's not just the newfound freedom that drives the sudden bouts of stubbornness. It's that walking turns the toddlers' world upside down—or vertical, as the case may be. Change, even change for the better, taxes the emotional reserves of human beings of all ages and is therefore stressful.

Shortly after learning to walk, toddlers are likely to:

- Repeatedly dissolve into tears over small frustrations
- Strike out when they are angry
- Be stubborn and uncooperative
- Have a hard time falling asleep

- Wake up crying during the night
- Show other signs of stress, such as more frequent infections

Don't worry that you've created a monster. You can expect the sunnier personality to reappear when the novelty of walking wears off and your toddler has adjusted to the many changes mobility has introduced into her life. Then during the "terrible twos" (or "terrific twos," depending on your point of view), conflict heats up in earnest as struggles over autonomy take center stage.

But when the terrible twos are successfully negotiated, toddlers trust themselves as well as their parents. At that point, youngsters will still dislike many of their parents' limits and rules. They may fuss some and try to get them to change their minds. But even if they're at a loss to understand the reasons for many of their parents' more disappointing decisions, they comply more often than not.

Experience as Teacher

Between ages one and three toddlers make great strides in mastering their careening emotions. In this case, "familiarity breeds content," so toddlers encounter fewer new things that inspire fear. They know what to expect and how to behave in many situations, and they have learned to follow most of the family routines and rules. Still, even older toddlers may become upset when confronting events they find especially distressing—for instance, when Mom and Dad leave them with a sitter and walk out the door. If the toddlers have been raised in a secure and stable environment, experience will have taught them that they are not being abandoned. Although youngsters nearing their third birthday still break lots of household rules and resist routines at times, they bump into fewer unexpected no-nos while toddling through the house each day. That alone makes parenting far easier.

Growing Bodies

The increased maturity of the frontal lobes of the brain plays a role in children's ever-improving emotional control, too. These physical changes render older toddlers less impulsive and more able to plan ahead, tolerate frustration, and delay gratification. Further, as youngsters develop physically, their skin becomes somewhat less sensitive, their digestive system works better, and their sleep patterns stabilize. Perhaps hunger pangs don't strike with such intensity at age three as at age one, so a minute spent waiting seems less like a year . . . and more like only half a year!

Baby Basics

Emotional development during the toddler years means that as they approach age three, they shouldn't routinely dissolve into tears while having to wait to have their needs and desires satisfied. Although waiting is still hard for them, they react less intensely to small stresses but still frequently become overwhelmed and remain overly emotional by adult standards.

PLAYING WITH YOUR BABY AND TODDLER

One of the biggest joys of parenthood is playing with your baby. The smiles and giggles your little one gives will delight you to no end. Becoming a parent reminds you of all the fun kids can have and how much they actually learn through play. The essential skills your baby will learn in the first year are foundations of lifelong learning. While these foundations are vital, they are also lots of fun. As your child's first playmate and teacher, do all you can to enrich her early life.

Talk to Your Baby

One of the best ways to play with your baby is to talk to her. Through hearing your voice, she will learn a lot about language and other rhythmic patterns in speech far before she can use these skills herself. She will also pick up tone and emotion in your voice.

The question is, what do you have to talk about with a newborn? If she can't respond, how can you make effective conversation? For many new parents, talking to their babies does not come easily at first. To ease into it, just try giving her a rundown of her daily activities: "It's bath time! Let's get you undressed. First we take off your shirt. Now it's time for your diaper. Feel the warm water? Do you like the water?"

Over time, the conversations will become more natural and your baby will seem more and more interested in the words you say. Your baby will learn to understand not only patterns of speech, but schedules as well. Soon she'll associate all your babbling about getting undressed with bath time.

Sing to Your Baby

When it comes to your baby, there are no singing lessons needed. Your baby doesn't care if you hit the notes or get the words right; she simply wants to hear the musical quality of your voice. Babies love to be sung to sleep with a soft lullaby or hear a playful tune while they bounce on your knee. Don't get embarrassed about singing to your baby. You'll soon find it's even easier than singing in the shower.

In addition to making silly faces, try overexaggerating different emotions to teach your baby about feelings. Show her what a huge grin looks like and then say "happy." Show her looks of anger, surprise, and sadness, too. Your baby will get a huge kick out of watching your one-man show, and may even try to mimic you right away.

Read to Your Baby

With a very young baby, simply sit him on your lap. Open the book and rest it on your knees at a comfortable viewing height and distance for your baby. As your baby ages, let him help you turn the pages. He will enjoy the feel of the pages, as well as any special textures that are included in the book. Putting his hands on the book will also give him a sense of ownership.

Choosing Toys

Nowadays, there are overwhelming possibilities when it comes to buying toys for your baby. From different materials to different technologies, boys and girls today have far more options than the simple truck or doll of years past. However, this doesn't mean you have to give your child one of everything. In fact, simple is often better when it comes to your child's playthings.

Parenting Pointer

Babies under one year of age really don't care much about characters. They aren't into marketing, and they don't know about the latest movie or fad. Any colorful toy with various textures is fine for this age, so don't get tricked into emptying your wallet for the hottest toy on eBay.

Keep It Simple

There are very few rules to keep in mind when buying toys for your baby. The main one is that the toys need to be safe. Look out for removable parts that can be swallowed, long strings or cords that can be choking hazards, and other potentially dangerous aspects. The truth is, the simpler the toy, the better it is for a baby. Your little one is more likely to show interest in the box a toy comes in than in the toy itself.

A basic, soft ball is a classic toy for your baby. Even very small babies love to watch a ball roll around. It's great for babies to become acquainted with this common shape early on. An unbreakable mirror is also a great toy. Remember, babies love to look at faces, and they become especially infatuated with their own reflections. Your baby may also start to hold the mirror up to you as he learns what a reflection is. And of course, simple toys that make noise, like bells and rattles, are big favorites. Balls, mirrors, and rattles will all give your baby his first lesson on cause and effect.

Baby Basics

Some studies show that newborns see high contrast best. This information has led to the creation of lots of red, black, and white toys, which are supposedly more interesting to a baby. Use your judgment before spending a lot on these special toys.

It's also nice for baby to have a stuffed animal or doll to play with. However, until your child is out of a crib, he shouldn't take this toy to bed with him. Older babies and toddlers love to play with stuffed toys and dolls and pretend to care for them like pets or children.

The Basics

Here are some of the toys that have entertained generations of babies:

- **Rattles.** Even a very young baby, who instinctively grasps anything put into his hand, can wave a rattle.
- **Nesting cups that fit inside each other.** This will be your baby's first puzzle. These cups can also stack, pour, be sorted into colors, and be counted. They let him experiment with the ideas of inside and outside and bigger and smaller.
- **Stacking toys**—plastic or wooden rings that stack up on a post, preferably not in graduated sizes until he's older. You'll also need lots of blocks—for touching, tasting, and banging together. Eventually, they might even be used for stacking.
- **Toys that react when a button or lever is pushed** (a train spins around, a funny man pops up). These teach cause and effect.
- **Toys that imitate your activities**—bowls, spoons, a little stove, a toy telephone, dolls, a mop, and and a toddler-sized stroller or shopping cart are all good choices.

What you don't need are "educational" toys designed to turn your baby into a child genius. Your baby has a huge curriculum he's covering in his first year as it is. Your job is to simply expose him to life, not drill him in his numbers. Sometimes it is hard to resist, so go ahead and teach. Just remember that he'll be better off learning his academics at a more developmentally appropriate time. Brain growth, recent research shows, does not stop in early childhood, as used to be thought. It continues throughout life, so there really is no rush.

Parenting Pointer

As an optional toy safety measure, avoid phthalates. (Phthalates are used in plastic toys, particularly teethers, to make the plastic soft.) Although public interest groups raised a concern about the use of the chemical diisononyl phthalate in baby toys, an independent panel of experts, as well as the CPSC, reported that concerns over phthalates are unwarranted. However, many major toy manufacturers have, since 1999, removed phthalates from their products.

Tactile Stimulation

Tactile stimulation, or appealing to the baby's sense of touch, is a great thing for even a small child. You don't have to spend lots of money on fancy toys—you can make your own tactile toys. For instance, put a few different objects with different textures into a paper bag. You can choose cotton balls, cereal pieces, one of your baby's socks, or whatever else you have around. Let your baby reach in and hand you an object. Talk to him about the object that he's pulled out. Your baby will love choosing objects and hearing your voice as you explain them.

Toy Safety

To be safe, be sure your baby's playthings meet these criteria:

- The paint is nontoxic.

- It has no small detachable parts.
- None of the edges or corners are sharp.
- No bells and whistles are at excessive decibels (some toy trucks emit siren noises that rival those from real fire trucks).
- No "bean-bag" stuffing (the pellets that stuff them are a choking hazard so stick to cuddlers stuffed with fluff).
- The toy doesn't have long or loose cords, strings, or ribbons (avoid anything, including necklaces, that your baby can get tangled around herself—especially her throat).
- No cords are more than twelve inches long.
- The toy, and any detachable parts, should be too large to fit inside a toilet-paper tube (smaller pieces are choking hazards).
- The toy has no lead in it.
- No recall has been announced for that version of the toy.

Outdoor Play

Playing outside is essential for children and parents. Fresh air and sunshine; room to run, yell, and tumble; and all sorts of things to explore make the out-of-doors a whole new world. Playing outside is also an opportunity to teach yard and street safety, and boundaries. The following games can be modified for city or suburban play as needed:

- Have your toddler lie down on the sidewalk. Trace his outline with nontoxic sidewalk chalk. Then have him draw in the eyes, ears, nose, and mouth.
- Place a series of parallel sticks on the ground spaced eight to twelve inches apart. See if your toddler can walk through them without stepping on any.
- Play follow-the-leader: walk with one or both hands on your hips, above your head, while swinging your arms.

- Blow tufts off the head of a dandelion.
- Collect leaves and line them up on the sidewalk in a long chain.

Invest in a small shopping cart or toy stroller that your child can push. He might love to use a tricycle or riding toy. Finally, don't underestimate the hours of fun he can have with a wagon.

The Dreaded Cleanup

There are a number of compelling reasons that your toddler needs to learn to pick up her toys—and not just to fulfill your desire for a neat house. Not only will toddlers break the toys by walking on them, but they can possibly hurt themselves tripping or stumbling amid the rubble. In the process of learning to care for their possessions, toddlers learn to sort and organize. Little ones won't know how to do that, so plan on doing most of the work for quite some time.

··

Parenting Pointer

Because toddlers slow things down to a snail's pace, it's often easier for parents to pick up everything. But when parents look ahead and consider that playthings will need to be picked up every day for the next eighteen years, they'll realize how important it is to work actively on teaching this skill now.

··

Toddlers do like to go back and forth between toys, playing with one for a while, moving on to another one, then returning to the first, so the strategy of insisting that one toy be put up before the next is taken out is too rigid. But to hold the chaos in check (which makes many toddlers, like many adults, feel scattered), to keep toys from becoming trampled on and broken, and to teach organizational skills, consider these guidelines:

- Only allow two or three different toys out at once, not counting that special truck, doll, or ball he wants to keep close at hand at all times.
- Keep the quantity down to items that can be carried to his room or piled into a container he can drag to the toy storage area in a single trip.
- Store toys that aren't being used much in the closet. Bring them out for a rainy day surprise.

Cleanup Games

When your toddler is looking for something new to play with, say, "Let's pick these up and find you a new toy." Then make the picking up of toys into a game. Ask, "How many of these can you carry?" Place one toy in her right hand, one in her left, tuck one under her arm, and another under her neck if she's a practiced walker. Keep up the fun by giving a quick tummy tickle and seeing if she can manage not to drop them.

If you're putting away toys in a carrier that a toddler can drag from room to room, toss a toy inside and then hand her one to toss inside and continue taking turns. Count aloud as you alternate placing toys in her box. Have a race and see who can pick up toys the fastest. Make the trek to her room pleasurable—this is a great time for a hiking song or a chorus of "Ten Little Indians"—though you might want to hold it to four Indians for such a short trip.

A GROWING TRUST

As they learn to play and interact with others, babies and toddlers begin to learn trust. Being able to trust caregivers enough to accept their comfort, help, rules, and guidance is critical for toddlers' overall emotional well-being. This foundation of trust should have been established during infancy through the unwavering love and nurturing devotion of parents and other caregivers. Toddlers' growing trust in themselves complicates their trust in parents, which wanes as toddlers put more trust in their own feelings, thoughts, and ideas. Emotional swings intensify as youngsters try to balance their trust in themselves and in their parents.

To maintain a strong relationship when trust wanes during the toddler years:

- Be true to your word.
- Invite toddlers to participate in decisions that affect them by giving them choices.
- Soothe upsets by cuddling, kissing, and speaking kindly .
- Communicate your understanding that some rules and limits are upsetting.
- Let your child's upset be her own. Don't let the situation escalate by becoming upset yourself.
- Let your child know you love him even if you dislike some of the things he does (criticize the behavior, not the child).
- Show with your actions that your love and respect for her continue even when you are angry with her.
- Apologize if you become harsh and critical—this will help your child learn that it is okay to make mistakes and to apologize for them.
- Understand that if you are the recipient of your child's worst scenes, it is because you are the person she trusts most.

THE PROBLEM WITH PRAISE

Brian was contentedly munching his cereal when his mother breezed by the table and gave him the thumbs-up sign. "Good job," she said. Brian's smile faded as he bleakly surveyed his brimming cereal bowl. He was already full, and he'd barely dented it. He wanted to please his mother, but knew he was going to have to let her down.

Just as parents use expressions like "No-no" or "That's not okay" to mean "Stop" or "Don't," they use expressions like "Good job!" or "Way to go" to mean "Yes, that's what I want you to do." If Brian's mother had said, "It looks like you're enjoying that cereal," he could have said "yes" without feeling obligated to eat more.

Parenting Pointer

Contrary to popular opinion, praising youngsters doesn't necessarily improve their self-esteem. Praise encourages them to focus on their success at pleasing adults and at measuring up to other people's expectations, rather than the achievement itself.

Certainly both praise and admonishments can be appropriate, depending on the circumstances. However, both are directive and controlling. Praise can make toddlers feel pressured to perform.

Children with good self-esteem feel pleased with themselves. When evaluating their own behavior, they feel they measure up to their personal expectations. But praise can actually serve to undermine self-esteem. First-born children, whose parents are apt to applaud each small gurgle and coo and record each new accomplishment in their bulging baby book, tend to be the least emotionally secure and suffer more problems with self-esteem than the rest of the brood whose successes receive far less attention. Meanwhile, the middle child, typically lost in a no-man's land between the accomplished older sibling and the darling baby, has a harder time finding ways to impress. Yet youngsters sandwiched in the middle of the pack tend to be more self-confident.

The following parent comments point out some of the pitfalls of praise:

- "I like the bright colors in your drawing" suggests to the child that to please the parent, he should use bright colors. Expressing interest and asking a neutral question such as, "What did you draw?" or "Tell me about your picture" enables the child to share his drawing and his feelings about it without having his choice of crayons judged.
- If the parent exclaims, "Good catch!" when the ball lands in her toddler's arms, it's understandable why the child becomes upset when it lands on the floor on subsequent tries: The youngster assumes they are "bad" catches.

- "Good boy!" the parent says when the toddler uses the potty by himself. This kind of evaluation—"You're good because you did what I wanted"— can cause toddlers who are in the throes of a struggle over independence to respond by refusing to use the potty thereafter. Instead, try, "You should be proud of yourself." Although that still conveys your opinion, it encourages the child to evaluate himself in a positive light rather than to focus exclusively on your opinion.

PRAISING ACCOMPLISHMENTS

After an hour or so has gone by without a repetition of a particular behavior problem, parents should make it a point to praise their child's accomplishment. Because toddlers get into so many things and break so many rules, it's easy to spend more time focusing on what they do wrong than on what they do right.

If, when you say, "I'm so glad you've left the TV off," the child runs toward it, hurry on over but try to give her the benefit of the doubt. There's a good chance she'll look at the controls without touching them and announce that it's a no-no, or wait for you to frown and shake your head and discuss this no-no with her once again. If so, she's making fabulous progress! Give her a hug and try to let her know you share the delight in her accomplishment. It's important for toddlers to realize that they really are capable of learning self-control and pleasing their parents. And parents will feel much better knowing that the child is making strides in learning to keep herself safe.

STRANGER ANXIETY

Shy, fearful behavior around strangers (meaning anyone other than the immediate family and trusted caregivers) intensifies around twelve months of age. It gradually lessens and disappears by age three except in the shiest youngsters. Negative reactions during this period tend to be more pronounced toward men than women, and least pronounced toward other children.

When a child is distressed about a "stranger" (who can actually be a relative or neighbor the child has met many times before), hold her on your lap to help her feel safe and don't pressure her to interact. Once out of the limelight and given time to observe, most toddlers grow bolder about approaching household guests. Tell Aunt Emily and Uncle Bob not to take the rejection personally.

This is not the time to teach toddlers about "dangerous" strangers, or "good" versus "bad" touching. They're too young to understand these concepts, and emphasizing the issue may make them more afraid of people than they already are. Instead, begin teaching limits by helping children ward off *any* intrusive actions, including hugs and kisses from "strangers," like Aunt Tanya and Great-grandpa David, and either kisses or blows from a toddler friend.

··

Parenting Pointer

Support your child's desire not to be touched by saying, "He doesn't want to be touched right now. He'll let you know when he's ready." Give your child the words to hold others at bay by instructing him, "Can you say, 'I don't like that. Please stop.' Can you say, 'Stop'?"

··

COMFORT OBJECTS

It's common for toddlers to become so attached to a particular object they can't bear to be separated from it. The object doesn't have to be something soft, like a blanket. Some youngsters develop affection for a toy truck or flashlight. What matters is the bond the child has formed with it. These special objects help toddlers cope with situations that require a separation from their parent, such as going to day care or to bed.

Parents may be frustrated if their toddler insists on having the same toy at his side every moment of the day and sleeps with it at night. As the months go by and their child's grip on Mr. Teddy or his "blankie" remains as tight as ever, they begin to picture their toddler walking up to the podium at high school graduation clutching the bedraggled toy under his arm.

Fortunately, no such incident has ever been recorded, and there's no reason to believe your darling will be the first! The social pressures of kindergarten can be counted on to bring a quick end to the love affair with an inanimate object—at least in public. Lots of teens still cuddle their teddy at night, so don't worry about your child's need for a comfort object, and don't push your child to relinquish it. If your child seems overly attached to a comfort object, try to give him more hugs and spend more time cuddling.

FEELINGS 101

Much of the improvement in emotional control that takes place during the toddler years is due to youngsters' enhanced ability to communicate. As toddlers become more adept at labeling their feelings and communicating their needs, they react less impulsively. Youngsters who cannot talk out their feelings can only act them out. As they are more able to express their feelings in words, they don't have to rely on crying to signal their hunger, thirst, need for a diaper change, desire to be held, or wish to play with a particular toy. Toddlers are not able to identify their feelings with much accuracy. They simply experience a physical or psychological discomfort and they react. Parents and other caregivers need to teach toddlers to recognize their emotional and physical states and to use the vocabulary of feelings to express discomfort.

These are toddlers' first steps in learning to express themselves appropriately and to resolve troublesome emotions. What is obvious to an adult is not at all obvious to a little person. Parents need to make it a habit to tell toddlers what they are feeling before attempting to help with whatever is upsetting them:

- "You're sad that I'm leaving." ("But I'll be back soon.")
- "You're frustrated with that puzzle." ("Do you want some help?")
- "You're happy that Daddy is home." ("Stay inside. He'll come inside in a minute.")

- "You're afraid of that clown." ("But he's just a man with makeup and paint on his face.")
- "You're angry because I won't let you play in the sandbox." ("We need to think of some other fun thing for you to do.")

Unhappy Feelings

Unhappy feelings serve a useful purpose. They let human beings know that something is wrong or that something needs to be changed. These feelings help people determine the source of their distress with greater precision. Once they know exactly what is wrong, they are in a better position to figure out how to get their needs met and desires fulfilled.

Unhappy feelings indicate that something is wrong, but toddlers may not know what that something is. They may be bored but think they are hungry. They may be tired but think they are angry at a toy. They may be feeling ill and think they are sad because their parent is talking on the telephone.

Parents must constantly provide corrections:

- "I don't think it's your brother that's upsetting you. I think you're tired."
- "Instead of a snack, I bet a diaper change will help you feel better."
- "Your new tooth is coming in. That's why so many things are bothering you today."

Once they are able to correctly identify their feelings, toddlers will be more able to figure out what to do to feel better.

DEVELOPING INITIATIVE

Young toddlers may experience innate urges to explore and grow and master their environment, but some youngsters become so discouraged by the difficulties they encounter they begin to back away from hard tasks. When the many things toddlers do that anger their parents are added to all the things that frustrate toddlers because they can't do them well, failure can begin to seem like the inevitable outcome of anything they try. Some youngsters become so overwhelmed by their own inadequacies that, instead of continuing to try to please their parents and develop their skills and abilities, they give up.

How toddlers view themselves—their self-concept and self-esteem—depends in large part on what their caregivers tell them about themselves. Toddlers need help to understand that most of their inadequacies stem from their age and lack of maturity and practice. If toddlers believe their incompetence stems from a basic deficiency or defect, they will lose confidence and give up readily when things are difficult for them, backing away from challenges instead of trying to overcome them.

Psychologists consider the need to develop initiative the central emotional task of the toddler years. "Failure" at this task means that shame and guilt swamp initiative. Children who feel ashamed and guilty respond to difficult tasks by raging, becoming destructive, crying, quickly giving up, and blaming others for their failings.

To help toddlers take initiative, parents need to be supportive of little ones' efforts to do things by themselves. Parents should focus on teaching, refrain from criticizing, and respond with kindness and compassion to their child's frustrations.

DELAYING GRATIFICATION

It isn't easy for toddlers to put off until tomorrow what they want right this minute. From age twelve to thirty-six months, toddlers should get much better at managing the tension born of wanting something now and not being able to have it. Being able to delay gratification at the end of the toddler years means:

- Not grabbing a cookie from the counter when Mom steps out of the kitchen even though the chocolate calls to her insistently
- Protesting but not falling apart when a parent says he can't have a ride on the mechanical pony in the department store lobby
- Confining herself to some whining and foot-dragging when her father says it's time to leave the park

- Handling his anger over being forbidden to play with a toy by pleading and pouting

Being able to delay gratification means that toddlers may whimper some, whine a bit, cry a few tears, argue, and drag their feet before forging ahead. It does not mean that they continue whining until parents want to smack them, wail to the point that they have to be carried kicking and screaming from the store, argue until parents give up and give in, or fall to the floor in a tantrum. (At least, children close to age three should not be doing these things *often*.)

Learning to Wait

How do you teach a toddler to hold it together and wait? Here are some tips:

- **Be calm, not angry.** Parental anger triggers more emotional upset in tots, making difficult situations all the more taxing for them. Remember that there is nothing wrong with a child *wanting* something.
- **Don't anticipate trouble!** When parents anticipate a scene and react to what they *think* will happen next, they become tense and may then overreact to a simple request.
- **Be a role model.** Let your toddler see how you handle yourself: "Oh, doesn't that cake look good! I'd really love a piece right now. But no, that will spoil my appetite. I need to wait until after supper." Soon your toddler will be able to discharge some of the tension of having to wait by talking, too.
- **Give reasons.** Explain why your toddler must wait. It is all too easy for toddlers to conclude that their parent is withholding things and privileges capriciously. That compounds their frustration.

Furthermore, reasonable explanations enable toddlers to apply what they learn in one situation to another. Tots in church may not understand when a parent says, "You must be quiet now. People are talking to God with their hearts and you're disturbing them. You can talk later." But as their language skills improve and they continue to hear explanations, they will eventually understand. Then they can use their knowledge to figure out how to act in other situations where people are concentrating, such as at a live performance, instead of needing an adult to tell them what to do at every moment.

Sometimes parents can't give explanations because they aren't clear about the reasons for certain rules themselves. They only know they must be observed. If you can't supply a reason at the moment, think about it later. When you come up with a reason, share it with your toddler: "Remember yesterday when I said you couldn't watch TV until later? That's because too much TV isn't good for kids. Kids need to play to exercise their bodies and minds." There is sometimes a benefit to sharing reasons later rather than during a contentious moment. Children are more able to listen and consider the parents' words more objectively.

Here are some other things to consider:

- If after thinking about a conflict, you can't come up with a reason that your toddler needed to wait, it's time to hold the mirror up to yourself and consider whether you actually needed to deny your child's request.
- Hold bullying to a minimum. Every parent will have to use the "No, because I said so" line from time to time. Still, it is a power play. Children who are regularly bullied learn to bully others—including their parents when they get big enough.
- When you promise your toddler she can do it "later," "tomorrow," or "next week," be as good as your word! It's true that if you don't remind your toddler of your promise to let him finger-paint later in the afternoon, he may forget. But trusting that when the parent says "later," that time will actually arrive makes waiting more tolerable.
- Help your child manage the time spent waiting. When children are excitedly anticipating something, their play may become unfocused and their concentration may deteriorate. Suggest an alternate activity.

If children are admonished when they have difficulty waiting and hear nothing when they do wait patiently, they won't recognize that they are capable of delaying gratification of their wants and desires. When your toddler finally calms down after a scene over wanting something *now*, remember to point out her accomplishment. An hour after calm is restored, say, "I'm proud you were able to stop crying when I told you that you couldn't paint until after lunch. I'll make sure you get to do it after we eat."

Maybe your child's tantrum was so violent you were still trembling an hour later. Maybe complimenting your toddler for waiting seems like complimenting Dracula for having such a charming effect on women. But toddlers need to know they are in fact capable of waiting. They prove it every time their wish isn't gratified and they live to tell the tale!

Baby Basics

When pointing out a child's success at delaying gratification, focus on his achievement. Save the "thank yous" for when your child has done *you* a favor. Children aren't doing their parents a favor by developing patience. This is a hard-won gift they are giving to themselves!

Appendix
DEVELOPMENTAL GUIDELINES

THE FIRST YEAR

0 to 3 Months

- If this is your first child, sleep when the baby sleeps. These catnaps may be the only chance for sleep you get for some time.
- Always use a car seat whenever you take your baby in a car.
- Your baby should sleep on his back to reduce the risks of sudden infant death syndrome (SIDS).
- Be sure not to let your baby get too warm. One light layer more than you would wear is plenty.
- Talk to your baby often to stimulate brain development.
- Always support your baby's head when holding or carrying him.
- Never leave your baby on a couch or other high surface, as he could easily roll off.
- The human face is very interesting to your baby; give him lots of face time.
- Tummy time is a very important part of play. Your baby should spend some time on his belly every day to help build her neck muscles.

4 to 6 Months

- Be wary of toys that put weight on your baby's legs, as they may cause strain on undeveloped muscles.
- Do not start solid foods yet, as they may cause food allergies.
- Start babyproofing, if you haven't already. Mobility isn't too far off.
- You can't spoil your baby with attention. Remember to respond to her needs immediately so she will feel confident and comfortable when alone.
- Consider learning some simple sign language to teach your baby how to communicate before language abilities are developed.
- Make time every day to read to your baby, even if it's simply talking through a picture book.
- Have a car seat checkup. Your baby may have outgrown the car seat you've chosen.
- Juice is not recommended for babies. It simply leads to obesity and doesn't really offer any nutritional value to your baby's diet.

7 to 9 Months

- When starting solid foods, try one food at a time for several days to note any allergic reactions, like rashes or irritability.
- Before moving your baby into a forward-facing car seat, check with your pediatrician to ensure that your baby is heavy and long enough for this to be safe.
- Check your home for low-hanging cords and unprotected electrical outlets. Your baby will be drawn to these at this age.
- Some sunscreens are safe for use on infants. Just be careful not to get any in your baby's eyes or mouth.
- Without going overboard, keep your baby's environment clean. Babies are very tempted to put things in their mouth at this age.

- Slings and backpacks are still great for getting around with your little one.
- Enjoy music with your baby. Different genres will inspire your little one to move and wiggle.
- Around this time, diaper changes may get a bit more hectic, as your baby won't want to be changed. Give your baby a special toy to play with to distract him during changes.

10 to 12 Months

- Zoos and petting farms are great treats for budding toddlers. Take your little one for a trip and tell her the names of all the animals. Just remember the importance of hand washing after touching animals.
- Babyproofing takes on a whole new meaning as your baby becomes more mobile. Take another look around your home for safety issues.
- Slings work well for carrying an older baby or toddler. They are also easier on your back than other carriers.
- Dry cereal is a mom's best friend during travel. Always carry a container of baby-friendly cereal with you in case hunger (or boredom) crops up.
- Don't be concerned if your almost-one-year-old is not yet walking. Many toddlers don't take their first steps until well after the first year.
- Play dates are great for older babies, but don't be discouraged if your baby doesn't want to play with a friend. At this age, you typically see parallel play, where the babies play next to each other with minimal interaction.
- Another car seat safety check is in order. Do you need a larger car seat now? Do you know how to use your new car seat?
- Go through your medicine chest. Do you have expired medications? Do you need to buy any new emergency meds to have on hand? Talk to your pediatrician about what medications you should keep at home.

MOTOR MILESTONES IN THE FIRST YEAR OR SO	
Age	**Milestone**
Birth–1 month	side to side head turn
2–4 months	mini push-up
2–5 months	swipes at object
2–5 months	brings both hands together
3–7 months	rolls over
3–7 months	grasps objects
5–9 months	sits unsupported
6–12 months	crawls (or somehow travels on four limbs)
7–13 months	pulls up to a stand
8–16 months	walks

AGE TWELVE TO EIGHTEEN MONTHS

Language

- Responds to own name
- Knows the meaning of "mama," "dada," and "no"
- Repeats words and imitates sounds
- Jabbers, hums, and "sings"
- Communicates needs by pointing and making sounds
- Points to a part of the body
- Responds to one-step commands (e.g., "Come here.")
- Identifies two pictures in books

Cognitive/Intellectual

- Understands that a hidden object still exists
- Explores via touch and taste
- Dumps things out
- Takes things out of a container and puts them back in again
- Tears paper
- Repeats actions to learn cause and effect
- Sorts simple objects by shape
- Does 3-D puzzles (e.g., inserts a block into a square hole)
- Remembers some things they saw or heard hours or days ago

Physical/Motor

- Stands alone
- Lowers himself from standing to sitting
- Walks alone
- Walks while carrying toys
- Bends over and picks something up
- Claps
- Points with index finger
- Picks up small objects with thumb and index finger
- Puts an object in a container
- Scribbles
- Opens drawers and cabinets
- Tosses or rolls a ball
- Throws a ball
- Stacks two to four blocks
- Stirs with a spoon
- Climbs 1–2 foot objects

Social

- Imitates demonstrations
- Initiates simple games
- Looks to caregiver for praise
- Is proud of accomplishments
- Signals a need for help
- Waves "bye-bye"
- Shows affection
- Smiles at favored objects and people

Self-Care

- Washes her hands
- Takes off an article of clothing
- Drinks from a cup with a lid
- Uses a spoon

AGE EIGHTEEN TO TWENTY-FOUR MONTHS

Language

- Understands the meaning of "don't"
- Knows names for familiar people and objects
- Uses fifty words (if talking)
- Makes two-word sentences ("Go bye-bye")
- Identifies four pictures in a book with words (if talking)
- Speaks in gibberish that has the cadence and rhythm of speech
- Listens to short books and nursery rhymes
- Points to six parts of the body when asked
- Follows a two-step command ("Get your coat and come here.")

Cognitive/Intellectual

- Categories (e.g., "toys," "books," "foods," "people")
- Points to specific pictures in books when asked
- Tries different ways to do something
- Figures out how to do things by trying different strategies
- Learns from looking at books
- Pretends (e.g., the piece of Play-Doh is a snake)
- Focuses on an activity for five minutes
- Chooses (between two things)
- Inspects something by looking (not tasting or touching)

Physical/Motor

- Runs
- Stacks six blocks
- Rides a toy by pushing on the floor with alternating feet
- Walks up steps
- Kicks a ball forward

Social

- Has an impact by saying "no" or resisting
- Feels concerned when someone is crying
- Tries to comfort someone who is very upset
- Handles simple responsibilities
- Is interested in other children
- Feeds a doll

Self-Care

- Drinks from a cup without a lid
- Uses a spoon and fork (still has trouble turning the hand)
- Puts arms and legs through holes when being dressed
- Takes off some clothes
- Puts on an article of clothing
- Washes and dry hands

AGE TWENTY-FOUR TO THIRTY MONTHS

Language

- Speaks in two-to-three-word sentences (if talking)
- Has short conversations (if talking)

Cognitive/Intellectual

- Listens to books with simple stories
- Understands the concepts "one" and "two"
- Identifies one color
- Plays make-believe and fantasy games

Physical/Motor

- Draws
- Matches objects that are the same
- Makes Play Dough or clay snakes and balls
- Stands on tiptoes
- Stacks eight blocks
- Uses a tricycle
- Jumps forward

- Kicks a ball forward
- Throws a ball
- Stands on one foot (briefly)
- Climbs low ladders
- Leans forward without falling
- Pedals a tricycle
- Goes up and down stairs using alternate feet

Social
- Plays next to other children
- Categorizes people as "boy" or "girl"
- Participates in interactive games
- Identifies a friend

Self-Care
- Puts on a pull-over shirt
- Puts on or pulls up pants

AGE THIRTY TO THIRTY-SIX MONTHS AND OLDER

Language
- Says the names of pictures in a book when asked (if talking)
- Names six body parts (if talking)
- Describes what two objects are used for (if talking)
- Makes three- to four-word sentences (if talking)
- Speaks so that others understand him most of the time (if talking)
- Says fifty words (if talking)
- Understands most of what is said to him

Cognitive/Intellectual

- Follows a two-step command ("Find your hat and put it on")
- Reasons through problems herself
- Counts to two
- Identifies four colors

Physical/Motor

- Copies a straight line
- Copies a circle
- Confines coloring to the paper
- Balances on one foot (two seconds)
- Stacks eight blocks

Social

- Says "please" and "thank-you" when prompted
- Takes turns (with guidance)
- Asserts rights with peers
- Knows not to bully other children
- Contributes to joint activities and discussions
- Negotiates and compromises
- Asks for information
- Approaches other children to play in daily care setting
- Plays with other children

Self-Care

- Uses the potty
- Eats with minimal assistance
- Dresses themselves
- Fixes a bowl of cereal

INDEX

A

Acetaminophen, 313, 314, 324
Advice, handling, 21–23
Allergies, food, 124, 127, 131, 136, 158
Allergies, pollen, 321–22
APGAR scoring, 54
Artificial respiration, 285–86
Aspirin, 319, 324
Asthma, 301, 322
Attachment parenting, 17, 67, 202. See also Parenting styles

B

Baby
    basic care of, 58–60
    bathing, 328–33
    bonding with, 51–52
    bringing home, 57–59
    care of, 58–60
    delivery of, 50–52
    developmental guidelines for, 375–78
    first meeting, 50–52
    gender differences, 70–72
    holding, 67, 76–78
    milestones for, 378
    naming, 48–49
    newborn tests, 53–54
    playing with, 67, 357–62
    preparing home for, 41–43
    siblings of, 63–64
    sleep cycles of, 27–28, 201, 203, 224
    temperament of, 66–67
    toys for, 359–62
    understanding, 66–86
    weight of, 54–55, 62, 318
The Baby Book, 202
Baby boys, 71–72
Baby carriages, 36–37
Baby clothes, 40–41
Baby food. See also Solids
    allergic reactions to, 131, 136
    amount to feed, 125, 138–39
    artificial additives, 132
    cereals, 124, 127, 133–34, 138–39
    chunkier foods, 133–34
    eggs, 136
    feeding, 125–26, 137
    finger foods, 133–37, 139
    first solids, 124, 127
    foods to avoid, 131, 135
    fruits, 127–28
    homemade foods, 128, 130
    honey, 136
    label-reading, 132

meats, 130
nitrates in, 129
organic foods, 128–29
recipes for, 140–55
safety tips for, 130
storing, 130
vegetables, 127–29
Baby girls, 70–71
Baby names, 48–49
Baby powder, 242
Baby slings, 38–39
Baby supplies
    bargains on, 41
    bassinets, 32–33
    bouncer seats, 37
    car seats, 30–32
    carriages, 36–37
    carriers, 38–39
    clothing, 40–41
    co-sleepers, 33
    cradles, 32–33
    cribs, 33–34
    front packs, 39, 76
    slings, 38–39
    stationary jumpers, 37–38
    strollers, 34–35
    swings, 36–37
Baby-proofing home, 41–43, 264–65,
    279–90. See also Safety basics
Barrett, Judi, 165
Bassinets, 32–33, 193
Bathing baby
    daily baths, 323
    ear care, 330
    eye care, 330
    first baths, 328
    hair shampoo, 330, 334
    intimate care, 243–45

scalp issues, 333
sponge baths, 329–31
supplies for, 328–29
tips for, 332–33
tub baths, 331–33
water temperature, 331–32
Bathroom safety, 280–81, 331–33. See also
    Safety basics
Bedtime routines, 195–96, 200–202,
    217–18, 228. See also Sleep, for babies;
    Sleep, for toddlers
Bedwetting, 258
Bee stings, 276, 283
Bilirubin, 56–57
Binky, 81. See also Pacifiers
Birth expenses, 47
Birth plan, 51
Bleeding, stopping, 277
Blood work, 54–55
Bottle-feeding
    bottle types, 112–13
    burping baby and, 120
    choices for, 112–13
    equipment for, 112–15
    formula for, 115–17
    introduction of, 120–21
    microwaves and, 118
    milk-based formula, 115–16
    mistakes with, 118
    nipples for, 113–14
    positions for, 119–20
    preparing bottles, 117
    soy-based formula, 115–16
    sterilizing bottles, 117–18
    temperature for, 117–18
    weaning from, 121
Bouncer seats, 37
Bowel movements

constipation, 129, 260, 318–19
diarrhea, 69, 84, 233, 273, 294, 303, 309, 317–18
meconium, 56, 61, 96, 233
number of, 61, 233, 309
potty training and, 247, 258–61
Boynton, Sandra, 218
Breast milk
    benefits of, 88–89
    cost savings of, 91
    defrosting, 110
    digesting, 91
    freezing, 110
    microwaves and, 118
    ounces per day, 138–39
    storing, 110, 120
    supply of, 89, 96, 102
Breast pumps, 99, 101, 108–9, 111
Breastfeeding
    benefits of, 88–91, 98
    biting and, 107
    breast favoritism, 106
    breast infections, 105
    breast pads, 101, 103
    breast pumps, 99, 101, 108–9
    breast shells, 101–2
    burping baby and, 95–96
    cabbage compresses, 100, 171
    clogged milk duct, 104
    clothing for, 101–2
    cradle hold position, 93
    cross-cradle hold position, 93
    difficulties with, 60–61
    ease of, 90
    first feeding, 52, 91–92
    football hold position, 94
    frequency of, 89, 96, 100
    growth spurts and, 102–3
    help with, 98, 107–8

    in hospital, 56–57
    inverted nipples, 106
    for jaundice cases, 56–57
    lactation consultants, 98
    leakage, 103
    let-down reflex, 100, 105
    mastitis, 105
    milk flow, 100, 105–7
    milk supply for, 89, 96, 102
    ounces per day, 138–39
    positions for, 93–94
    post-cesarean, 98–99
    problems with, 107–8
    in public, 108
    recommendations for, 89
    rejection of, 107
    side-lying hold position, 94
    sore nipples, 103–4
    step-by-step technique for, 92
    thrush and, 105, 326
    tips for, 97–98, 102–3
    for twins, 94
    weaning from, 121, 170–71
    workplace and, 110–12
Breathing difficulties, 55–56, 285–88
Bronchiolitis, 320
Bronchitis, 320
Brown, Margaret Wise, 217–18
Bug bites, 272, 276, 278, 283
Burns, 275
Burping baby, 95–96

C

Car safety, 31–32, 289–90
Car seats, 30–32, 289–90
Carbon monoxide detectors, 42–43, 281
Cardiopulmonary resuscitation, 268–69, 284–88

Carle, Eric, 165

Carriages, 36–37

Carriers, 38–39, 76

Cesarean section, 47, 51

Chest compressions, 286–87

Chickenpox, 325–26

Chickenpox vaccine, 303

Childproofing home, 41–43, 264–65, 279–90. *See also* Safety basics

Choking, first aid, 268, 285, 287–88

Choking, preventing, 268–69

Chronic conditions, 301, 322, 323. *See also* Illnesses

Circumcision, 71, 244–45

Cleanliness. *See also* Hygiene

   bath supplies, 328–29

   bathing baby, 328–33

   cradle cap, 334

   daily baths, 323

   ear care, 330

   eye care, 330

   hair shampoo, 330, 334

   nail trimming, 334–35

   scalp issues, 333

   sponge baths, 329–31

   tips for, 332–33

   tub baths, 331–33

Cloth diapers, 233–35. *See also* Diapers

Cloudy with a Chance of Meatballs, 165

Cognitive/intellectual skills, 248, 379, 381–82, 384

Colds, 319–20, 327

Colic, 84–86

Colostrum, 56, 88, 96, 98–99

Combination vaccines, 304

Comfort objects, 200–201, 208, 368–69

Constipation, 129, 260, 318–19

Cord blood banking, 43–44

Cord stump, 69–70

Co-sleepers, 33, 193, 202–4, 216–17

Cosmetics ingestion, 283

Coughs, 319–21

CPR skills, 268–69, 284–88

Cradle cap, 334

Cradles, 32–33

Crawling, 264, 273, 305, 378

Cribs, 33–34, 193, 224–29

Croup, 320–21

Crying baby

   colic and, 84–86

   distracting, 80

   holding, 67, 78–80

   pacifiers for, 81

   rocking, 80–81

   singing to, 79

   soothing, 78–81, 85–86

   swaddling, 73, 81–84

   temperature and, 79

   understanding, 74–75

   walking with, 79

Cups, drinking from, 121, 126, 132–33, 139

Cuthbertson, Joanne, 205

Cuts/scrapes, 275, 277, 278

D

Dad

   adjustments for, 23–25

   emotions of, 23–25

   expectations for, 23–25

   nighttime awakenings, 208–9

   parenting styles, 19–20

   prioritizing time, 25–26

   qualities of, 26–27

   role of, 24–27, 208–9

   sleep basics, 208–9

   supporting new mom, 64–65

Dehydration, 19, 69, 117, 309, 313, 317–18

Developmental delays, 305
Developmental guidelines
    for babies, 375–78
    milestones, 378
    for toddlers, 378–84
Diaper rash, 232, 235–36, 238, 240–43
Diapers
    blood in, 232, 243–44
    changing how-to, 238–45
    changing stations, 238
    changing tables, 238–40
    cloth diapers, 233–35
    diaper rash, 232, 235–36, 238, 240–43
    diapering basics, 232–41
    diapering how-to, 238–45
    diapering tips, 240–45
    dirty diapers, 233
    disposable diapers, 233, 235–38
    intimate care and, 243–45
    wet diaper numbers, 61, 100, 107, 232
Diarrhea
    causes of, 317–18
    colic and, 84
    dehydration and, 69, 309, 317–18
    illnesses and, 294, 303
    instances of, 327
    salmonella and, 273
    treating, 315, 317
Discipline
    for dangerous situations, 345–46
    distractions as, 343
    meaning of, 340–41
    redirection as, 344–45
    spankings, 348–50
    for tantrums, 350–54
    teaching "no-no," 341–43
    time-outs, 347–48
Disposable diapers, 233, 235–38. See also
    Diapers

Doctor visits. See also Pediatricians
    preparing for, 298–301
    schedule for, 299–300
    sick-child visits, 306–27
    vaccinations, 301–5
    well-child checkups, 298–305
Dr. Seuss, 218
Drownings, 272–73, 280, 285
DTaP vaccine, 302

E

Ear care, 330
Ear infections, 294, 303, 307, 324–25
Eating disorders, 167–68
Eating habits, 167–68
Eczema, 301, 323
Emergency numbers, 267, 287
Emergency room, 287, 318, 321
Emotional control, 369–70
Expenses, budgeting, 47–48
Eye care, 330
Eye medications, 316–17
Eyes, sand in, 276
Eyesight, 51, 55

F

Family and Medical Leave Act (FMLA),
    46–47
Family bed, 193, 202–4, 214–17
Febrile convulsions, 313–14
Feedings
    breastfeeding, 88–94
    difficulties with, 60–62
    first feeding, 52, 91–92
    formula feedings, 112–20
    nighttime feedings, 57, 118, 191–92, 207

positions for, 93
solids, 125–26
technique for, 92
Feelings, understanding, 369–71
Ferber, Dr. Richard, 201–2
"Ferberizing," 201–2
Fevers. *See also* Illnesses
calling doctor about, 309–10
convulsions, 313–14
high fevers, 310–11
purpose of, 311
seizures, 313–14
taking temperature, 312–13
treating, 313
Fifth disease, 326–27
Financial considerations, 45–48
Finger foods, 133–37, 139, 159. *See also*
Toddler foods
Fire safety, 42–43
Firearms safety, 282–83
Fireplace safety, 281
First aid, 268, 274–78, 285, 287–88
First aid kit, 274
Flu shots, 303–4
Fontanel, 68–69
Food preparation, 161–64
Food struggles, 165–70
Formula feedings. *See also* Bottle-feeding
bottle types, 112–13
burping baby and, 120
difficulties with, 61–62
equipment for, 112–15
formula for, 115–17
formula types, 115–16
microwaves and, 118
milk-based formula, 115–16
mistakes with, 118
nipples for, 112–13
ounces per day, 138–39

positions for, 119–20
preparing bottles, 117
soy-based formula, 115–16
sterilizing bottles, 117–18
temperature for, 117–18
Fox, Mem, 218
Freud, Sigmund, 246
Front packs, 39, 76
Fussy baby
colic and, 84–86
cries of, 74–75
distracting, 80
holding, 67, 78–80
pacifiers for, 81
rocking, 80–81
settling, 78–81
singing to, 79
soothing, 78–81, 85–86
swaddling, 73, 81–84
temperature and, 79
walking with, 79
white noise for, 78

G

Galactosemia, 115–16
Games, 256, 362, 364, 380, 382–83
Garage safety, 281–82
Gastroenteritis, 294
Gender matters, 70–71
Germs, 53, 88
The Going to Bed Book, 218
Goodnight Moon, 218
Grandparents, 21–22, 49
Grasp reflex, 72
Grasping objects, 134, 139, 360, 378
Gratification, delaying, 371–74
Growth spurts, 102–3, 162
Guide to Your Child's Sleep, 201

H

Hair, washing, 330, 334
Hand, foot, and mouth disease (HFMD), 324
Head, supporting, 68
Health problems. *See also* Illnesses
    breathing difficulties, 55–56
    at home, 60–63
    in hospital, 55–57
    jaundice, 56–57, 63
    meconium staining, 56
    poor weight gain, 62
Healthy Sleep Habits, Happy Child, 204
Hearing screenings, 55
Helping Your Child Sleep Through the Night, 205
Hepatitis B vaccine, 302
Herbal safety, 289
Hib vaccine, 303
Highchairs, 126
Hives, 323
Holding baby, 67, 76–78
Holiday safety tips, 283–84
Home
    bringing baby home, 57–59
    carbon monoxide detectors, 42–43
    caring for siblings, 63–64
    childproofing, 41–43, 264–65, 279–90
    fire safety, 42–43
    health problems at, 60–63
    hot water temperature, 41
    safety precautions, 41–43
    secondhand smoke, 41–42
    smoke detectors, 42–43
Hospital
    breastfeeding in, 56–57
    common problems in, 55–57
    expectations for, 50–55

procedures in, 53–55
rooming-in, 57
taking baby home, 57–59
tests in, 53–54
visitors at, 52–53
Hot water precautions, 41, 331–32
Houseplants, poisonous, 282
Hygiene. *See also* Cleanliness
    bathing baby, 328–33
    cradle cap, 334
    daily baths, 323
    diapering tips, 243–44
    ear care, 330
    eye care, 330
    hair shampoo, 330, 334
    intimate care, 243–44
    nail trimming, 334–35
    for potty training, 254–55
    scalp issues, 333
    sponge baths, 329–31
    tips for, 332–33
    tub baths, 331–33

I

Ibuprofen, 313, 315, 324
Illnesses
    common illnesses, 317–27
    doctor visits, 306–27
    fevers, 309–14
    during first month, 309–10
    medications for, 314–18
    in older baby, 310
    questions about, 307–8
    taking temperature, 312–13
Immunizations, 301–5
Independence, gaining, 355–73. *See also* Toddler years
Initiative, developing, 370–71

Injuries and treatments
    bee stings, 276
    bleeding, 277
    burns, 275
    cuts, 277
    insect bites, 272, 276, 278, 283
    poison ingestion, 266–68, 275
    sand in eyes, 276
    scrapes, 275, 278
    splinters, 277
    sunburns, 276–77
    tick bites, 276
Insect repellents, 271–72
Insurance plans, 292, 296
IPV vaccine, 302

J

Jaundice, 56–57, 63
Jealousy, 25, 63–64

K

Kitchen safety, 279–80. *See also* Safety
    basics

L

La Leche League, 98
Lactation consultants, 98
Lactose intolerance, 115–16
Lead poisoning, 267–68
Lifesaving skills, 268–69, 284–88

M

Mastitis, 105
Maternity leave, 46–47
Meal preparation, 161–64
Meconium, 56, 61, 96, 233
Medical decisions, 43–44, 244, 292–93
Medical problems. *See also* Sicknesses
    breathing difficulties, 55–56
    at home, 60–63
    in hospital, 55–57
    jaundice, 56–57, 63
    meconium staining, 56
    poor weight gain, 62
Medications
    administering, 315–18
    for colic, 85
    eye medications, 316–17
    for fevers, 313
    for illnesses, 314–18
    safety tips for, 288–89
Metabolic disorders, 54–55
Milestones for babies, 378
MMR vaccine, 303
Moro reflex, 72–73
Motherhood myths, 27–28
Motor skills, 159, 378–79, 381–84

N

Nails, trimming, 334–35
Naptime, 199, 204, 205–6, 210–11, 226–27
Neonatal intensive care unit (NICU), 52,
    99
Nightmares, 223–24
Nighttime awakenings, 208–9
Nighttime feedings, 57, 118, 191–92, 207
Nighttime Parenting, 202
The No-Cry Sleep Solution, 204

"No-no's," 341–43. *See also* Discipline
Nursing baby, 88–112. *See also*
 Breastfeeding
Nursing bra, 101
Nursing dress, 101
Nursing pillow, 101
Nursing stool, 101

O

Oxygen, lack of, 55–56, 285–88

P

Pacifiers, 81, 197, 202, 207, 325, 326
Palmar grasp reflex, 72
Pantley, Elizabeth, 204
Parachute reflex, 72
Parenthood
 caring for siblings, 63–64
 dads as parents, 24–27
 excitement of, 29
 moms as parents, 27–29
 parenting styles, 16–20
 stay-at-home parent, 47–48
Parenting styles
 advice from others, 21–23
 attachment parenting, 17, 67, 202
 developing, 16–17
 differences in, 19–20, 23–24
 pediatrician-directed parenting, 17–18
 scheduled parenting, 18–19
Paternity leave, 46–47
Patience, developing, 371–74
Peanuts/peanut butter, 131
Pediatrician-directed parenting, 17–18
Pediatricians. *See also* Doctor visits
 choosing, 292–97
 expectations for, 294

insurance and, 296
interviewing, 296–97
new parent consultation, 297
practice of, 295–96
questions for, 296
recommendations for, 293
selection process, 292–97
sick-child visits, 306–27
style of, 294
well-child checkups, 298–305
Pertussis, 321
Pets, 273
Phenylketonuria, 54
Phthalates, 361
Physical/motor skills, 159, 378–79, 381–84
Plantar grasp reflex, 72
Plants, poisonous, 282
Playtime, 67, 357–62
Poison control, 266–68, 275
Poison ingestion, 266 68, 275
Poisonous chemicals, 283
Poisonous insects, 283
Poisonous plants, 282
Pool safety, 272–73
Potty training
 bedwetting and, 258
 bladder control and, 247–48
 bowel control and, 247, 258–61
 demonstration of, 250–52
 games for, 256
 hygiene and, 254–55
 musical potties, 257
 praise during, 255–56
 public facilities and, 251
 readiness for, 247–50
 rewards and, 255–56
 toilet seats for, 251–53
 tracking progress of, 256–57
 training pants, 253, 257, 261

Praise, 255–56, 365–67
Prevnar vaccine, 303
Product recalls, 41, 269–70

R

Rashes, 276, 311, 322–23, 326–27. *See also*
   Diaper rash
Recipes
   Apple, Sweet Potato, and Cinnamon
      Purée, 151
   Apple Purée, 143
   Arrounce Verde con Frijoles Negro, 184
   Avocado Mash, 144
   Banana Bread, 175
   Banana Mash, 144
   Barley, 148
   Beef Stew Mash, 153
   Black Bean Mash, 150
   Blackberry Frozen Yogurt, 180
   Blueberry Mini Muffins, 174
   Brown Rice, 148
   Chicken and Mango Purée, 152–53
   Chicken Noodle Soup, 173
   Chicken Pot Pie Muffins, 183
   Chicken with Cherries and Brown Rice,
      152
   Cream Cheese Frosting, 187
   Farmer's Pie, 177
   Fish and Carrots, 155
   Happy Birthday Vanilla Cake, 181
   Happy Second Birthday Carrot Cake,
      186
   Hummus, 180
   Kasha, 149
   Lentils, 150
   Oatmeal, 149
   Papaya Purée, 146
   Peach and Avocado Mash, 147
   Peach Purée, 146
   Pear Purée, 145
   Plum Purée, 145
   Pork Chop with Applesauce, 154
   Potato Mash, 151
   Pumpkin Pear Rice Cereal, 147
   Pumpkin Purée, 142
   Quinoa, 148–49
   Rice Cereal, 140
   Spinach Tomato Scramble, 182
   Squash Purée, 142
   Sweet Pea and Apple Purée, 147
   Sweet Pea Purée, 141
   Sweet Potato Purée, 143
   Thumbprint Cookies, 185
   Tofu Bites, 176
   Tomato and Orzo Soup, 176
   Turkey Chili, 178
   Vegetable Rice Soup, 172
   Whole-Wheat Rotini with Bolognese
      Sauce, 179
Reflexes, 71–73
Respiratory syncytial virus (RSV), 320
Rocking baby, 80–81
Rooting reflex, 72
Roseola, 326
Rotavirus vaccines, 303

S

Safety basics
   baby-proofing home, 41–43, 264–65,
      279–90
   bathroom safety, 280–81
   child-safe items, 265–66
   choking, first aid, 268, 285, 287–88
   choking, prevention, 268–69
   cosmetics safety, 283
   CPR skills, 268–69, 284–88

discipline for, 345–46
emergency numbers, 267
firearms safety, 282–83
fireplace safety, 281
first aid, 268, 274–78
garage safety, 281–82
holiday safety tips, 283–84
houseplants, 282
injuries and treatments, 275–78
insect repellents, 271–72
kitchen safety, 279–80
lead poisoning, 267–68
lifesaving skills, 268–69, 284–88
pet safety, 273
poison control, 266–68, 275
poisonous chemicals, 283
poisonous insects, 283
poisonous plants, 282
pool safety, 272–73
product recalls, 269–70
room-by-room safety, 279–82
sun exposure, 270–71, 276–77
sunscreen, 270–71
swimming lessons, 273
toy chests, 282–83
water safety, 272–73
Scalp issues, 333–34
Scheduled parenting style, 18–19
Schevill, Susie, 205
Scrapes/cuts, 275, 277, 278
Sears, Dr. William, 17, 193, 202–3
Secondhand smoke, 41–42
Security objects, 200–201, 208, 368–69
Seizures, 313–14
Self-care skills, 380, 382–84
Separation anxiety, 195, 217, 220, 356
Sexually transmitted infection (STI), 55
Siblings, 63–64
Sickle cell disease, 44, 54

Sicknesses
common sicknesses, 317–27
doctor visits, 306–27
fevers, 309–14
during first month, 309–10
medications for, 314–18
in older baby, 310
questions about, 307–8
taking temperature, 312–13
Size of baby, 54–55
Skin-to-skin contact, 80
Sleep, 211
Sleep, for babies
area for sleeping, 192–93
back-sleep position, 60, 73, 196–98
basics of, 190–91
bassinets, 32–33, 193
bedtime routines, 195–96, 200–202
co-sleeping, 33, 193, 202–4
cribs, 33–34, 193
dads and, 208–9
falling asleep, 195–96, 200–202
family bed, 193, 202–4
naptime, 199, 204–6, 226–27
nighttime feedings, 57, 118, 191–92, 207, 209
patterns of sleep, 73–74, 190–91, 194–98, 204–5
position for sleep, 60, 73, 196–98
sleep cycles, 27–28, 201, 203, 224
sleep problems, 206–8
sleep programs, 200–205
sleep requirements, 73–74
sleep strategies, 198–201
sleeping through night, 194–98, 204–5
swaddling baby, 73
Sleep, for toddlers
attention seekers, 223
beds, 224–29

bedtime routines, 217–18, 228
bottle and, 219
cribs, 224–29
falling asleep, 206–7, 211–12, 218–19
family bed, 214–17
fears and, 223–24
firmness for, 220–21
healthy sleep skills, 218–19
hysteria issues, 221
independent toddlers, 222–29
naptime, 210–11
nightmares and, 223–24
patterns of sleep, 214
resisting sleep, 217, 222, 227–29
role of parents, 219–20
schedules for, 213–14
signals for, 213
sleep requirements, 210–11
sleep terrors, 224
sleep-deprived toddlers, 229
sleepiness, 212
sleeping alone, 214–17
tiredness, 212
wakeups, 221–22
winding-down time, 217–18
Sleep Book, 218
Sleep cycles, 27–28, 201, 203, 224
Sleep patterns, 73–74, 190–91, 194–98, 204–5, 214
Sleep problems, 206–8, 214–17, 221–22, 227–29
Sleep programs, 200–205
Sleep requirements, 73–74, 210–11
Sleep strategies, 198–201
Sleep terrors, 224
Slings, 38–39, 76, 101
Smiles, 317, 380
Smoke detectors, 42–43, 281
Social skills, 380–81, 383–84

Soft spot, 68–69
Solids. See also Toddler foods
allergic reactions to, 124, 127, 131, 136
amount to feed, 125, 138–39
artificial additives, 132
cereals, 124, 127, 133–34, 138–39
chunkier foods, 133–34
constipation and, 129
eggs, 136
feeding, 125–26, 137
finger foods, 133–37, 139
first solids, 124, 127
food processor, 126
foods to avoid, 131, 135
fruits, 127–28
homemade foods, 128, 130
honey, 136
introduction of, 122–26
label-reading, 132
meats, 130
nitrates in, 129
organic foods, 128–29
peanuts/peanut butter, 131
ready for, 123–24
recipes for, 140–55
rice cereal, 124, 127
safety tips for, 130
storing, 130
supplies for, 126–27
vegetables, 127–29
waiting to introduce, 122–24
Solve Your Child's Sleep Problems, 201
Spankings, 348–50. See also Discipline
Splinters, 277
Spoiling concerns, 67
Startle reflex, 72–73
Stationary jumpers, 37–38
Stem cells, 43–44
Stools

blood in, 232
consistency of, 91, 100, 233, 309
constipation, 129, 260, 318–19
diarrhea, 69, 84, 233, 273, 294, 303, 309, 317–18
meconium, 56, 61, 96, 233
number of bowel movements, 61, 233, 309
Stranger anxiety, 367–68
Strep throat, 324
Strollers, 34–35
Sudden Infant Death Syndrome (SIDS)
family bed and, 193
room-sharing and, 204
secondhand smoke and, 42
security objects and, 208
sleep positions and, 60, 73, 196–97, 375
Sun exposure, 270–71
Sunburns, 276–77
Sundlof, Dr. Stephen, 116
Sunscreen, 270–71
Swaddling baby, 73, 81–84
Swimming lessons, 273
Swimming pool safety, 272–73
Swings, 36–37

T

Tactile stimulation, 361
Talking, 378, 380, 382–83
Tantrums, 350–54. *See also* Discipline
Teething, 336–37
Telogen effluvium, 333
Temperament, 66–67
Temperature, taking, 312–13
"Terrible twos," 222–23, 355–56
Thermometers, 312–13
Thrush, 105, 326

Time, prioritizing, 25–26
Time for Bed, 218
Time-outs, 347–48. *See also* Discipline
Toddler bed, 224–29
Toddler foods
allergic reactions to, 158
chewing, 158
creative concoctions, 161
dipping, 158–59
dos and don'ts, 160
eating disorders, 166–68
eating habits, 167–68
eating jags, 166
fats, 157
finger foods, 159
fruits, 161
growing own foods, 162
guidelines for, 156–57
healthy foods, 160–62, 168
helping prepare, 162–64
junk foods, 166, 169
nutritional concerns, 158
portions, 156–57
recipes for, 172–87
self-feeding, 159
serving sizes, 156–57
snacks, 165–68
struggles with, 165–70
sweets, 169
trying new foods, 161–62
vegetables, 160–61
vitamin supplements, 166
well-balanced meals, 165–69
Toddler years
cleanup time, 363–64
comfort objects, 368–69
developmental changes, 356–57
developmental guidelines for, 378–84
emotional control, 369–70

foods for toddlers, 156–87
frustration during, 370–71
gratification, delaying, 371–74
independence, gaining, 355–73
initiative, developing, 370–71
outdoor play, 362–63
patience, developing, 371–74
playing with child, 357–63
praise during, 365–67
reading to child, 358
singing to child, 358
sleep for toddlers, 218–29
stranger anxiety, 367–68
talking with child, 357–58, 365–70
"terrible twos," 222–23, 355–56
toys for child, 359–62
trust, gaining, 364–65
Tonic neck reflex, 73
Tonsillitis, 324
Tooth/gum care, 335–37
Toy chests, 282–83
Toy safety, 361–62
Toys, choosing, 359–62
Training pants, 253, 257, 261. See also
Potty training
Trust, gaining, 364–65
Twelve-month vaccines, 303

U

Umbilical cord, 43–44
Umbilical cord stump, 69–70
Upper respiratory tract infection, 294,
321–22, 326–27

V

Vaccinations, 301–5
Vehicle safety, 31–32, 289–90
The Very Hungry Caterpillar, 165
Visitors, seeing, 52–53
Vitamin supplements, 166
Vomiting, 69, 84, 273, 294, 303, 310, 317

W

Walkers, 37, 268
Walking, 305, 345, 355–56, 377–78
Water safety, 272–73
Weight of baby, 54–55, 62, 318
Weissbluth, Dr. Marc, 204
Well-child checkups, 298–305. See also
Doctor visits
Whooping cough, 321
Will, making, 45

ABOUT THE EXPERTS

Advice on baby's first year

Marian Edelman Borden is the author of ten nonfiction books. Her work includes *The Pocket Idiot's Guide to Play Groups*; *Smart Start: The Parents' Complete Guide to Preschool Education*; and *The Baffled Parent's Guide to Sibling Rivalry*. She is also the former editor of *New Family: First Year Guide*; *Every Baby*; *Parents Expecting*; *Parents Baby*; and *Parents FAQ*. She is the mother of four children.

Advice on the toddler years

Ellen Bowers, PhD, the mother of a daughter, has a doctorate degree in psychology and a master's of science degree in education and psychology. As former owner and director of a preschool focused on exposing toddlers and preschoolers to the arts, she has an extensive background in early childhood education. Dr. Bowers also worked as a teacher in a program that focused on language development in toddlers.

Advice for dad on baby's first year

Vincent Iannelli, MD, is a board-certified pediatrician, a fellow of the American Academy of Pediatricians, and an associate professor of pediatrics at the University of Texas Southwestern Medical Center. He is also the Pediatrics Guide at About.com and is the president of Keep Kids Healthy, LLC, a parenting advice website. Dr. Iannelli has four children and lives in Heath, TX.

Advice for mom on baby's first year

Robin Elise Weiss, MPH, CLC, LCCE, is a well-known expert in the pregnancy field including her many books and work at pregnancy.about.com. She is a doula and childbirth educator certified by Lamaze International, DONA International, and ICEA. She's the mother of eight and lives in Louisville, KY. You can find her at robineliseweiss.com or on Twitter at @RobinPregnancy.

Advice on toddler activities

Joni Levine, MEd, a mother of a child with special needs, has been working with young children and their families as a daycare provider and consultant since 1981. She writes articles for both parents and child-care professionals on *www.childcarelounge.com*. Levine is also the author of *The Everything® Toddler Activities Book, 2nd Edition, The Everything® Parent's Guide to Tantrums,* and *365 Toddler Activities That Inspire Creativity*. She resides in Dormont, PA.

Advice on cooking for baby and toddler

Kim Lutz is the author of *Welcoming Kitchen: 200 Delicious Allergen & Gluten-Free Vegan Recipes* and the website Welcoming Kitchen. Kim is also the coauthor with Megan Hart of *The Everything® Organic Cooking for Baby & Toddler Book* and *The Everything® Guide to Cooking for Children with Autism*. Kim lives with her husband and two sons.

Megan Hart, MS, RD, is a specialist in pediatric nutrition. She currently works as a clinical dietitian at Rainbow Babies & Children's Hospital in Cleveland, Ohio. Ms. Hart has over a decade of experience working with families to develop creative strategies to meet their special dietary needs and has coauthored several specialty-diet cookbooks. Megan Hart also consults with Kim Lutz on the allergy-friendly food blog Welcoming Kitchen. Ms. Hart lives in Chagrin Falls, Ohio, with her husband and son.